Praise for Programming TypeScript

This is the right book to help you learn TypeScript in depth. *Programming TypeScript* shows all the benefits of using a type system on top of JavaScript and provides deep insight into how to master the language.

—*Minko Gechev, Engineer, Angular Team at Google*

Programming TypeScript onboarded me to the TypeScript tooling and overall ecosystem quickly and efficiently. Every usage question I had was covered by concise, real-world examples. The "Advanced Types" chapter breaks down terminology I usually stumble over, and shows how to leverage TypeScript to create extremely safe code that's still pleasant to use.

—*Sean Grove, Cofounder of OneGraph*

Boris has provided a comprehensive guide to TypeScript. Read this for the 10,000-foot view all the way back down to Earth, and then some.

—*Blake Embrey, Engineer at Opendoor, author of* TypeScript Node and Typings

Programming TypeScript
Making Your JavaScript Applications Scale

Boris Cherny

Beijing · Boston · Farnham · Sebastopol · Tokyo

Programming TypeScript

by Boris Cherny

Copyright © 2019 Boris Cherny. All rights reserved.

Published by O'Reilly Media, Inc., 1005 Gravenstein Highway North, Sebastopol, CA 95472.

O'Reilly books may be purchased for educational, business, or sales promotional use. Online editions are also available for most titles (*http://oreilly.com*). For more information, contact our corporate/institutional sales department: 800-998-9938 or *corporate@oreilly.com*.

Development Editor: Angela Rufino	**Indexer:** Ellen Troutman
Acquisitions Editor: Jennifer Pollock	**Interior Designer:** David Futato
Production Editor: Katherine Tozer	**Cover Designer:** Karen Montgomery
Copyeditor: Rachel Head	**Illustrator:** Rebecca Demarest
Proofreader: Charles Roumeliotis	

May 2019:   First Edition

Revision History for the First Edition

2019-04-18:   First Release
2019-08-09:   Second Release

See *http://oreilly.com/catalog/errata.csp?isbn=9781492037651* for release details.

The O'Reilly logo is a registered trademark of O'Reilly Media, Inc. *Programming TypeScript*, the cover image, and related trade dress are trademarks of O'Reilly Media, Inc.

The views expressed in this work are those of the author, and do not represent the publisher's views. While the publisher and the author have used good faith efforts to ensure that the information and instructions contained in this work are accurate, the publisher and the author disclaim all responsibility for errors or omissions, including without limitation responsibility for damages resulting from the use of or reliance on this work. Use of the information and instructions contained in this work is at your own risk. If any code samples or other technology this work contains or describes is subject to open source licenses or the intellectual property rights of others, it is your responsibility to ensure that your use thereof complies with such licenses and/or rights.

978-1-492-03765-1

[LSI]

To Sasha and Michael, who might also fall in love with types, someday.

Table of Contents

Preface

This is a book for programmers of all walks: professional JavaScript engineers, C# people, Java sympathizers, Python lovers, Ruby aficionados, Haskell nerds. Whatever language(s) you write in, so long as you have some experience programming and know the basics of functions, variables, classes, and errors, this book is for you. Some experience with JavaScript, including a basic knowledge of the Document Object Model (DOM) and the network, will help you along the way—while we don't dive deep into these concepts, they are a wellspring of excellent examples, and if you're not familiar with them the examples might not make as much sense.

Regardless of what programming languages you've used in the past, what unites all of us is our shared experience of tracking down exceptions, tracing through code line by line to figure out what went wrong and how we can fix it. This is the experience that TypeScript helps prevent by examining your code automatically and pointing out the mistakes you may have missed.

It's OK if you haven't worked with a statically typed language before. I'll teach you about types and how to use them effectively to make your programs crash less, document your code better, and scale your applications across more users, engineers, and servers. I'll try to avoid big words when I can, and explain ideas in a way that's intuitive, memorable, and practical, using lots of examples along the way to help keep things concrete.

That's the thing about TypeScript: unlike a lot of other typed languages, TypeScript is intensely practical. It invents completely new concepts so you can speak more concisely and precisely, letting you write applications in a way that's fun, modern, and safe.

How This Book Is Organized

This book has two aims: to give you a deep understanding of how the TypeScript language works (theory) and provide bucketfuls of pragmatic advice about how to write production TypeScript code (practice).

Because TypeScript is such a practical language, theory quickly turns to practice, and most of this book ends up being a mix of the two, with the first couple of chapters almost entirely theory, and the last few almost completely practice.

I'll start with the basics of what compilers, typecheckers, and types are. I'll then give a broad overview of the different types and type operators in TypeScript, what they're for, and how you use them. Using what we've learned, I'll cover some advanced topics like TypeScript's most sophisticated type system features, error handling, and asynchronous programming. Finally, I'll wrap up with how to use TypeScript with your favorite frameworks (frontend and backend), migrating your existing JavaScript project to TypeScript, and running your TypeScript application in production.

Most chapters come with a set of exercises at the end. Try to do these yourself—they'll give you a deeper intuition for what we cover than just reading would. Answers for chapter exercises are available online, at *https://github.com/bcherny/ programming-typescript-answers*.

Style

Throughout this book, I tried to stick to a single code style. Some aspects of this style are deeply personal—for example:

- I only use semicolons when necessary.
- I indent with two spaces.
- I use short variable names like a, f, or _ where the program is a quick snippet, or where the structure of the program is more important than the details.

Some aspects of the code style, however, are things that I think you should do too. A few of these are:

- You should use the latest JavaScript syntax and features (the latest JavaScript version is usually just called "esnext"). This will keep your code in line with the latest standards, improving interoperability and Googleability, and it can help reduce ramp-up time for new hires. It also lets you take advantage of powerful, modern JavaScript features like arrow functions, promises, and generators.

- You should keep your data structures immutable with spreads (...) most of the time.[1]
- You should make sure everything has a type, inferred when possible. Be careful not to abuse explicit types; this will help keep your code clear and terse, and improve safety by surfacing incorrect types rather than bandaiding over them.
- You should keep your code reusable and generic. Polymorphism (see "Polymorphism" on page 64) is your best friend.

Of course, these ideas are hardly new. But TypeScript works especially well when you stick to them. TypeScript's built-in downlevel compiler, support for read-only types, powerful type inference, deep support for polymorphism, and completely structural type system encourage good coding style, while the language remains incredibly expressive and true to the underlying JavaScript.

A couple more notes before we begin.

JavaScript doesn't expose pointers and references; instead it has value and reference types. Values are immutable, and include things like strings, numbers, and booleans, while references point to often-mutable data structures like arrays, objects, and functions. When I use the word "value" in this book, I usually mean it loosely to refer to either a JavaScript value or a reference.

Lastly, you might find yourself writing less-than-ideal TypeScript code in the wild when interoperating with JavaScript, or incorrectly typed third-party libraries, or legacy code, or if you're in a rush. This book largely presents how you *should* write TypeScript, and makes an argument for why you should try really hard not to make compromises. But in practice, how correct your code is is up to you and your team.

Conventions Used in This Book

The following typographical conventions are used in this book:

Italic
> Indicates new terms, URLs, email addresses, filenames, and file extensions.

`Constant width`
> Used for program listings, as well as within paragraphs to refer to program elements such as variable or function names, data types, environment variables, statements, and keywords.

---

1 If you're not coming from JavaScript, here's an example: if you have an object o, and you want to add a property k to it with the value 3, you can either mutate o directly—`o.k = 3`—or you can apply your change to o, creating a *new* object as a result—`let p = {...o, k: 3}`.

Constant width italic

Shows text that should be replaced with user-supplied values or by values determined by context.

This element signifies a tip or suggestion.

This element signifies a general note.

This element indicates a warning or caution.

Using Code Examples

Supplemental material (code examples, exercises, etc.) is available for download at *https://github.com/bcherny/programming-typescript-answers*.

This book is here to help you get your job done. In general, if example code is offered with this book, you may use it in your programs and documentation. You do not need to contact us for permission unless you're reproducing a significant portion of the code. For example, writing a program that uses several chunks of code from this book does not require permission. Selling or distributing a CD-ROM of examples from O'Reilly books does require permission. Answering a question by citing this book and quoting example code does not require permission. Incorporating a significant amount of example code from this book into your product's documentation does require permission.

We appreciate, but do not require, attribution. An attribution usually includes the title, author, publisher, and ISBN. For example: "*Programming TypeScript* by Boris Cherny (O'Reilly). Copyright 2019 Boris Cherny, 978-1-492-03765-1."

If you feel your use of code examples falls outside fair use or the permission given above, feel free to contact us at *permissions@oreilly.com*.

O'Reilly Online Learning

O'REILLY® For almost 40 years, *O'Reilly Media* has provided technology and business training, knowledge, and insight to help companies succeed.

Our unique network of experts and innovators share their knowledge and expertise through books, articles, conferences, and our online learning platform. O'Reilly's online learning platform gives you on-demand access to live training courses, in-depth learning paths, interactive coding environments, and a vast collection of text and video from O'Reilly and 200+ other publishers. For more information, please visit *http://oreilly.com*.

How to Contact Us

Please address comments and questions concerning this book to the publisher:

O'Reilly Media, Inc.
1005 Gravenstein Highway North
Sebastopol, CA 95472
800-998-9938 (in the United States or Canada)
707-829-0515 (international or local)
707-829-0104 (fax)

We have a web page for this book, where we list errata, examples, and any additional information. You can access this page at *https://oreil.ly/programming-typescript*.

To comment or ask technical questions about this book, send email to *bookques-tions@oreilly.com*.

For more information about our books, courses, conferences, and news, see our website at *http://www.oreilly.com*.

Find us on Facebook: *http://facebook.com/oreilly*

Follow us on Twitter: *http://twitter.com/oreillymedia*

Watch us on YouTube: *http://www.youtube.com/oreillymedia*

Acknowledgments

This book is the product of years' worth of snippets and doodles, followed by a year's worth of early mornings and nights and weekends and holidays spent writing.

Thank you to O'Reilly for the opportunity to work on this book, and to my editor Angela Rufino for the support throughout the process. Thank you to Nick Nance for his contribution in "Typesafe APIs" on page 210, and to Shyam Seshadri for his contribution in "Angular" on page 207. Thanks to my technical editors: Daniel Rosenwasser of the TypeScript team, who spent an unreasonable amount of time reading through this manuscript and guiding me through the nuances of TypeScript's type system, and Jonathan Creamer, Yakov Fain, and Paul Buying, and Rachel Head for technical edits and feedback. Thanks to my family—Liza and Ilya, Vadim, Roza and Alik, Faina and Yosif—for encouraging me to pursue this project.

Most of all, thanks to my partner Sara Gilford, who supported me throughout the writing process, even when it meant calling off weekend plans, late nights writing and coding, and far too many unprompted conversations about the ins and outs of type systems. I couldn't have done it without you, and I'm forever grateful for your support.

## CHAPTER 1

Introduction

So, you decided to buy a book about TypeScript. Why?

Maybe it's because you're sick of those weird `cannot read property blah of undefined` JavaScript errors. Or maybe you heard TypeScript can help your code scale better, and wanted to see what all the fuss is about. Or you're a C# person, and have been thinking of trying out this whole JavaScript thing. Or you're a functional programmer, and decided it was time to take your chops to the next level. Or your boss was so fed up with your code causing production issues that they gave you this book as a Christmas present (stop me if I'm getting warm).

Whatever your reasons are, what you've heard is true. TypeScript is the language that will power the next generation of web apps, mobile apps, NodeJS projects, and Internet of Things (IoT) devices. It will make your programs safer by checking for common mistakes, serve as documentation for yourself and future engineers, make refactoring painless, and make, like, half of your unit tests unnecessary ("What unit tests?"). TypeScript will double your productivity as a programmer, and it will land you a date with that cute barista across the street.

But before you go rushing across the street, let's unpack all of that a little bit, starting with this: what exactly do I mean when I say "safer"? What I am talking about, of course, is *type safety*.

> **Type safety**
>
> Using types to prevent programs from doing invalid things.[1]

---

1 Depending on which statically typed language you use, "invalid" can mean a range of things, from programs that will crash when you run them to things that won't crash but are clearly nonsensical.

Here are a few examples of things that are invalid:

- Multiplying a number and a list
- Calling a function with a list of strings when it actually needs a list of objects
- Calling a method on an object when that method doesn't actually exist on that object
- Importing a module that was recently moved

There are some programming languages that try to make the most of mistakes like these. They try to figure out what you really meant when you did something invalid, because hey, you do what you can, right? Take JavaScript, for example:

```
3 + []                 // Evaluates to the string "3"

let obj = {}
obj.foo                // Evaluates to undefined

function a(b) {
  return b/2
}
a("z")                 // Evaluates to NaN
```

Notice that instead of throwing exceptions when you try to do things that are obviously invalid, JavaScript tries to make the best of it and avoids exceptions whenever it can. Is JavaScript being helpful? Certainly. Does it make it easier for you to catch bugs quickly? Probably not.

Now imagine if JavaScript threw more exceptions instead of quietly making the best of what we gave it. We might get feedback like this instead:

```
3 + []                 // Error: Did you really mean to add a number and an array?

let obj = {}
obj.foo                // Error: You forgot to define the property "foo" on obj.

function a(b) {
  return b/2
}
a("z")                 // Error: The function "a" expects a number,
                       // but you gave it a string.
```

Don't get me wrong: trying to fix our mistakes for us is a neat feature for a programming language to have (if only it worked for more than just programs!). But for JavaScript, this feature creates a disconnect between when you make a mistake in your code, and when you *find out* that you made a mistake in your code. Often, that means that the first time you hear about your mistake will be from someone else.

So here's a question: when exactly does JavaScript tell you that you made a mistake?

Right: when you actually *run* your program. Your program might get run when you test it in a browser, or when a user visits your website, or when you run a unit test. If you're disciplined and write plenty of unit tests and end-to-end tests, smoke test your code before pushing it, and test it internally for a while before shipping it to users, you will hopefully find out about your error before your users do. But what if you don't?

That's where TypeScript comes in. Even cooler than the fact that TypeScript gives you helpful error messages is *when* it gives them to you: TypeScript gives you error messages *in your text editor, as you type*. That means you don't have to rely on unit tests or smoke tests or coworkers to catch these sorts of issues: TypeScript will catch them for you and warn you about them as you write your program. Let's see what TypeScript says about our previous example:

```
3 + []              // Error TS2365: Operator '+' cannot be applied to types '3'
                    // and 'never[]'.

let obj = {}
obj.foo             // Error TS2339: Property 'foo' does not exist on type '{}'.

function a(b: number) {
  return b / 2
}
a("z")              // Error TS2345: Argument of type '"z"' is not assignable to
                    // parameter of type 'number'.
```

In addition to eliminating entire classes of type-related bugs, this will actually change the way you write code. You will find yourself sketching out a program at the type level before you fill it in at the value level;[2] you will think about edge cases as you design your program, not as an afterthought; and you will design programs that are simpler, faster, easier to understand, and easier to maintain.

Are you ready to begin the journey? Let's go!

---

2 If you're not sure what "type level" means here, don't worry. We'll go over it in depth in later chapters.

TypeScript: A 10_000 Foot View

Over the next few chapters, I'll introduce the TypeScript language, give you an overview of how the TypeScript Compiler (TSC) works, and take you on a tour of TypeScript's features and the patterns you can develop with them. We'll start with the compiler.

The Compiler

Depending on what programming languages you worked with in the past (that is, before you decided to buy this book and commit to a life of type safety), you'll have a different understanding of how programs work. The way TypeScript works is unusual compared to other mainstream languages like JavaScript or Java, so it's important that we're on the same page before we go any further.

Let's start broad: programs are files that contain a bunch of text written by you, the programmer. That text is parsed by a special program called a *compiler*, which transforms it into an *abstract syntax tree (AST)*, a data structure that ignores things like whitespace, comments, and where you stand on the tabs versus spaces debate. The compiler then converts that AST to a lower-level representation called *bytecode*. You can feed that bytecode into another program called a *runtime* to evaluate it and get a result. So when you run a program, what you're really doing is telling the runtime to evaluate the bytecode generated by the compiler from the AST parsed from your source code. The details vary, but for most languages this is an accurate high-level view.

Once again, the steps are:

1. Program is parsed into an AST.
2. AST is compiled to bytecode.

3. Bytecode is evaluated by the runtime.

Where TypeScript is special is that instead of compiling straight to bytecode, Type-Script compiles to… JavaScript code! You then run that JavaScript code like you normally would—in your browser, or with NodeJS, or by hand with a paper and pen (for anyone reading this after the machine uprising has begun).

At this point you may be thinking: "Wait! In the last chapter you said TypeScript makes my code safer! When does that happen?"

Great question. I actually skipped over a crucial step: after the TypeScript Compiler generates an AST for your program—but before it emits code—it *typechecks* your code.

Typechecker

A special program that verifies that your code is typesafe.

This typechecking is the magic behind TypeScript. It's how TypeScript makes sure that your program works as you expect, that there aren't obvious mistakes, and that the cute barista across the street really will call you back when they said they would. (Don't worry, they're probably just busy.)

So if we include typechecking and JavaScript emission, the process of compiling TypeScript now looks roughly like Figure 2-1:

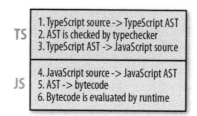

Figure 2-1. Compiling and running TypeScript

Steps 1–3 are done by TSC, and steps 4–6 are done by the JavaScript runtime that lives in your browser, NodeJS, or whatever JavaScript engine you're using.

 JavaScript compilers and runtimes tend to be smushed into a single program called an *engine*; as a programmer, this is what you'll normally interact with. It's how V8 (the engine powering NodeJS, Chrome, and Opera), SpiderMonkey (Firefox), JSCore (Safari), and Chakra (Edge) work, and it's what gives JavaScript the appearance of being an *interpreted* language.

In this process, steps 1–2 use your program's types; step 3 does not. That's worth reiterating: *when TSC compiles your code from TypeScript to JavaScript, it won't look at your types*. That means your program's types will never affect your program's generated output, and are only used for typechecking. This feature makes it foolproof to play around with, update, and improve your program's types, without risking breaking your application.

The Type System

Modern languages have all sorts of different *type systems*.

> **Type system**
>
> A set of rules that a typechecker uses to assign types to your program.

There are generally two kinds of type systems: type systems in which you have to tell the compiler what type everything is with explicit syntax, and type systems that infer the types of things for you automatically. Both approaches have trade-offs.[1]

TypeScript is inspired by both kinds of type systems: you can explicitly annotate your types, or you can let TypeScript infer most of them for you.

To explicitly signal to TypeScript what your types are, use annotations. Annotations take the form *value: type* and tell the typechecker, "Hey! You see this *value* here? Its type is *type*." Let's look at a few examples (the comments following each line are the actual types inferred by TypeScript):

```
let a: number = 1            // a is a number
let b: string = 'hello'      // b is a string
let c: boolean[] = [true, false] // c is an array of booleans
```

And if you want TypeScript to infer your types for you, just leave them off and let TypeScript get to work:

```
let a = 1                    // a is a number
let b = 'hello'              // b is a string
let c = [true, false]        // c is an array of booleans
```

Right away, you'll notice how good TypeScript is at inferring types for you. If you leave off the annotations, the types are the same! Throughout this book, we will use

---

1 There are languages all over this spectrum: JavaScript, Python, and Ruby infer types at runtime; Haskell and OCaml infer and check missing types at compile time; Scala and TypeScript require some explicit types and infer and check the rest at compile time; and Java and C need explicit annotations for almost everything, which they check at compile time.

annotations only when necessary, and let TypeScript work its inference magic for us whenever possible.

 In general, it is good style to let TypeScript infer as many types as it can for you, keeping explicitly typed code to a minimum.

TypeScript Versus JavaScript

Let's take a deeper look at TypeScript's type system, and how it compares to JavaScript's type system. Table 2-1 presents an overview. A good understanding of the differences is key to building a mental model of how TypeScript works.

Table 2-1. Comparing JavaScript's and TypeScript's type systems

Type system feature	JavaScript	TypeScript
How are types bound?	Dynamically	Statically
Are types automatically converted?	Yes	No (mostly)
When are types checked?	At runtime	At compile time
When are errors surfaced?	At runtime (mostly)	At compile time (mostly)

How are types bound?

Dynamic type binding means that JavaScript needs to actually run your program to know the types of things in it. JavaScript doesn't know your types before running your program.

TypeScript is a *gradually typed* language. That means that TypeScript works best when it knows the types of everything in your program at compile time, but it doesn't have to know every type in order to compile your program. Even in an untyped program TypeScript can infer some types for you and catch some mistakes, but without knowing the types for everything, it will let a lot of mistakes slip through to your users.

This gradual typing is really useful for migrating legacy codebases from untyped JavaScript to typed TypeScript (more on that in "Gradually Migrating from JavaScript to TypeScript" on page 236), but unless you're in the middle of migrating your codebase, you should aim for 100% type coverage. That is the approach this book takes, except where explicitly noted.

Are types automatically converted?

JavaScript is weakly typed, meaning if you do something invalid like add a number and an array (like we did in Chapter 1), it will apply a bunch of rules to figure out what you really meant so it can do the best it can with what you gave it. Let's walk through the specific example of how JavaScript evaluates 3 + [1]:

1. JavaScript notices that 3 is a number and [1] is an array.
2. Because we're using +, it assumes we want to concatenate the two.
3. It implicitly converts 3 to a string, yielding "3".
4. It implicitly converts [1] to a string, yielding "1".
5. It concatenates the results, yielding "31".

We could do this more explicitly too (so JavaScript avoids doing steps 1, 3, and 4):

```
3 + [1];                        // evaluates to "31"

(3).toString() + [1].toString() // evaluates to "31"
```

While JavaScript tries to be helpful by doing clever type conversions for you, TypeScript complains as soon as you do something invalid. When you run that same JavaScript code through TSC, you'll get an error:

```
3 + [1];                        // Error TS2365: Operator '+' cannot be applied to
                                // types '3' and 'number[]'.

(3).toString() + [1].toString() // evaluates to "31"
```

If you do something that doesn't seem right, TypeScript complains, and if you're explicit about your intentions, TypeScript gets out of your way. This behavior makes sense: who in their right mind would try to add a number and an array, expecting the result to be a string (of course, besides Bavmorda the JavaScript witch who spends her time coding by candlelight in your startup's basement)?

The kind of implicit conversion that JavaScript does can be a really hard-to-track-down source of errors, and is the bane of many JavaScript programmers. It makes it hard for individual engineers to get their jobs done, and it makes it even harder to scale code across a large team, since every engineer needs to understand the implicit assumptions your code makes.

In short, if you must convert types, do it explicitly.

When are types checked?

In most places JavaScript doesn't care what types you give it, and it instead tries to do its best to convert what you gave it to what it expects.

TypeScript, on the other hand, typechecks your code at compile time (remember step 2 in the list at the beginning of this chapter?), so you don't need to actually run your code to see the Error from the previous example. TypeScript *statically analyzes* your code for errors like these, and shows them to you before you run it. If your code doesn't compile, that's a really good sign that you made a mistake and you should fix it before you try to run the code.

Figure 2-2 shows what happens when I type the last code example into VSCode (my code editor of choice).

```
1   3 + [1]

2   [ts] Operator '+' cannot be applied to types
3   '3' and 'number[]'. [2365]
4
```

Figure 2-2. TypeError reported by VSCode

With a good TypeScript extension for your preferred code editor, the error will show up as a red squiggly line under your code *as you type it*. This dramatically speeds up the feedback loop between writing code, realizing that you made a mistake, and updating the code to fix that mistake.

When are errors surfaced?

When JavaScript throws exceptions or performs implicit type conversions, it does so at runtime.[2] This means you have to actually run your program to get a useful signal back that you did something invalid. In the best case, that means as part of a unit test; in the worst case, it means an angry email from a user.

TypeScript throws both syntax-related errors and type-related errors at compile time. In practice, that means those kinds of errors will show up in your code editor, right as you type—it's an amazing experience if you've never worked with an incrementally compiled statically typed language before.[3]

That said, there are lots of errors that TypeScript can't catch for you at compile time —things like stack overflows, broken network connections, and malformed user inputs—that will still result in runtime exceptions. What TypeScript does is make compile-time errors out of most errors that would have otherwise been runtime errors in a pure JavaScript world.

---

2 To be sure, JavaScript surfaces syntax errors and a few select bugs (like multiple const declarations with the same name in the same scope) after it parses your program, but before it runs it. If you parse your JavaScript as part of your build process (e.g., with Babel), you can surface these errors at build time.

3 Incrementally compiled languages can be quickly recompiled when you make a small change, rather than having to recompile your whole program (including the parts you didn't touch).

Code Editor Setup

Now that you have some intuition for how the TypeScript Compiler and type system work, let's get your code editor set up so we can start diving into some real code.

Start by downloading a code editor to write your code in. I like VSCode because it provides a particularly nice TypeScript editing experience, but you can also use Sublime Text, Atom, Vim, WebStorm, or whatever editor you like. Engineers tend to be really picky about IDEs, so I'll leave it to you to decide. If you do want to use VSCode, follow the instructions on the website (*https://code.visualstudio.com/*) to get it set up.

TSC is itself a command-line application written in TypeScript,[4] which means you need NodeJS to run it. Follow the instructions on the official NodeJS website (*https://nodejs.org*) to get NodeJS up and running on your machine.

NodeJS comes with NPM, a package manager that you will use to manage your project's dependencies and orchestrate your build. We'll start by using it to install TSC and TSLint (a linter for TypeScript). Start by opening your terminal and creating a new folder, then initializing a new NPM project in it:

```
# Create a new folder
mkdir chapter-2
cd chapter-2

# Initialize a new NPM project (follow the prompts)
npm init

# Install TSC, TSLint, and type declarations for NodeJS
npm install --save-dev typescript tslint @types/node
```

tsconfig.json

Every TypeScript project should include a file called *tsconfig.json* in its root directory. This *tsconfig.json* is where TypeScript projects define things like which files should be compiled, which directory to compile them to, and which version of JavaScript to emit.

---

4 This puts TSC in the mystical class of compilers known as *self-hosting compilers*, or compilers that compile themselves.

Create a new file called *tsconfig.json* in your root folder (`touch tsconfig.json`),[5] then pop it open in your code editor and give it the following contents:

```
{
  "compilerOptions": {
    "lib": ["es2015"],
    "module": "commonjs",
    "outDir": "dist",
    "sourceMap": true,
    "strict": true,
    "target": "es2015"
  },
  "include": [
    "src"
  ]
}
```

Let's briefly go over some of those options and what they mean (Table 2-2):

Table 2-2. tsconfig.json options

Option	Description
`include`	Which folders should TSC look in to find your TypeScript files?
`lib`	Which APIs should TSC assume exist in the environment you'll be running your code in? This includes things like ES5's `Function.prototype.bind`, ES2015's `Object.assign`, and the DOM's `document.querySelector`.
`module`	Which module system should TSC compile your code to (CommonJS, SystemJS, ES2015, etc.)?
`outDir`	Which folder should TSC put your generated JavaScript code in?
`strict`	Be as strict as possible when checking for invalid code. This option enforces that all of your code is properly typed. We'll be using it for all of the examples in the book, and you should use it for your TypeScript project too.
`target`	Which JavaScript version should TSC compile your code to (ES3, ES5, ES2015, ES2016, etc.)?

These are just a few of the available options—*tsconfig.json* supports dozens of options, and new ones are added all the time. You won't find yourself changing these much in practice, besides dialing in the `module` and `target` settings when switching to a new module bundler, adding `"dom"` to `lib` when writing TypeScript for the browser (you'll learn more about this in Chapter 12), or adjusting your level of `strict`ness when migrating your existing JavaScript code to TypeScript (see "Gradually Migrating from JavaScript to TypeScript" on page 236). For a complete and up-to-date list of supported options, head over to the official documentation on the TypeScript website (*http://bit.ly/2JWfsgY*).

---

5 For this exercise, we're creating a *tsconfig.json* manually. When you set up TypeScript projects in the future, you can use TSC's built-in initialize command to generate one for you: `./node_modules/.bin/tsc --init`.

Note that while using a *tsconfig.json* file to configure TSC is handy because it lets us check that configuration into source control, you can set most of TSC's options from the command line too. Run `./node_modules/.bin/tsc --help` for a list of available command-line options.

tslint.json

Your project should also have a *tslint.json* file containing your TSLint configuration, codifying whatever stylistic conventions you want for your code (tabs versus spaces, etc.).

 Using TSLint is optional, but it's strongly recommend for all Type-Script projects to enforce a consistent coding style. Most importantly, it will save you from arguing over code style with coworkers during code reviews.

The following command will generate a *tslint.json* file with a default TSLint configuration:

```
./node_modules/.bin/tslint --init
```

You can then add overrides to this to conform with your own coding style. For example, my *tslint.json* looks like this:

```
{
  "defaultSeverity": "error",
  "extends": [
    "tslint:recommended"
  ],
  "rules": {
    "semicolon": false,
    "trailing-comma": false
  }
}
```

For the full list of available rules, head over to the TSLint documentation (*https://palantir.github.io/tslint/rules/*). You can also add custom rules, or install extra presets (like for ReactJS (*https://www.npmjs.com/package/tslint-react*)).

index.ts

Now that you've set up your *tsconfig.json* and *tslint.json*, create a *src* folder containing your first TypeScript file:

```
mkdir src
touch src/index.ts
```

Your project's folder structure should now look this:

```
chapter-2/
├─node_modules/
├─src/
|  └─index.ts
├─package.json
├─tsconfig.json
└─tslint.json
```

Pop open *src/index.ts* in your code editor, and enter the following TypeScript code:

```
console.log('Hello TypeScript!')
```

Then, compile and run your TypeScript code:

```
# Compile your TypeScript with TSC
./node_modules/.bin/tsc

# Run your code with NodeJS
node ./dist/index.js
```

If you've followed all the steps here, your code should run and you should see a single log in your console:

```
Hello TypeScript!
```

That's it—you just set up and ran your first TypeScript project from scratch. Nice work!

 Since this might have been your first time setting up a TypeScript project from scratch, I wanted to walk through each step so you have a sense for all the moving pieces. There are a couple of shortcuts you can take to do this faster next time:

- Install ts-node (*https://npmjs.org/package/ts-node*), and use it to compile and run your TypeScript with a single command.

- Use a scaffolding tool like typescript-node-starter (*https://github.com/Microsoft/TypeScript-Node-Starter*) to quickly generate your folder structure for you.

Exercises

Now that your environment is set up, open up *src/index.ts* in your code editor. Enter the following code:

```
let a = 1 + 2
let b = a + 3
let c = {
  apple: a,
  banana: b
}
let d = c.apple * 4
```

Now hover over a, b, c, and d, and notice how TypeScript infers the types of all your variables for you: a is a number, b is a number, c is an object with a specific shape, and d is also a number (Figure 2-3).

```
 6   let a = 1 + 2
 7   let b = a + 3
 8   let c = {
 9     apple: a,
10     banana: b
11   }   let d: number
12   let d = c.apple * 4
```

Figure 2-3. TypeScript inferring types for you

Play around with your code a bit. See if you can:

- Get TypeScript to show a red squiggly when you do something invalid (we call this "throwing a TypeError").
- Read the TypeError, and try to understand what it means.
- Fix the TypeError and see the red squiggly disappear.

If you're ambitious, try to write a piece of code that TypeScript is unable to infer the type for.

## CHAPTER 3

All About Types

In the last chapter I introduced the idea of type systems, but I never defined what the *type* in type system really means.

Type

A set of values and the things you can do with them.

If that sounds confusing, let me give a few familiar examples:

- The `boolean` type is the set of all booleans (there are just two: `true` and `false`) and the operations you can perform on them (like `||`, `&&`, and `!`).

- The `number` type is the set of all numbers and the operations you can perform on them (like `+`, `-`, `*`, `/`, `%`, `||`, `&&`, and `?`), including the methods you can call on them like `.toFixed`, `.toPrecision`, `.toString`, and so on.

- The `string` type is the set of all strings and the operations you can perform on them (like `+`, `||`, and `&&`), including the methods you can call on them like `.concat` and `.toUpperCase`.

When you see that something is of type `T`, not only do you know that it's a `T`, but you also know *exactly what you can do* with that `T` (and what you can't). Remember, the whole point is to use the typechecker to stop you from doing invalid things. And the way the typechecker knows what's valid and what's not is by looking at the types you're using and how you're using them.

In this chapter we'll take a tour of the types available in TypeScript and cover the basics of what you can do with each of them. Figure 3-1 gives an overview.

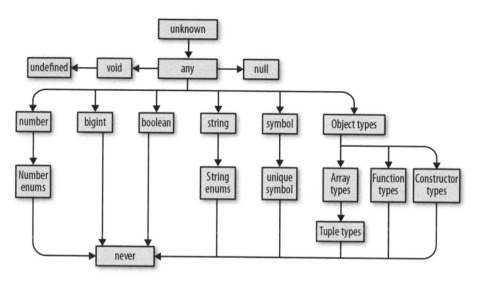

Figure 3-1. TypeScript's type hierarchy

Talking About Types

When programmers talk about types, they share a precise, common vocabulary to describe what they mean. We're going to use this vocabulary throughout this book.

Say you have a function that takes some value and returns that value multiplied by itself:

```
function squareOf(n) {
  return n * n
}
squareOf(2)     // evaluates to 4
squareOf('z')   // evaluates to NaN
```

Clearly, this function will only work for numbers—if you pass anything besides a number to `squareOf`, the result will be invalid. So what we do is explicitly *annotate* the parameter's type:

```
function squareOf(n: number) {
  return n * n
}
squareOf(2)     // evaluates to 4
squareOf('z')   // Error TS2345: Argument of type '"z"' is not assignable to
                // parameter of type 'number'.
```

Now if we call `squareOf` with anything but a number, TypeScript will know to complain right away. This is a trivial example (we'll talk a lot more about functions in the next chapter), but it's enough to introduce a couple of concepts that are key to talking about types in TypeScript. We can say the following things about the last code example:

1. squareOf's parameter n is *constrained to* number.
2. The type of the value 2 is *assignable to* (equivalently: *compatible with*) number.

Without a type annotation, squareOf is unconstrained in its parameter, and you can pass any type of argument to it. Once we constrain it, TypeScript goes to work for us verifying that every place we call our function, we call it with a compatible argument. In this example the type of 2 is number, which is assignable to squareOf's annotation number, so TypeScript accepts our code; but 'z' is a string, which is not assignable to number, so TypeScript complains.

You can also think of it in terms of *bounds*: we told TypeScript that n's *upper bound* is number, so any value we pass to squareOf has to be at most a number. If it's anything more than a number (like, if it's a value that might be a number or might be a string), then it's not assignable to n.

I'll define assignability, bounds, and constraints more formally in Chapter 6. For now, all you need to know is this is the language that we use to talk about whether or not a type can be used in a place where we require a certain type.

The ABCs of Types

Let's take a tour of the types TypeScript supports, what values they contain, and what you can do with them. We'll also cover a few basic language features for working with types: type aliases, union types, and intersection types.

any

any is the Godfather of types. It does anything for a price, but you don't want to ask any for a favor unless you're completely out of options. In TypeScript everything needs to have a type at compile time, and any is the default type when you (the programmer) and TypeScript (the typechecker) can't figure out what type something is. It's a last resort type, and you should avoid it when possible.

Why should you avoid it? Remember what a type is? (It's a set of values and the things you can do with them.) any is the set of *all* values, and you can do *anything* with any. That means that if you have a value of type any you can add to it, multiply by it, call .pizza() on it—anything.

any makes your value behave like it would in regular JavaScript, and totally prevents the typechecker from working its magic. When you allow any into your code you're flying blind. Avoid any like fire, and use it only as a very, very last resort.

On the rare occasion that you do need to use it, you do it like this:

```
let a: any = 666          // any
let b: any = ['danger']   // any
let c = a + b             // any
```

Notice how the third type should report an error (why are you trying to add a number and an array?), but doesn't because you told TypeScript that you're adding two anys. If you want to use any, you have to be explicit about it. When TypeScript infers that some value is of type any (for example, if you forgot to annotate a function's parameter, or if you imported an untyped JavaScript module), it will throw a compile-time exception and toss a red squiggly at you in your editor. By explicitly annotating a and b with the any type (: any), you avoid the exception—it's your way of telling TypeScript that you know what you're doing.

TSC Flag: noImplicitAny

By default, TypeScript is permissive, and won't complain about values that it infers as any. To get TypeScript to complain about implicit anys, be sure to enable the noImplicitAny flag in your *tsconfig.json*.

noImplicitAny is part of the strict family of TSC flags, so if you already enabled strict in your *tsconfig.json* (as we did in "tsconfig.json" on page 11), you're good to go.

unknown

If any is the Godfather, then unknown is Keanu Reeves as undercover FBI agent Johnny Utah in *Point Break*: laid back, fits right in with the bad guys, but deep down has a respect for the law and is on the side of the good guys. For the few cases where you have a value whose type you really don't know ahead of time, don't use any, and instead reach for unknown. Like any, it represents any value, but TypeScript won't let you use an unknown type until you refine it by checking what it is (see "Refinement" on page 126).

What operations does unknown support? You can compare unknown values (with ==, ===, ||, &&, and ?), negate them (with !), and refine them (like you can any other type) with JavaScript's typeof and instanceof operators. Use unknown like this:

```
let a: unknown = 30       // unknown
let b = a === 123         // boolean
let c = a + 10            // Error TS2571: Object is of type 'unknown'.
if (typeof a === 'number') {
  let d = a + 10          // number
}
```

This example should give you a rough idea of how to use unknown:

1. TypeScript will never infer something as unknown—you have to explicitly annotate it (a).[1]

2. You can compare values to values that are of type unknown (b).

3. But, you can't do things that assume an unknown value is of a specific type (c); you have to prove to TypeScript that the value really is of that type first (d).

boolean

The boolean type has two values: true and false. You can compare them (with ==, ===, ||, &&, and ?), negate them (with !), and not much else. Use boolean like this:

```
let a = true            // boolean
var b = false           // boolean
const c = true          // true
let d: boolean = true   // boolean
let e: true = true      // true
let f: true = false     // Error TS2322: Type 'false' is not assignable
                        // to type 'true'.
```

This example shows a few ways to tell TypeScript that something is a boolean:

1. You can let TypeScript infer that your value is a boolean (a and b).

2. You can let TypeScript infer that your value is a specific boolean (c).

3. You can tell TypeScript explicitly that your value is a boolean (d).

4. You can tell TypeScript explicitly that your value is a specific boolean (e and f).

In general, you will use the first or second way in your programs. Very rarely, you'll use the fourth way—only when it buys you extra type safety (I'll show you examples of that throughout this book). You will almost never use the third way.

The second and fourth cases are particularly interesting because while they do something intuitive, they're supported by surprisingly few programming languages and so might be new to you. What I did in that example was say, "Hey TypeScript! See this variable e here? e isn't just any old boolean—it's the specific boolean true." By using a value as a type, I essentially limited the possible values for e and f from all booleans to one specific boolean each. This feature is called *type literals*.

---

1 Almost. When unknown is part of a union type, the result of the union will be unknown. You'll read more about union types in "Union and intersection types" on page 32.

> **Type literal**
>
> A type that represents a single value and nothing else.

In the fourth case I explicitly annotated my variables with type literals, and in the second case TypeScript inferred a literal type for me because I used `const` instead of `let` or `var`. Because TypeScript knows that once a primitive is assigned with `const` its value will never change, it infers the most narrow type it can for that variable. That's why in the second case TypeScript inferred c's type as `true` instead of as `boolean`. To learn more about why TypeScript infers different types for `let` and `const`, jump ahead to "Type Widening" on page 122.

We will revisit type literals throughout this book. They are a powerful language feature that lets you squeeze out extra safety all over the place. Type literals make TypeScript unique in the language world and are something you should lord over your Java friends.

number

`number` is the set of all numbers: integers, floats, positives, negatives, `Infinity`, `NaN`, and so on. Numbers can do, well, numbery things, like addition (+), subtraction (-), modulo (%), and comparison (<). Let's look at a few examples:

```
let a = 1234              // number
var b = Infinity * 0.10   // number
const c = 5678            // 5678
let d = a < b             // boolean
let e: number = 100       // number
let f: 26.218 = 26.218    // 26.218
let g: 26.218 = 10        // Error TS2322: Type '10' is not assignable
                          // to type '26.218'.
```

Like in the `boolean` example, there are four ways to type something as a `number`:

1. You can let TypeScript infer that your value is a `number` (a and b).

2. You can use `const` so TypeScript infers that your value is a specific `number` (c).[2]

3. You can tell TypeScript explicitly that your value is a `number` (e).

4. You can tell TypeScript explicitly that your value is a specific `number` (f and g).

And just like with `booleans`, you're usually going to let TypeScript infer the type for you (the first way). Once in a while you'll do some clever programming that requires

---

2 At the time of writing, you can't use `NaN`, `Infinity`, or `-Infinity` as type literals.

your number's type to be restricted to a specific value (the second or fourth way). There is no good reason to explicitly type something as a number (the third way).

When working with long numbers, use numeric separators to make those numbers easier to read. You can use numeric separators in both type and value positions:

```
let oneMillion = 1_000_000 // Equivalent to 1000000
let twoMillion: 2_000_000 = 2_000_000
```

bigint

bigint is a newcomer to JavaScript and TypeScript: it lets you work with large integers without running into rounding errors. While the number type can only represent whole numbers up to 2^{53}, bigint can represent integers bigger than that too. The bigint type is the set of all BigInts, and supports things like addition (+), subtraction (-), multiplication (*), division (/), and comparison (<). Use it like this:

```
let a = 1234n          // bigint
const b = 5678n        // 5678n
var c = a + b          // bigint
let d = a < 1235       // boolean
let e = 88.5n          // Error TS1353: A bigint literal must be an integer.
let f: bigint = 100n   // bigint
let g: 100n = 100n     // 100n
let h: bigint = 100    // Error TS2322: Type '100' is not assignable
                       // to type 'bigint'.
```

Like with boolean and number, there are four ways to declare bigints. Try to let TypeScript infer your bigint's type when you can.

At the time of writing, bigint is not yet natively supported by every JavaScript engine. If your application relies on bigint, be careful to check whether or not it's supported by your target platform.

string

string is the set of all strings and the things you can do with them like concatenate (+), slice (.slice), and so on. Let's see some examples:

```
let a = 'hello'          // string
var b = 'billy'          // string
const c = '!'            // '!'
let d = a + ' ' + b + c  // string
let e: string = 'zoom'   // string
let f: 'john' = 'john'   // 'john'
```

```
let g: 'john' = 'zoe'        // Error TS2322: Type "zoe" is not assignable
                             // to type "john".
```

Like `boolean` and `number`, there are four ways to declare `string` types, and you should let TypeScript infer the type for you whenever you can.

symbol

`symbol` is a relatively new language feature that arrived with one of the latest major JavaScript revisions (ES2015). Symbols don't come up often in practice; they are used as an alternative to string keys in objects and maps, in places where you want to be extra sure that people are using the right well-known key and didn't accidentally set the key—think setting a default iterator for your object (`Symbol.iterator`), or overriding at runtime whether or not your object is an instance of something (`Symbol.hasInstance`). Symbols have the type `symbol`, and there isn't all that much you can do with them:

```
let a = Symbol('a')          // symbol
let b: symbol = Symbol('b')  // symbol
var c = a === b              // boolean
let d = a + 'x'              // Error TS2469: The '+' operator cannot be applied
                             // to type 'symbol'.
```

The way `Symbol('a')` works in JavaScript is by creating a new `symbol` with the given name; that `symbol` is unique, and will not be equal (when compared with `==` or `===`) to any other `symbol` (even if you create a second `symbol` with the same exact name!). Similarly to how the value 27 is inferred to be a `number` when declared with `let` but the specific number 27 when you declare it with `const`, symbols are inferred to be of type `symbol` but can be explicitly typed as `unique symbol`:

```
const e = Symbol('e')               // typeof e
const f: unique symbol = Symbol('f') // typeof f
let g: unique symbol = Symbol('f')   // Error TS1332: A variable whose type is a
                                     // 'unique symbol' type must be 'const'.
let h = e === e              // boolean
let i = e === f              // Error TS2367: This condition will always return
                             // 'false' since the types 'unique symbol' and
                             // 'unique symbol' have no overlap.
```

This example shows off a few ways to create unique symbols:

1. When you declare a new `symbol` and assign it to a `const` variable (not a `let` or `var` variable), TypeScript will infer its type as `unique symbol`. It will show up as typeof *yourVariableName*, not `unique symbol`, in your code editor.

2. You can explicitly annotate a `const` variable's type as `unique symbol`.

3. A `unique symbol` is always equal to itself.

4. TypeScript knows at compile time that a `unique symbol` will never be equal to any other `unique symbol`.

Think of `unique symbols` like other literal types, like 1, `true`, or `"literal"`. They're a way to create a type that represents a particular inhabitant of `symbol`.

Objects

TypeScript's object types specify the shapes of objects. Notably, they can't tell the difference between simple objects (like the kind you make with {}) and more complicated ones (the kind you create with `new Blah`). This is by design: JavaScript is generally *structurally typed*, so TypeScript favors that style of programming over a *nominally typed* style.

> ### Structural typing
>
> A style of programming where you just care that an object has certain properties, and not what its name is (nominal typing). Also called *duck typing* in some languages (or, not judging a book by its cover).

There are a few ways to use types to describe objects in TypeScript. The first is to declare a value as an `object`:

```
let a: object = {
  b: 'x'
}
```

What happens when you access b?

```
a.b   // Error TS2339: Property 'b' does not exist on type 'object'.
```

Wait, that's not very useful! What's the point of typing something as an `object` if you can't do anything with it?

Why, that's a great point, aspiring TypeScripter! In fact, `object` is a little narrower than `any`, but not by much. `object` doesn't tell you a lot about the value it describes, just that the value is a JavaScript object (and that it's not `null`).

What if we leave off the explicit annotation, and let TypeScript do its thing?

```
let a = {
  b: 'x'
}           // {b: string}
a.b         // string

let b = {
  c: {
```

```
    d: 'f'
  }
}                 // {c: {d: string}}
```

Voilà! You've just discovered the second way to type an object: object literal syntax (not to be confused with type literals). You can either let TypeScript infer your object's shape for you, or explicitly describe it inside curly braces({}):

```
let a: {b: number} = {
  b: 12
}                 // {b: number}
```

Type Inference When Declaring Objects with const

What would have happened if we'd used const to declare the object instead?

```
const a: {b: number} = {
  b: 12
}                 // Still {b: number}
```

You might be surprised that TypeScript inferred b as a number, and not as the literal 12. After all, we learned that when declaring numbers or strings, our choice of const or let affects how TypeScript infers our types.

Unlike the primitive types we've looked at so far—boolean, number, bigint, string, and symbol—declaring an object with const won't hint to TypeScript to infer its type more narrowly. That's because JavaScript objects are mutable, and for all TypeScript knows you might update their fields after you create them.

We explore this idea more deeply—including how to opt into narrower inference—in "Type Widening" on page 122.

Object literal syntax says, "Here is a thing that has this shape." The thing might be an object literal, or it might be a class:

```
let c: {
  firstName: string
  lastName: string
} = {
  firstName: 'john',
  lastName: 'barrowman'
}

class Person {
  constructor(
    public firstName: string,    // public is shorthand for
                                 // this.firstName = firstName
    public lastName: string
  ) {}
}
c = new Person('matt', 'smith') // OK
```

`{firstName: string, lastName: string}` describes the *shape* of an object, and both the object literal and the class instance from the last example satisfy that shape, so TypeScript lets us assign a `Person` to c.

Let's explore what happens when we add extra properties, or leave out required ones:

```
let a: {b: number}

a = {}  // Error TS2741: Property 'b' is missing in type '{}'
        // but required in type '{b: number}'.

a = {
  b: 1,
  c: 2  // Error TS2322: Type '{b: number; c: number}' is not assignable
}       // to type '{b: number}'. Object literal may only specify known
        // properties, and 'c' does not exist in type '{b: number}'.
```

Definite Assignment

This is the first example we've looked at where we first declare a variable (a), then initialize it with values ({} and {b: 1, c: 2}). This is a common JavaScript pattern, and it's supported by TypeScript too.

When you declare a variable in one place and initialize it later, TypeScript will make sure that your variable is *definitely assigned* a value by the time you use it:

```
let i: number
let j = i * 3  // Error TS2454: Variable 'i' is used
               // before being assigned.
```

And don't worry, TypeScript enforces this for you even if you leave off the explicit type annotation:

```
let i
let j = i * 3  // Error TS2532: Object is possibly
               // 'undefined'.
```

By default, TypeScript is pretty strict about object properties—if you say the object should have a property called b that's a number, TypeScript expects b and only b. If b is missing, or if there are extra properties, TypeScript will complain.

Can you tell TypeScript that something is optional, or that there might be more properties than you planned for? You bet:

```
let a: {
  b: number  ❶
  c?: string  ❷
  [key: number]: boolean  ❸
}
```

❶ a has a property b that's a number.

❷ a might have a property c that's a string. And if c is set, it might be undefined.

❸ a might have any number of numeric properties that are booleans.

Let's see what types of objects we can assign to a:

```
a = {b: 1}
a = {b: 1, c: undefined}
a = {b: 1, c: 'd'}
a = {b: 1, 10: true}
a = {b: 1, 10: true, 20: false}
a = {10: true}          // Error TS2741: Property 'b' is missing in type
                        // '{10: true}'.
a = {b: 1, 33: 'red'}   // Error TS2741: Type 'string' is not assignable
                        // to type 'boolean'.
```

Index Signatures

The `[key: T]: U` syntax is called an *index signature*, and this is the way you tell TypeScript that the given object might contain more keys. The way to read it is, "For this object, all keys of type T must have values of type U." Index signatures let you safely add more keys to an object, in addition to any keys that you explicitly declared.

There is one rule to keep in mind for index signatures: the index signature key's type (T) must be assignable to either `number` or `string`.[3]

Also note that you can use any word for the index signature key's name—it doesn't have to be `key`:

```
let airplaneSeatingAssignments: {
  [seatNumber: string]: string
} = {
  '34D': 'Boris Cherny',
  '34E': 'Bill Gates'
}
```

Optional (?) isn't the only modifier you can use when declaring object types. You can also mark fields as read-only (that is, you can declare that a field can't be modified after it's assigned an initial value—kind of like `const` for object properties) with the `readonly` modifier:

---

3 Objects in JavaScript use strings for keys; arrays are special kinds of objects that use numerical keys.

```
let user: {
  readonly firstName: string
} = {
  firstName: 'abby'
}

user.firstName // string
user.firstName =
  'abbey with an e' // Error TS2540: Cannot assign to 'firstName' because it
                    // is a read-only property.
```

Object literal notation has one special case: empty object types ({}). Every type—except null and undefined—is assignable to an empty object type, which can make it tricky to use. Try to avoid empty object types when possible:

```
let danger: {}
danger = {}
danger = {x: 1}
danger = []
danger = 2
```

As a final note on objects, it's worth mentioning one last way of typing something as an object: Object. This is pretty much the same as using {}, and is best avoided. [4]

To summarize, there are four ways to declare objects in TypeScript:

1. Object literal notation (like {a: string}), also called a *shape*. Use this when you know which fields your object could have, or when all of your object's values will have the same type.

2. Empty object literal notation ({}). Try to avoid this.

3. The object type. Use this when you just want an object, and don't care about which fields it has.

4. The Object type. Try to avoid this.

In your TypeScript programs, you should almost always stick to the first way and the third way. Be careful to avoid the second and fourth ways—use a linter to warn about them, complain about them in code reviews, print posters—use your team's preferred tool to keep them far away from your codebase.

---

4 There's one minor technical difference: {} lets you define whatever types you want for built-in methods on the Object prototype, like .toString and .hasOwnProperty (head over to MDN (*https://mzl.la/2VSuDJz*) to learn more about prototypes), while Object enforces that the types you declare are assignable to those on Object's prototype. For example, this code typechecks: let a: {} = {toString() { return 3 }}. But if you change the type annotation to Object, TypeScript complains: let b: Object = {toString() { return 3 }} results in Error TS2322: Type 'number' is not assignable to type 'string'.

Table 3-1 is a handy reference for options 2–4 in the previous list.

Table 3-1. Is the value a valid object?

Value	{}	object	Object
{}	Yes	Yes	Yes
['a']	Yes	Yes	Yes
function () {}	Yes	Yes	Yes
new String('a')	Yes	Yes	Yes
'a'	Yes	No	Yes
1	Yes	No	Yes
Symbol('a')	Yes	No	Yes
null	No	No	No
undefined	No	No	No

Intermission: Type Aliases, Unions, and Intersections

You are quickly becoming a grizzled TypeScript programmer. You have seen several types and how they work, and are now familiar with the concepts of type systems, types, and safety. It's time we go deeper.

As you know, if you have a value, you can perform certain operations on it, depending on what its type permits. For example, you can use + to add two numbers, or .toUpperCase to uppercase a string.

If you have a *type*, you can perform some operations on it too. I'm going to introduce a few type-level operations here—there are more to come later in the book, but these are so common that I want to introduce them as early as possible.

Type aliases

Just like you can use variable declarations (let, const, and var) to declare a variable that aliases a value, you can declare a type alias that points to a type. It looks like this:

```
type Age = number

type Person = {
  name: string
  age: Age
}
```

Age is but a number. It can also help make the definition of the Person shape easier to understand. Aliases are never inferred by TypeScript, so you have to type them explicitly:

```
let age: Age = 55

let driver: Person = {
  name: 'James May'
  age: age
}
```

Because Age is just an alias for number, that means it's also assignable to number, so we can rewrite this as:

```
let age = 55

let driver: Person = {
  name: 'James May'
  age: age
}
```

Wherever you see a type alias used, you can substitute in the type it aliases without changing the meaning of your program.

Like JavaScript variable declarations (let, const, and var), you can't declare a type twice:

```
type Color = 'red'
type Color = 'blue'  // Error TS2300: Duplicate identifier 'Color'.
```

And like let and const, type aliases are block-scoped. Every block and every function has its own scope, and inner type alias declarations shadow outer ones:

```
type Color = 'red'

let x = Math.random() < .5

if (x) {
  type Color = 'blue'  // This shadows the Color declared above.
  let b: Color = 'blue'
} else {
  let c: Color = 'red'
}
```

Type aliases are useful for DRYing up repeated complex types,[5] and for making it clear what a variable is used for (some people prefer descriptive type names to descriptive variable names!). When deciding whether or not to alias a type, use the

---

5 The acronym DRY stands for "Don't Repeat Yourself"—the idea that code shouldn't be repetitive. It was introduced by Andrew Hunt and David Thomas in their book *The Pragmatic Programmer: From Journeyman to Master* (Addison-Wesley).

same judgment as when deciding whether or not to pull a value out into its own variable.

Union and intersection types

If you have two things A and B, the *union* of those things is their sum (everything in A or B or both), and the *intersection* is what they have in common (everything in both A and B). The easiest way to think about this is with sets. In Figure 3-2 I represent sets as circles. On the left is the union, or *sum*, of the two sets; on the right is their intersection, or *product*.

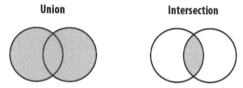

Union   **Intersection**

Figure 3-2. Union (|) and intersection (&)

TypeScript gives us special type operators to describe unions and intersections of types: | for union and & for intersection. Since types are a lot like sets, we can think of them in the same way:

```
type Cat = {name: string, purrs: boolean}
type Dog = {name: string, barks: boolean, wags: boolean}
type CatOrDogOrBoth = Cat | Dog
type CatAndDog = Cat & Dog
```

If something is a CatOrDogOrBoth, what do you know about it? You know that it has a name property that's a string, and not much else. On the flip side, what can you assign to a CatOrDogOrBoth? Well, a Cat, a Dog, or both:

```
// Cat
let a: CatOrDogOrBoth = {
  name: 'Bonkers',
  purrs: true
}

// Dog
a = {
  name: 'Domino',
  barks: true,
  wags: true
}

// Both
a = {
  name: 'Donkers',
  barks: true,
  purrs: true,
```

```
  wags: true
}
```

This is worth reiterating: a value with a union type (|) isn't necessarily one specific member of your union; in fact, it can be both members at once![6]

On the other hand, what do you know about CatAndDog? Not only does your canine-feline hybrid super-pet have a name, but it can purr, bark, and wag:

```
let b: CatAndDog = {
  name: 'Domino',
  barks: true,
  purrs: true,
  wags: true
}
```

Unions come up naturally a lot more often than intersections do. Take this function, for example:

```
function trueOrNull(isTrue: boolean) {
  if (isTrue) {
    return 'true'
  }
  return null
}
```

What is the type of the value this function returns? Well, it might be a string, or it might be null. We can express its return type as:

```
type Returns = string | null
```

How about this one?

```
function(a: string, b: number) {
  return a || b
}
```

If a is truthy then the return type is string, and otherwise it's number: in other words, string | number.

The last place where unions come up naturally is in arrays (specifically the heterogeneous kind), which we'll talk about next.

Arrays

Like in JavaScript, TypeScript arrays are special kinds of objects that support things like concatenation, pushing, searching, and slicing. It's example time:

---

6 Jump ahead to "Discriminated union types" on page 128 to learn how to hint to TypeScript that your union is disjoint and a value of that union's type has to be one or the other, and not both.

```
let a = [1, 2, 3]             // number[]
var b = ['a', 'b']            // string[]
let c: string[] = ['a']       // string[]
let d = [1, 'a']              // (string | number)[]
const e = [2, 'b']            // (string | number)[]

let f = ['red']
f.push('blue')
f.push(true)                  // Error TS2345: Argument of type 'true' is not
                              // assignable to parameter of type 'string'.

let g = []                    // any[]
g.push(1)                     // number[]
g.push('red')                 // (string | number)[]

let h: number[] = []          // number[]
h.push(1)                     // number[]
h.push('red')                 // Error TS2345: Argument of type '"red"' is not
                              // assignable to parameter of type 'number'.
```

TypeScript supports two syntaxes for arrays: `T[]` and `Array<T>`.
They are identical both in meaning and in performance. This book
uses `T[]` syntax for its terseness, but you should pick whichever
style you like for your own code.

As you read through these examples, notice that everything but c and h is implicitly typed. You'll also notice that TypeScript has rules about what you can and can't put in an array.

The general rule of thumb is to keep arrays *homogeneous*. That is, don't mix apples and oranges and numbers in a single array—try to design your programs so that every element of your array has the same type. The reason is that otherwise, you're going to have to do more work to prove to TypeScript that what you're doing is safe.

To see why things are easier when your arrays are homogeneous, take a look at example f. I initialized an array with the string `'red'` (at the point when I declared the array it contained just strings, so TypeScript inferred that it must be an array of strings). I then pushed `'blue'` onto it; `'blue'` is a string, so TypeScript let it pass. Then I tried to push `true` onto the array, but that failed! Why? Because f is an array of strings, and `true` is not a string.

On the other hand, when I initialized d I gave it a `number` and a `string`, so TypeScript inferred that it must be an array of type `number | string`. Because each element might be either a number or a string, you have to check which it is before using it. For example, say you want to map over that array, converting every letter to uppercase and tripling every number:

```
let d = [1, 'a']

d.map(_ => {
  if (typeof _ === 'number') {
    return _ * 3
  }
  return _.toUpperCase()
})
```

You have to query the type of each item with `typeof`, checking if it's a `number` or a `string` before you can do anything with it.

Like with objects, creating arrays with `const` won't hint to TypeScript to infer their types more narrowly. That's why TypeScript inferred both `d` and `e` to be arrays of `number | string`.

`g` is the special case: when you initialize an empty array, TypeScript doesn't know what type the array's elements should be, so it gives you the benefit of the doubt and makes them `any`. As you manipulate the array and add elements to it, TypeScript starts to piece together your array's type. Once your array leaves the scope it was defined in (for example, if you declared it in a function, then returned it), TypeScript will assign it a final type that can't be expanded anymore:

```
function buildArray() {
  let a = []              // any[]
  a.push(1)               // number[]
  a.push('x')             // (string | number)[]
  return a
}

let myArray = buildArray()  // (string | number)[]
myArray.push(true)          // Error 2345: Argument of type 'true' is not
                            // assignable to parameter of type 'string | number'.
```

So as far as uses of `any` go, this one shouldn't make you sweat too much.

Tuples

Tuples are subtypes of `array`. They're a special way to type arrays that have fixed lengths, where the values at each index have specific, known types. Unlike most other types, tuples have to be explicitly typed when you declare them. That's because the JavaScript syntax is the same for tuples and arrays (both use square brackets), and TypeScript already has rules for inferring array types from square brackets:

```
let a: [number] = [1]

// A tuple of [first name, last name, birth year]
let b: [string, string, number] = ['malcolm', 'gladwell', 1963]

b = ['queen', 'elizabeth', 'ii', 1926]  // Error TS2322: Type 'string' is not
                                        // assignable to type 'number'.
```

Tuples support optional elements too. Just like in object types, ? means "optional":

```
// An array of train fares, which sometimes vary depending on direction
let trainFares: [number, number?][] = [
  [3.75],
  [8.25, 7.70],
  [10.50]
]

// Equivalently:
let moreTrainFares: ([number] | [number, number])[] = [
  // ...
]
```

Tuples also support rest elements, which you can use to type tuples with minimum lengths:

```
// A list of strings with at least 1 element
let friends: [string, ...string[]] = ['Sara', 'Tali', 'Chloe', 'Claire']

// A heterogeneous list
let list: [number, boolean, ...string[]] = [1, false, 'a', 'b', 'c']
```

Not only do tuple types safely encode heterogeneous lists, but they also capture the length of the list they type. These features buy you significantly more safety than plain old arrays—use them often.

Read-only arrays and tuples

While regular arrays are mutable (meaning you can .push onto them, .splice them, and update them in place), which is probably what you want most of the time, sometimes you want an immutable array—one that you can update to produce a new array, leaving the original unchanged.

TypeScript comes with a `readonly` array type out of the box, which you can use to create immutable arrays. Read-only arrays are just like regular arrays, but you can't update them in place. To create a read-only array, use an explicit type annotation; to update a read-only array, use nonmutating methods like .concat and .slice instead of mutating ones like .push and .splice:

```
let as: readonly number[] = [1, 2, 3]      // readonly number[]
let bs: readonly number[] = as.concat(4)  // readonly number[]
let three = bs[2]                          // number
as[4] = 5              // Error TS2542: Index signature in type
                       // 'readonly number[]' only permits reading.
as.push(6)             // Error TS2339: Property 'push' does not
                       // exist on type 'readonly number[]'.
```

Like `Array`, TypeScript comes with a couple of longer-form ways to declare read-only arrays and tuples:

```
type A = readonly string[]              // readonly string[]
type B = ReadonlyArray<string>          // readonly string[]
type C = Readonly<string[]>             // readonly string[]

type D = readonly [number, string]      // readonly [number, string]
type E = Readonly<[number, string]>     // readonly [number, string]
```

Which syntax you use—the terser `readonly` modifier, or the longer-form `Readonly` or `ReadonlyArray` utilities—is a matter of taste.

Note that while read-only arrays can make your code easier to reason about in some cases by avoiding mutability, they are backed by regular JavaScript arrays. That means even small updates to an array result in having to copy the original array first, which can hurt your application's runtime performance if you're not careful. For small arrays this overhead is rarely noticeable, but for bigger arrays, the overhead can become significant.

 If you plan to make heavy use of immutable arrays, consider reaching for a more efficient implementation, like Lee Byron's excellent `immutable` (*https://www.npmjs.com/package/immutable*).

null, undefined, void, and never

JavaScript has two values to represent an absence of something: `null` and `undefined`. TypeScript supports both of these as values, and it also has types for them—any guess what they're called? You got it, the types are called `null` and `undefined` too.

They're both special types, because in TypeScript the only thing of type `undefined` is the value `undefined`, and the only thing of type `null` is the value `null`.

JavaScript programmers usually use the two interchangeably, though there is a subtle semantic difference worth mentioning: `undefined` means that something hasn't been defined yet, and `null` means an absence of a value (like if you tried to compute a value, but ran into an error along the way). These are just conventions and Type-Script doesn't hold you to them, but it can be a useful distinction to make.

In addition to `null` and `undefined`, TypeScript also has `void` and `never`. These are really specific, special-purpose types that draw even finer lines between the different kinds of things that don't exist: `void` is the return type of a function that doesn't explicitly return anything (for example, `console.log`), and `never` is the type of a function that never returns at all (like a function that throws an exception, or one that runs forever):

```
// (a) A function that returns a number or null
function a(x: number) {
  if (x < 10) {
```

```
    return x
  }
  return null
}

// (b) A function that returns undefined
function b() {
  return undefined
}

// (c) A function that returns void
function c() {
  let a = 2 + 2
  let b = a * a
}

// (d) A function that returns never
function d() {
  throw TypeError('I always error')
}

// (e) Another function that returns never
function e() {
  while (true) {
    doSomething()
  }
}
```

(a) and (b) explicitly return `null` and `undefined`, respectively. (c) returns `undefined`, but it doesn't do so with an explicit `return` statement, so we say it returns `void`. (d) throws an exception, and (e) runs forever—neither will ever return, so we say their return type is `never`.

If `unknown` is the supertype of every other type, then `never` is the subtype of every other type. We call it a *bottom type*. That means it's assignable to every other type, and a value of type `never` can be used anywhere safely. This has mostly theoretical significance,[7] but is something that will come up when you talk about TypeScript with other language nerds.

Table 3-2 summarizes how the four absence types are used.

---

7 The way to think about a bottom type is as a type that has no values. A bottom type corresponds to a mathematical proposition that's always false.

Table 3-2. Types that mean an absence of something

Type	Meaning
null	Absence of a value
undefined	Variable that has not been assigned a value yet
void	Function that doesn't have a `return` statement
never	Function that never returns

Strict null Checking

In older versions of TypeScript (or with TSC's `strictNullChecks` option set to `false`), null behaves a little differently: it is a subtype of all types, except never. That means every type is nullable, and you can never really trust the type of anything without first checking if it's null or not. For example, if someone passes the variable pizza to your function and you want to call the method .addAnchovies on it, you first have to check if your pizza is null before you can add delicious tiny fish to it. In practice this is really tedious to do with every single variable, so people often forget to actually check first. Then, when something really is null, you get a dreaded null pointer exception at runtime:

```
function addDeliciousFish(pizza: Pizza) {
  return pizza.addAnchovies()  // Uncaught TypeError: Cannot read
}                              // property 'addAnchovies' of null

// TypeScript lets this fly with strictNullChecks = false
addDeliciousFish(null)
```

null has been called the "billion dollar mistake" (*http://bit.ly/2WEdZNO*) by the guy that introduced it in the 1960s. The problem with null is it's something that most languages' type systems can't express and don't check for; so when a programmer tries to do something with a variable that they thought was defined but it actually turns out to be null at runtime, the code throws a runtime exception!

Why? Don't ask me, I'm just the guy writing this book. But languages are coming around to encoding null in their type systems, and TypeScript is a great example of how to do it right. If the goal is to catch as many bugs as possible at compile time before your users encounter them, then being able to check for null in the type system is indispensable.

Enums

Enums are a way to *enumerate* the possible values for a type. They are unordered data structures that map keys to values. Think of them like objects where the keys are

```
let d = Language[6]        // Error TS2476: A const enum member can only be
                           // accessed using a string literal.
```

A const enum doesn't let you do reverse lookups, and so behaves a lot like a regular JavaScript object. It also doesn't generate any JavaScript code by default, and instead inlines the enum member's value wherever it's used (for example, TypeScript will replace every occurrence of Language.Spanish with its value, 1).

 TSC Flag: preserveConstEnums

const enum inlining can lead to safety issues when you import a const enum from someone else's TypeScript code: if the enum author updates their const enum after you've compiled your Type-Script code, then your version of the enum and their version might point to different values at runtime, and TypeScript will be none the wiser.

If you use const enums, be careful to avoid inlining them and to only use them in TypeScript programs that you control: avoid using them in programs that you're planning to publish to NPM, or to make available for others to use as a library.

To enable runtime code generation for const enums, switch the preserveConstEnums TSC setting to true in your *tsconfig.json*:

```
{
  "compilerOptions": {
    "preserveConstEnums": true
  }
}
```

Let's see how we use const enums:

```
const enum Flippable {
  Burger,
  Chair,
  Cup,
  Skateboard,
  Table
}

function flip(f: Flippable) {
  return 'flipped it'
}

flip(Flippable.Chair)    // 'flipped it'
flip(Flippable.Cup)      // 'flipped it'
flip(12)                 // 'flipped it' (!!!)
```

Everything looks great—Chairs and Cups work exactly as you expect... until you realize that all numbers are also assignable to enums! That behavior is an unfortunate consequence of TypeScript's assignability rules, and to fix it you have to be extra careful to only use string-valued enums:

```
const enum Flippable {
  Burger = 'Burger',
  Chair = 'Chair',
  Cup = 'Cup',
  Skateboard = 'Skateboard',
  Table = 'Table'
}

function flip(f: Flippable) {
  return 'flipped it'
}

flip(Flippable.Chair)    // 'flipped it'
flip(Flippable.Cup)      // 'flipped it'
flip(12)                 // Error TS2345: Argument of type '12' is not
                         // assignable to parameter of type 'Flippable'.
flip('Hat')              // Error TS2345: Argument of type '"Hat"' is not
                         // assignable to parameter of type 'Flippable'.
```

All it takes is one pesky numeric value in your enum to make the whole enum unsafe.

Because of all the pitfalls that come with using enums safely, I recommend you stay away from them—there are plenty of better ways to express yourself in TypeScript.

And if a coworker insists on using enums and there's nothing you can do to change their mind, be sure to ninja-merge a few TSLint rules while they're out to warn about numeric values and non-const enums.

Summary

In short, TypeScript comes with a bunch of built-in types. You can let TypeScript infer types for you from your values, or you can explicitly type your values. `const` will infer more specific types, `let` and `var` more general ones. Most types have general and more specific counterparts, the latter subtypes of the former (see Table 3-3).

Table 3-3. Types and their more specific subtypes

Type	Subtype
boolean	Boolean literal
bigint	BigInt literal
number	Number literal
string	String literal

Type	Subtype
symbol	unique symbol
object	Object literal
Array	Tuple
enum	const enum

Exercises

1. For each of these values, what type will TypeScript infer?

   a. `let a = 1042`

   b. `let b = 'apples and oranges'`

   c. `const c = 'pineapples'`

   d. `let d = [true, true, false]`

   e. `let e = {type: 'ficus'}`

   f. `let f = [1, false]`

   g. `const g = [3]`

   h. `let h = null` (try this out in your code editor, then jump ahead to "Type Widening" on page 122 if the result surprises you!)

2. Why does each of these throw the error it does?

   a.

   ```
   let i: 3 = 3
   i = 4 // Error TS2322: Type '4' is not assignable to type '3'.
   ```

   b.

   ```
   let j = [1, 2, 3]
   j.push(4)
   j.push('5') // Error TS2345: Argument of type '"5"' is not
               // assignable to parameter of type 'number'.
   ```

   c.

   ```
   let k: never = 4 // Error TSTS2322: Type '4' is not assignable
                    // to type 'never'.
   ```

   d.

   ```
   let l: unknown = 4
   let m = l * 2 // Error TS2571: Object is of type 'unknown'.
   ```

## CHAPTER 4

Functions

In the last chapter we covered the basics of TypeScript's type system: primitive types, objects, arrays, tuples, and enums, as well as the basics of TypeScript's type inference and how type assignability works. You are now ready for TypeScript's pièce de résistance (or raison d'être, if you're a functional programmer): functions. A few of the topics we'll cover in this chapter are:

- The different ways to declare and invoke functions in TypeScript
- Signature overloading
- Polymorphic functions
- Polymorphic type aliases

Declaring and Invoking Functions

In JavaScript, functions are first-class objects. That means you can use them exactly like you would any other object: assign them to variables, pass them to other functions, return them from functions, assign them to objects and prototypes, write properties to them, read those properties back, and so on. There is a lot you can do with functions in JavaScript, and TypeScript models all of those things with its rich type system.

Here's what a function looks like in TypeScript (this should look familiar from the last chapter):

```
function add(a: number, b: number) {
  return a + b
}
```

You will usually explicitly annotate function parameters (a and b in this example)—TypeScript will always infer types throughout the body of your function, but in most cases it won't infer types for your parameters, except for a few special cases where it can infer types from context (more on that in "Contextual Typing" on page 58). The return type *is* inferred, but you can explicitly annotate it too if you want:

```
function add(a: number, b: number): number {
  return a + b
}
```

 Throughout this book I'll explicitly annotate return types where it helps you, the reader, understand what the function does. Otherwise I'll leave the annotations off because TypeScript already infers them for us, and why would we want to repeat work?

The last example used *named function syntax* to declare the function, but JavaScript and TypeScript support at least five ways to do this:

```
// Named function
function greet(name: string) {
  return 'hello ' + name
}

// Function expression
let greet2 = function(name: string) {
  return 'hello ' + name
}

// Arrow function expression
let greet3 = (name: string) => {
  return 'hello ' + name
}

// Shorthand arrow function expression
let greet4 = (name: string) =>
  'hello ' + name

// Function constructor
let greet5 = new Function('name', 'return "hello " + name')
```

Besides function constructors (which you shouldn't use unless you are being chased by bees because they are totally unsafe),[1] all of these syntaxes are supported by Type-

---

1 Why are they unsafe? If you enter that last example into your code editor, you'll see that its type is Function. What is this Function type? It's an object that is callable (you know, by putting () after it) and has all the prototype methods from Function.prototype. But its parameters and return type are untyped, so you can call the function with any arguments you want, and TypeScript will stand idly by, watching you do something that by all means should be illegal in whatever town you live in.

Script in a typesafe way, and they all follow the same rules around usually mandatory type annotations for parameters and optional annotations for return types.

 A quick refresher on terminology:

- A parameter is a piece of data that a function needs to run, declared as part of a function declaration. Also called a *formal parameter*.
- An argument is a piece of data that you passed to a function when invoking it. Also called an *actual parameter*.

When you invoke a function in TypeScript, you don't need to provide any additional type information—just pass in some arguments, and TypeScript will go to work checking that your arguments are compatible with the types of your function's parameters:

```
add(1, 2)          // evaluates to 3
greet('Crystal')   // evaluates to 'hello Crystal'
```

Of course, if you forgot an argument, or passed an argument of the wrong type, TypeScript will be quick to point it out:

```
add(1)          // Error TS2554: Expected 2 arguments, but got 1.
add(1, 'a')     // Error TS2345: Argument of type '"a"' is not assignable
                // to parameter of type 'number'.
```

Optional and Default Parameters

Like in object and tuple types, you can use ? to mark parameters as optional. When declaring your function's parameters, required parameters have to come first, followed by optional parameters:

```
function log(message: string, userId?: string) {
  let time = new Date().toLocaleTimeString()
  console.log(time, message, userId || 'Not signed in')
}

log('Page loaded') // Logs "12:38:31 PM Page loaded Not signed in"
log('User signed in', 'da763be') // Logs "12:38:31 PM User signed in da763be"
```

Like in JavaScript, you can provide default values for optional parameters. Semantically it's similar to making a parameter optional, in that callers no longer have to pass it in (a difference is that default parameters don't have to be at the end of your list of parameters, while optional parameters do).

For example, we can rewrite `log` as:

```
function log(message: string, userId = 'Not signed in') {
  let time = new Date().toISOString()
  console.log(time, message, userId)
}

log('User clicked on a button', 'da763be')
log('User signed out')
```

Notice how when we give `userId` a default value, we remove its optional annotation, `?`. We also don't have to type it anymore. TypeScript is smart enough to infer the parameter's type from its default value, keeping our code terse and easy to read.

Of course, you can also add explicit type annotations to your default parameters, the same way you can for parameters without defaults:

```
type Context = {
  appId?: string
  userId?: string
}

function log(message: string, context: Context = {}) {
  let time = new Date().toISOString()
  console.log(time, message, context.userId)
}
```

You'll find yourself using default parameters over optional parameters often.

Rest Parameters

If a function takes a list of arguments, you can of course simply pass the list in as an array:

```
function sum(numbers: number[]): number {
  return numbers.reduce((total, n) => total + n, 0)
}

sum([1, 2, 3]) // evaluates to 6
```

Sometimes, you might opt for a *variadic* function API—one that takes a variable number of arguments—instead of a *fixed-arity* API that takes a fixed number of arguments. Traditionally, that required using JavaScript's magic `arguments` object.

`arguments` is "magic" because your JavaScript runtime automatically defines it for you in functions, and assigns to it the list of arguments you passed to your function. Because `arguments` is only array-like, and not a true array, you first have to convert it to an array before you can call the built-in `.reduce` on it:

```
function sumVariadic(): number {
  return Array
    .from(arguments)
```

```
    .reduce((total, n) => total + n, 0)
}

sumVariadic(1, 2, 3) // evaluates to 6
```

But there's one big problem with using `arguments`: it's totally unsafe! If you hover over `total` or `n` in your text editor, you'll see output similar to that shown in Figure 4-1.

```
1
2
3    function sum() {
4      return Array
5        .from(arguments)
6        .reduce((total, n) => total + n, 0)
7    }
8
```

```
.reduce((total, n) => total + n, 0)
}

(parameter) n: any
```

Figure 4-1. arguments is unsafe

This means TypeScript inferred that both n and `total` are of type any, and silently let it pass—that is, until you try to use `sumVariadic`:

```
sumVariadic(1, 2, 3) // Error TS2554: Expected 0 arguments, but got 3.
```

Since we didn't declare that `sumVariadic` takes arguments, from TypeScript's point of view it doesn't take any arguments, so we get a `TypeError` when we try to use it.

So, how can we safely type variadic functions?

Rest parameters to the rescue! Instead of resorting to the unsafe `arguments` magic variable, we can instead use rest parameters to safely make our `sum` function accept any number of arguments:

```
function sumVariadicSafe(...numbers: number[]): number {
  return numbers.reduce((total, n) => total + n, 0)
}

sumVariadicSafe(1, 2, 3) // evaluates to 6
```

That's it! Notice that the only change between this variadic `sum` and our original single-parameter `sum` function is the extra `...` in the parameter list—nothing else has to change, and it's totally typesafe.

A function can have at most one rest parameter, and that parameter has to be the last one in the function's parameter list. For example, take a look at TypeScript's built-in declaration for `console.log` (if you don't know what an `interface` is, don't worry— we'll cover it in Chapter 5). `console.log` takes an optional `message`, and any number of additional arguments to log:

```
interface Console {
  log(message?: any, ...optionalParams: any[]): void
}
```

call, apply, and bind

In addition to invoking a function with parentheses (), JavaScript supports at least two other ways to call a function. Take add from earlier in the chapter:

```
function add(a: number, b: number): number {
  return a + b
}
```

```
add(10, 20)                // evaluates to 30
add.apply(null, [10, 20])  // evaluates to 30
add.call(null, 10, 20)     // evaluates to 30
add.bind(null, 10, 20)()   // evaluates to 30
```

apply binds a value to this within your function (in this example, we bind this to null), and spreads its second argument over your function's parameters. call does the same, but applies its arguments in order instead of spreading.

bind() is similar, in that it *binds* a this-argument and a list of arguments to your function. The difference is that bind does not invoke your function; instead, it returns a new function that you can then invoke with (), .call, or .apply, passing more arguments in to be bound to the so far unbound parameters if you want.

TSC Flag: strictBindCallApply

To safely use .call, .apply, and .bind in your code, be sure to enable the strictBindCallApply option in your *tsconfig.json* (it's automatically enabled if you already enabled strict mode).

Typing this

If you're not coming from JavaScript, you may be surprised to learn that in JavaScript the this variable is defined for every function, not just for those functions that live as methods on classes. this has a different value depending on how you called your function, which can make it notoriously fragile and hard to reason about.

For this reason, a lot of teams ban this everywhere except in class methods—to do this for your codebase too, enable the no-invalid-this TSLint rule.

The reason that this is fragile has to do with the way it's assigned. The general rule is that this will take the value of the thing to the left of the dot when invoking a method. For example:

```
let x = {
  a() {
    return this
  }
}
x.a() // this is the object x in the body of a()
```

But if at some point you reassign a before calling it, the result will change!

```
let a = x.a
a() // now, this is undefined in the body of a()
```

Say you have a utility function for formatting dates that looks like this:

```
function fancyDate() {
  return `${this.getDate()}/${this.getMonth}/${this.getFullYear()}`
}
```

You designed this API in your early days as a programmer (before you learned about function parameters). To use fancyDate, you have to call it with a Date bound to this:

```
fancyDate.call(new Date) // evaluates to "4/14/2005"
```

If you forget to bind a Date to this, you'll get a runtime exception!

```
fancyDate() // Uncaught TypeError: this.getDate is not a function
```

Though exploring all of the semantics of this is beyond the scope of this book,[2] this behavior—that this depends on the way you called a function, and not on the way that you declared it—can be surprising to say the least.

Thankfully, TypeScript has your back. If your function uses this, be sure to declare your expected this type as your function's first parameter (before any additional parameters), and TypeScript will enforce that this really is what you say it is at every call site. this isn't treated like other parameters—it's a reserved word when used as part of a function signature:

```
function fancyDate(this: Date) {
  return `${this.getDate()}/${this.getMonth()}/${this.getFullYear()}`
}
```

---

2 For a deep dive into this, check out Kyle Simpson's You Don't Know JS (*http://shop.oreilly.com/product/0636920033738.do*) series from O'Reilly.

Now here's what happens when we call `fancyDate`:

```
fancyDate.call(new Date) // evaluates to "6/13/2008"

fancyDate() // Error TS2684: The 'this' context of type 'void' is
            // not assignable to method's 'this' of type 'Date'.
```

We took a runtime error, and gave TypeScript enough information to warn about the error at compile time instead.

TSC Flag: noImplicitThis

To enforce that `this` types are always explicitly annotated in functions, enable the `noImplicitThis` setting in your *tsconfig.json*. `strict` mode includes `noImplicitThis`, so if you already have that enabled you're good to go.

Note that `noImplicitThis` doesn't enforce `this`-annotations for classes, or for functions on objects.

Generator Functions

Generator functions (*generators* for short) are a convenient way to, well, *generate* a bunch of values. They give the generator's consumer fine control over the pace at which values are produced. Because they're lazy—that is, they only compute the next value when a consumer asks for it—they can do things that can be hard to do otherwise, like generate infinite lists.

They work like this:

```
function* createFibonacciGenerator() { ❶
  let a = 0
  let b = 1
  while (true) { ❷
    yield a; ❸
    [a, b] = [b, a + b] ❹
  }
}

let fibonacciGenerator = createFibonacciGenerator() // IterableIterator<number>
fibonacciGenerator.next()   // evaluates to {value: 0, done: false}
fibonacciGenerator.next()   // evaluates to {value: 1, done: false}
fibonacciGenerator.next()   // evaluates to {value: 1, done: false}
fibonacciGenerator.next()   // evaluates to {value: 2, done: false}
fibonacciGenerator.next()   // evaluates to {value: 3, done: false}
fibonacciGenerator.next()   // evaluates to {value: 5, done: false}
```

❶ The asterisk (*) before a function's name makes that function a generator. Calling a generator returns an iterable iterator.

❷ Our generator can generate values forever.

❸ Generators use the `yield` keyword to, well, *yield* values. When a consumer asks for the generator's next value (for example, by calling `next`), `yield` sends a result back to the consumer and pauses execution until the consumer asks for the next value. In this way the `while(true)` loop doesn't immediately cause the program to run forever and crash.

❹ To compute the next Fibonacci number, we reassign a to b and b to a + b in a single step.

We called `createFibonacciGenerator`, and that returned an `IterableIterator`. Every time we call `next`, the iterator computes the next Fibonacci number and yields it back to us. Notice how TypeScript is able to infer the type of our iterator from the type of the value we `yield`ed.

You can also explicitly annotate a generator, wrapping the type it yields in an `Itera bleIterator`:

```
function* createNumbers(): IterableIterator<number> {
  let n = 0
  while (1) {
    yield n++
  }
}

let numbers = createNumbers()
numbers.next()            // evaluates to {value: 0, done: false}
numbers.next()            // evaluates to {value: 1, done: false}
numbers.next()            // evaluates to {value: 2, done: false}
```

We won't delve deeper into generators in this book—they're a big topic, and since this book is about TypeScript, I don't want to get sidetracked with JavaScript features. The short of it is they're a super cool JavaScript language feature that TypeScript supports too. To learn more about generators, head to their page on MDN (*https://mzl.la/2UitIk4*).

Iterators

Iterators are the flip side to generators: while generators are a way to produce a stream of values, iterators are a way to consume those values. The terminology can get pretty confusing, so let's start with a couple of definitions.

Iterable

Any object that contains a property called `Symbol.itera tor`, whose value is a function that returns an iterator.

Iterator

Any object that defines a method called `next`, which returns an object with the properties `value` and `done`.

When you create a generator (say, by calling `createFibonacciGenerator`), you get a value back that's *both* an iterable and an iterator—an *iterable iterator*—because it defines both a `Symbol.iterator` property and a `next` method.

You can manually define an iterator or an iterable by creating an object (or a class) that implements `Symbol.iterator` or `next`, respectively. For example, let's define an iterator that returns the numbers 1 through 10:

```
let numbers = {
  *[Symbol.iterator]() {
    for (let n = 1; n <= 10; n++) {
      yield n
    }
  }
}
```

If you type that iterator into your code editor and hover over it, you'll see what Type-Script infers as its type (Figure 4-2).

```
1
2    let numbers: {
3        [Symbol.iterator](): IterableIterator<num
4    ber>;
5    }
6    let numbers = {
7        *[Symbol.iterator]() {
8          for (let n = 1; n ≤ 10; n++) {
9            yield n
10         }
11       }
12   }
```

Figure 4-2. Manually defining an iterator

In other words, `numbers` is an iterable, and calling the generator function `num bers[Symbol.iterator]()` returns an iterable iterator.

Not only can you define your own iterators, but you can use JavaScript's built-in iterators for common collection types—Array, Map, Set, String,[3] and so on—to do things like:

```
// Iterate over an iterator with for-of
for (let a of numbers) {
  // 1, 2, 3, etc.
}

// Spread an iterator
let allNumbers = [...numbers] // number[]

// Destructure an iterator
let [one, two, ...rest] = numbers // [number, number, number[]]
```

Again, we won't go more deeply into iterators in this book. You can read more about iterators and async iterators on MDN (*https://mzl.la/2OAoy1o*).

TSC Flag: downlevelIteration

If you're compiling your TypeScript to a JavaScript version older than ES2015, you can enable custom iterators with the downlevelIteration flag in your *tsconfig.json*.

You may want to keep downlevelIteration disabled if your application is especially sensitive to bundle size: it takes a lot of code to get custom iterators working in older environments. For example, the previous numbers example generates nearly 1 KB of code (gzipped).

Call Signatures

So far, we've learned to type functions' parameters and return types. Now, let's switch gears and talk about how we can express the full types of functions themselves.

Let's revisit sum from the top of this chapter. As a reminder, it looks like this:

```
function sum(a: number, b: number): number {
  return a + b
}
```

What is the type of sum? Well, sum is a function, so its type is:

```
Function
```

---

3 Notably, Object and Number are not iterators.

The `Function` type, as you may have guessed, is not what you want to use most of the time. Like `object` describes all objects, `Function` is a catchall type for all functions, and doesn't tell you anything about the specific function that it types.

How else can we type `sum`? `sum` is a function that takes two `number`s and returns a `number`. In TypeScript we can express its type as:

```
(a: number, b: number) => number
```

This is TypeScript's syntax for a function's type, or *call signature* (also called a *type signature*). You'll notice it looks remarkably similar to an arrow function—this is intentional! When you pass functions around as arguments, or return them from other functions, this is the syntax you'll use to type them.

> The parameter names `a` and `b` just serve as documentation, and don't affect the assignability of a function with that type.

Function call signatures only contain *type-level* code—that is, types only, no values. That means function call signatures can express parameter types, `this` types (see "Typing this" on page 50), return types, rest types, and optional types, and they cannot express default values (since a default value is a value, not a type). And because they have no body for TypeScript to infer from, call signatures require explicit return type annotations.

Type Level and Value Level Code

People use the terms "type-level" and "value-level" a lot when talking about programming with static types, and it helps to have a common vocabulary.

Throughout this book, when I use the term *type-level code*, what I'm referring to is code that consists exclusively of types and type operators. Contrast that with *value-level code*, which is everything else. A rule of thumb is: if it's valid JavaScript code, then it's value-level; if it's valid TypeScript but not valid JavaScript, then it's type-level.[4]

To be extra sure that we're on the same page, let's look at an example—the bold terms here are type-level, and everything else is value-level:

```
function area(radius: number): number | null {
    if (radius < 0) {
```

---

4 The exceptions to this rule of thumb are enums, classes, and namespaces. Enums and classes each generate both a type and a value, and namespaces exist just at the value level. See Appendix C for a complete reference.

```
      return null
    }
    return Math.PI * (radius ** 2)
  }

  let r: number = 3
  let a = area(r)
  if (a !== null) {
    console.info('result:', a)
  }
```

The bold type-level terms are type annotations and the union type operator, |; every-thing else is a value-level term.

Let's go through a few of the examples of functions we've seen so far in this chapter, and pull out their types into standalone call signatures that we'll bind to type aliases:

```
// function greet(name: string)
type Greet = (name: string) => string

// function log(message: string, userId?: string)
type Log = (message: string, userId?: string) => void

// function sumVariadicSafe(...numbers: number[]): number
type SumVariadicSafe = (...numbers: number[]) => number
```

Getting the hang of it? The functions' call signatures look remarkably similar to their implementations. This is intentional, and is a language design choice that makes call signatures easier to reason about.

Let's make the relationship between call signatures and their implementations more concrete. If you have a call signature, how can you declare a function that implements that signature? You simply combine the call signature with a function expression that implements it. For example, let's rewrite Log to use its shiny new signature:

```
type Log = (message: string, userId?: string) => void

let log: Log = (  ❶
  message,  ❷
  userId = 'Not signed in'  ❸
) => {  ❹
  let time = new Date().toISOString()
  console.log(time, message, userId)
}
```

❶ We declare a function expression log, and explicitly type it as type Log.

❷ We don't need to annotate our parameters twice. Since `message` is already annotated as a `string` as part of the definition for `Log`, we don't need to type it again
here. Instead, we let TypeScript infer it for us from `Log`.

❸ We add a default value for `userId`, since we captured `userId`'s type in our signature for `Log`, but we couldn't capture the default value as part of `Log` because `Log`
is a type and can't contain values.

❹ We don't need to annotate our return type again, since we already declared it as
`void` in our `Log` type.

Contextual Typing

Notice that the last example was the first example we've seen where we didn't have to
explicitly annotate our function parameter types. Because we already declared that
`log` is of type `Log`, TypeScript is able to infer from context that `message` has to be of
type `string`. This is a powerful feature of TypeScript's type inference called *contextual typing*.

Earlier in this chapter, we touched on one other place where contextual typing comes
up: callback functions.[5]

Let's declare a function `times` that calls its callback `f` some number of times `n`, passing the current index to `f` each time:

```
function times(
  f: (index: number) => void,
  n: number
) {
  for (let i = 0; i < n; i++) {
    f(i)
  }
}
```

When you call `times`, you don't have to explicitly annotate the function you pass to
`times` if you declare that function inline:

```
times(n => console.log(n), 4)
```

TypeScript infers from context that `n` is a `number`—we declared that `f`'s argument
`index` is a `number` in `times`'s signature, and TypeScript is smart enough to infer that `n`
is that argument, so it must be a `number`.

---

5 If you haven't heard the term "callback" before, all it is is a function that you passed as an argument to
another function.

Note that if we didn't declare f inline, TypeScript wouldn't have been able to infer its type:

```
function f(n) { // Error TS7006: Parameter 'n' implicitly has an 'any' type.
  console.log(n)
}

times(f, 4)
```

Overloaded Function Types

The function type syntax we used in the last section—type Fn = (...) => ...—is a *shorthand call signature*. We can instead write it out more explicitly. Again taking the example of Log:

```
// Shorthand call signature
type Log = (message: string, userId?: string) => void

// Full call signature
type Log = {
  (message: string, userId?: string): void
}
```

The two are completely equivalent in every way, and differ only in syntax.

Would you ever want to use a full call signature over the shorthand? For simple cases like our Log function, you should prefer the shorthand; but for more complicated functions, there are a few good use cases for full signatures.

The first of these is *overloading* a function type. But first, what does it even mean to overload a function?

Overloaded function

A function with multiple call signatures.

In most programming languages, once you declare a function that takes some set of parameters and yields some return type, you can call that function with exactly that set of parameters, and you will always get that same return type back. Not so in JavaScript. Because JavaScript is such a dynamic language, it's a common pattern for there to be multiple ways to call a given function; not only that, but sometimes the output type will actually depend on the input type for an argument!

TypeScript models this dynamism—overloaded function declarations, and a function's output type depending on its input type—with its static type system. We might take this language feature for granted, but it's a really advanced feature for a type system to have!

You can use overloaded function signatures to design really expressive APIs. For example, let's design an API to book a vacation—we'll call it Reserve. Let's start by sketching out its types (with a full type signature this time):

```
type Reserve = {
  (from: Date, to: Date, destination: string): Reservation
}
```

Let's then stub out an implementation for Reserve:

```
let reserve: Reserve = (from, to, destination) => {
  // ...
}
```

So a user who wants to book a trip to Bali has to call our reserve API with a from date, a to date, and "Bali" as a destination.

We might repurpose our API to support one-way trips too:

```
type Reserve = {
  (from: Date, to: Date, destination: string): Reservation
  (from: Date, destination: string): Reservation
}
```

You'll notice that when you try to run this code, TypeScript will give you an error at the point where you implement Reserve (see Figure 4-3).

```
let reserve: Reserve = (from, to, destination) => {
  // ...
type }
  (f
  (f [ts] Type '(from: any, to: any, destination: any) => v
  } oid' is not assignable to type 'Reserve'.

  let reserve: Reserve
let reserve: Reserve = (from, to, destination) => {
  // ...
}
```

Figure 4-3. TypeError when missing a combined overload signature

This is because of the way call signature overloading works in TypeScript. If you declare a set of overload signatures for a function f, from a caller's point of view f's type is the union of those overload signatures. But from f's *implementation's* point of view, there needs to be a single, combined type that can actually be implemented. You need to manually declare this combined call signature when implementing f—it won't be inferred for you. For our Reserve example, we can update our reserve function like this:

```
type Reserve = {
  (from: Date, to: Date, destination: string): Reservation
  (from: Date, destination: string): Reservation
} ❶
```

```
let reserve: Reserve = (
  from: Date,
  toOrDestination: Date | string,
  destination?: string
) => { ❷
  // ...
}
```

❶ We declare two overloaded function signatures.

❷ The implementation's signature is the result of us manually combining the two
    overload signatures (in other words, we computed Signature1 | Signature2 by
    hand). Note that the combined signature isn't visible to functions that call
    reserve; from a consumer's point of view, Reserve's signature is:

```
type Reserve = {
  (from: Date, to: Date, destination: string): Reservation
  (from: Date, destination: string): Reservation
}
```

Notably, this doesn't include the combined signature we created:

```
// Wrong!
type Reserve = {
  (from: Date, to: Date, destination: string): Reservation
  (from: Date, destination: string): Reservation
  (from: Date, toOrDestination: Date | string,
    destination?: string): Reservation
}
```

Since reserve might be called in either of two ways, when you implement reserve
you have to prove to TypeScript that you checked how it was called:[6]

```
let reserve: Reserve = (
  from: Date,
  toOrDestination: Date | string,
  destination?: string
) => {
  if (toOrDestination instanceof Date && destination !== undefined) {
    // Book a one-way trip
  } else if (typeof toOrDestination === 'string') {
    // Book a round trip
```

---

6 To learn more, jump ahead to "Refinement" on page 126.

```
    }
  }
```

Overloads come up naturally in browser DOM APIs. The `createElement` DOM API,
for example, is used to create a new HTML element. It takes a string corresponding
to an HTML tag and returns a new HTML element of that tag's type. TypeScript
comes with built-in types for each HTML element. These include:

- `HTMLAnchorElement` for `<a>` elements
- `HTMLCanvasElement` for `<canvas>` elements

- HTMLTableElement for \<table\> elements

Overloaded call signatures are a natural way to model how createElement works. Think about how you might type createElement (try to answer this by yourself before you read on!).

The answer:

```
type CreateElement = {
  (tag: 'a'): HTMLAnchorElement ❶
  (tag: 'canvas'): HTMLCanvasElement
  (tag: 'table'): HTMLTableElement
  (tag: string): HTMLElement ❷
}

let createElement: CreateElement = (tag: string): HTMLElement => { ❸
  // ...
}
```

❶ We overload on the parameter's type, matching on it with string literal types.

❷ We add a catchall case: if the user passed a custom tag name, or a cutting-edge experimental tag name that hasn't made its way into TypeScript's built-in type declarations yet, we return a generic HTMLElement. Since TypeScript resolves overloads in the order they were declared,[7] when you call createElement with a string that doesn't have a specific overload defined (e.g., createEle ment('foo')), TypeScript will fall back to HTMLElement.

❸ To type the implementation's parameter, we combine all the types that parameter might have in createElement's overload signatures, resulting in 'a' | 'can vas' | 'table' | string. Since the three string literal types are all subtypes of string, the type reduces to just string.

---

7 Mostly—TypeScript hoists literal overloads above nonliteral ones, before resolving them in order. You might not want to depend on this feature, though, since it can make your overloads hard to understand for other engineers who aren't familiar with this behavior.

In all of the examples in this section we overloaded function expressions. But what if we want to overload a function declaration? As always, TypeScript has your back, with an equivalent syntax for function declarations. Let's rewrite our `createElement` overloads:

```
function createElement(tag: 'a'): HTMLAnchorElement
function createElement(tag: 'canvas'): HTMLCanvasElement
function createElement(tag: 'table'): HTMLTableElement
function createElement(tag: string): HTMLElement {
  // ...
}
```

Which syntax you use is up to you, and depends on what kind of function you're overloading (function expression or function declarations).

Full type signatures aren't limited to overloading how you call a function. You can also use them to model properties on functions. Since JavaScript functions are just callable objects, you can assign properties to them to do things like:

```
function warnUser(warning) {
  if (warnUser.wasCalled) {
    return
  }
  warnUser.wasCalled = true
  alert(warning)
}
warnUser.wasCalled = false
```

That is, we show the user a warning, and we don't show a warning more than once. Let's use TypeScript to type `warnUser`'s full signature:

```
type WarnUser = {
  (warning: string): void
  wasCalled: boolean
}
```

Not only is `warnUser` a function that can be called, but it also has a property `wasCalled` that's a `boolean`.

Polymorphism

So far in this book, we've been talking about the hows and whys of concrete types, and functions that use concrete types. What's a *concrete type*? It so happens that every type we've seen so far is concrete:

- `boolean`
- `string`

- Date[]
- {a: number} | {b: string}
- (numbers: number[]) => number

Concrete types are useful when you know precisely what type you're expecting, and want to verify that type was actually passed. But sometimes, you don't know what type to expect beforehand, and you don't want to restrict your function's behavior to a specific type!

As an example of what I mean, let's implement `filter`. You use `filter` to iterate over an array and refine it; in JavaScript, it might look like this:

```
function filter(array, f) {
  let result = []
  for (let i = 0; i < array.length; i++) {
    let item = array[i]
    if (f(item)) {
      result.push(item)
    }
  }
  return result
}

filter([1, 2, 3, 4], _ => _ < 3) // evaluates to [1, 2]
```

Let's start by pulling out `filter`'s full type signature, and adding some placeholder unknowns for the types:

```
type Filter = {
  (array: unknown, f: unknown) => unknown[]
}
```

Now, let's try to fill in the types with, say, `number`:

```
type Filter = {
  (array: number[], f: (item: number) => boolean): number[]
}
```

Typing the array's elements as `number` works well for this example, but `filter` is meant to be a generic function—you can filter arrays of numbers, strings, objects, other arrays, anything. The signature we wrote works for arrays of numbers, but it doesn't work for arrays of other types of elements. Let's try to use an overload to extend it to work on arrays of strings too:

```
type Filter = {
  (array: number[], f: (item: number) => boolean): number[]
  (array: string[], f: (item: string) => boolean): string[]
}
```

So far so good (though it might get messy to write out an overload for every type). What about arrays of objects?

```
type Filter = {
  (array: number[], f: (item: number) => boolean): number[]
  (array: string[], f: (item: string) => boolean): string[]
  (array: object[], f: (item: object) => boolean): object[]
}
```

This might look fine at first glance, but let's try to use it to see where it breaks down. If you implement a filter function with that signature (that is, filter: Filter), and try to use it, you'll get:

```
let names = [
  {firstName: 'beth'},
  {firstName: 'caitlyn'},
  {firstName: 'xin'}
]

let result = filter(
  names,
  _ => _.firstName.startsWith('b')
) // Error TS2339: Property 'firstName' does not exist on type 'object'.

result[0].firstName // Error TS2339: Property 'firstName' does not exist
                    // on type 'object'.
```

At this point, it should make sense why TypeScript is throwing this error. We told TypeScript that we might pass an array of numbers, strings, or objects to filter. We passed an array of objects, but remember that object doesn't tell you anything about the shape of the object. So each time we try to access a property on an object in the array, TypeScript throws an error, because we didn't tell it what specific shape the object has.

What to do?

If you come from a language that supports generic types, then by now you are rolling your eyes and shouting, "THAT'S WHAT GENERICS ARE FOR!" The good news is, you're spot on (the bad news is, you just woke up the neighbors' kid with your shouting).

In case you haven't worked with generic types before, I'll define them first, then give an example with our filter function.

Generic type parameter

A placeholder type used to enforce a type-level constraint in multiple places. Also known as *polymorphic type parameter*.

Going back to our `filter` example, here is what its type looks like when we rewrite it with a generic type parameter T:

```
type Filter = {
  <T>(array: T[], f: (item: T) => boolean): T[]
}
```

What we've done here is say: "This function `filter` uses a generic type parameter T; we don't know what this type will be ahead of time, so TypeScript if you can infer what it is each time we call `filter` that would be swell." TypeScript infers T from the type we pass in for `array`. Once TypeScript infers what T is for a given call to `filter`, it substitutes that type in for every T it sees. T is like a placeholder type, to be filled in by the typechecker from context; it *parameterizes* `Filter`'s type, which is why we call it a generic type *parameter*.

Because it's such a mouthful to say "generic type parameter" every time, people often shorten it to just "generic type," or simply "generic." I'll use the terms interchangeably throughout this book.

The funny-looking angle brackets, `<>`, are how you declare generic type parameters (think of them like the `type` keyword, but for generic types); where you place the angle brackets scopes the generics (there are just a few places you can put them), and TypeScript makes sure that within their scope, all instances of the generic type parameters are eventually bound to the same concrete types. Because of where the angle brackets are in this example, TypeScript will bind concrete types to our generic T when we call `filter`. And it will decide which concrete type to bind to T depending on what we called `filter` with. You can declare as many comma-separated generic type parameters as you want between a pair of angle brackets.

T is just a type name, and we could have used any other name instead: A, Zebra, or l33t. By convention, people use uppercase single-letter names starting with the letter T and continuing to U, V, W, and so on depending on how many generics they need.

If you're declaring a lot of generics in a row or are using them in a complicated way, consider deviating from this convention and using more descriptive names like Value or WidgetType instead.

Some people prefer to start at A instead of T. Different programming language communities prefer one or the other, depending on their heritage: functional language users prefer A, B, C, and so on because of their likeness to the Greek letters α, β, and γ that you might find in math proofs; object-oriented language users tend to use T for "Type." TypeScript, though it supports both programming styles, uses the latter convention.

Like a function's parameter gets re-bound every time you call that function, so each call to filter gets its own binding for T:

```
type Filter = {
  <T>(array: T[], f: (item: T) => boolean): T[]
}

let filter: Filter = (array, f) => // ...

// (a) T is bound to number
filter([1, 2, 3], _ => _ > 2)

// (b) T is bound to string
filter(['a', 'b'], _ => _ !== 'b')

// (c) T is bound to {firstName: string}
let names = [
  {firstName: 'beth'},
  {firstName: 'caitlyn'},
  {firstName: 'xin'}
]
filter(names, _ => _.firstName.startsWith('b'))
```

TypeScript infers these generic bindings from the types of the arguments we passed in. Let's walk through how TypeScript binds T for (a):

1. From the type signature for filter, TypeScript knows that array is an array of elements of some type T.

2. TypeScript notices that we passed in the array [1, 2, 3], so T must be number.

3. Wherever TypeScript sees a T, it substitutes in the number type. So the parameter `f: (item: T) => boolean` becomes `f: (item: number) => boolean`, and the return type `T[]` becomes `number[]`.

4. TypeScript checks that the types all satisfy assignability, and that the function we passed in as `f` is assignable to its freshly inferred signature.

Generics are a powerful way to say what your function does in a more general way than what concrete types allow. The way to think about generics is as *constraints*. Just like annotating a function parameter as `n: number` constrains the *value* of the parameter `n` to the type `number`, so using a generic T constrains the *type* of whatever type you bind to T to be the same type everywhere that T shows up.

Generic types can also be used in type aliases, classes, and interfaces—we'll use them copiously throughout this book. I'll introduce them in context as we cover more topics.

Use generics whenever you can. They will help keep your code general, reusable, and terse.

When Are Generics Bound?

The place where you declare a generic type doesn't just scope the type, but also dictates when TypeScript will bind a concrete type to your generic. From the last example:

```
type Filter = {
  <T>(array: T[], f: (item: T) => boolean): T[]
}

let filter: Filter = (array, f) =>
  // ...
```

Because we declared `<T>` as part of a call signature (right before the signature's opening parenthesis, `()`, TypeScript will bind a concrete type to T when we actually call a function of type `Filter`.

If we'd instead scoped T to the type alias `Filter`, TypeScript would have required us to bind a type explicitly when we used `Filter`:

```
type Filter<T> = {
  (array: T[], f: (item: T) => boolean): T[]
}

let filter: Filter = (array, f) => // Error TS2314: Generic type 'Filter'
  // ...                            // requires 1 type argument(s).

type OtherFilter = Filter          // Error TS2314: Generic type 'Filter'
                                   // requires 1 type argument(s).
```

```
let filter: Filter<number> = (array, f) =>
  // ...

type StringFilter = Filter<string>
let stringFilter: StringFilter = (array, f) =>
  // ...
```

Generally, TypeScript will bind concrete types to your generic when you use the generic: for functions, it's when you call them; for classes, it's when you instantiate them (more on that in "Polymorphism" on page 100); and for type aliases and interfaces (see "Interfaces" on page 91), it's when you use or implement them.

Where Can You Declare Generics?

For each of TypeScript's ways to declare a call signature, there's a way to add a generic type to it:

```
type Filter = { ❶
  <T>(array: T[], f: (item: T) => boolean): T[]
}
let filter: Filter = // ...

type Filter<T> = { ❷
  (array: T[], f: (item: T) => boolean): T[]
}
let filter: Filter<number> = // ...

type Filter = <T>(array: T[], f: (item: T) => boolean) => T[] ❸
let filter: Filter = // ...

type Filter<T> = (array: T[], f: (item: T) => boolean) => T[] ❹
let filter: Filter<string> = // ...

function filter<T>(array: T[], f: (item: T) => boolean): T[] { ❺
  // ...
}
```

❶ A full call signature, with T scoped to an individual signature. Because T is scoped to a single signature, TypeScript will bind the T in this signature to a concrete type when you call a function of type filter. Each call to filter will get its own binding for T.

❷ A full call signature, with T scoped to *all* of the signatures. Because T is declared as part of Filter's type (and not part of a specific signature's type), TypeScript will bind T when you declare a function of type Filter.

❸ Like ❶, but a shorthand call signature instead of a full one.

❹ Like ❷, but a shorthand call signature instead of a full one.

❺ A named function call signature, with T scoped to the signature. TypeScript will bind a concrete type to T when you call `filter`, and each call to `filter` will get its own binding for T.

As a second example, let's write a `map` function. `map` is pretty similar to `filter`, but instead of removing items from an array, it transforms each item with a mapping function. We'll start by sketching out the implementation:

```
function map(array: unknown[], f: (item: unknown) => unknown): unknown[] {
  let result = []
  for (let i = 0; i < array.length; i++) {
    result[i] = f(array[i])
  }
  return result
}
```

Before you go on, try to think through how you'd make `map` generic, replacing each unknown with some type. How many generics do you need? How do you declare your generics, and scope them to the `map` function? What should the types of `array`, `f`, and the return value be?

Ready? If you didn't try to do it yourself first, I encourage you to give it a shot. You can do it. Really!

OK, no more nagging. Here's the answer:

```
function map<T, U>(array: T[], f: (item: T) => U): U[] {
  let result = []
  for (let i = 0; i < array.length; i++) {
    result[i] = f(array[i])
  }
  return result
}
```

We need exactly two generic types: T for the type of the array members going in, and U for the type of the array members going out. We pass in an array of Ts, and a mapping function that takes a T and maps it to a U. Finally, we return an array of Us.

---

filter and map in the Standard Library

Our definitions for `filter` and `map` are awfully similar to the ones that ship with TypeScript:

```
interface Array<T> {
  filter(
    callbackfn: (value: T, index: number, array: T[]) => any,
    thisArg?: any
```

```
  ): T[]
  map<U>(
    callbackfn: (value: T, index: number, array: T[]) => U,
    thisArg?: any
  ): U[]
}
```

We haven't covered interfaces yet, but this definition says that `filter` and `map` are functions on an array of type T. They both take a function `callbackfn`, and a type for `this` inside of the function.

`filter` uses the generic T that's scoped to the entire `Array` interface. `map` uses T too, and adds a second generic U that's scoped just to the `map` function. That means TypeScript will bind a concrete type to T when you create an array, and every call to `filter` and `map` on that array will share that concrete type. Every time you call `map`, that call will get its own binding for U, in addition to having access to the already-bound T.

Many functions in the JavaScript standard library are generic, especially those on `Array`'s prototype. Arrays can contain values of any type, so we call that type T and can say things like ".push takes an argument of type T," or ".map maps from an array of Ts to an array of Us".

Generic Type Inference

In most cases, TypeScript does a great job of inferring generic types for you. When you call the `map` function we wrote earlier, TypeScript infers that T is `string` and U is `boolean`:

```
function map<T, U>(array: T[], f: (item: T) => U): U[] {
  // ...
}

map(
  ['a', 'b', 'c'],   // An array of T
  _ => _ === 'a'     // A function that returns a U
)
```

You can, however, explicitly annotate your generics too. Explicit annotations for generics are all-or-nothing; either annotate every required generic type, or none of them:

```
map    <string, boolean>(
  ['a', 'b', 'c'],
  _ => _ === 'a'
)

map    <string>( // Error TS2558: Expected 2 type arguments, but got 1.
  ['a', 'b', 'c'],
  _ => _ === 'a'
)
```

TypeScript will check that each inferred generic type is assignable to its corresponding explicitly bound generic; if it's not assignable, you'll get an error:

```
// OK, because boolean is assignable to boolean | string
map<string, boolean | string>(
  ['a', 'b', 'c'],
  _ => _ === 'a'
)

map<string, number>(
  ['a', 'b', 'c'],
  _ => _ === 'a'  // Error TS2322: Type 'boolean' is not assignable
)               // to type 'number'.
```

Since TypeScript infers concrete types for your generics from the arguments you pass into your generic function, sometimes you'll hit a case like this:

```
let promise = new Promise(resolve =>
  resolve(45)
)
promise.then(result => // Inferred as {}
  result * 4 // Error TS2362: The left-hand side of an arithmetic operation must
)            // be of type 'any', 'number', 'bigint', or an enum type.
```

What gives? Why did TypeScript infer result to be {}? Because we didn't give it enough information to work with—since TypeScript only uses the types of a generic function's arguments to infer a generic's type, it defaulted T to {}!

To fix this, we have to explicitly annotate Promises generic type parameter:

```
let promise = new Promise<number>(resolve =>
  resolve(45)
)
promise.then(result => // number
  result * 4
)
```

Generic Type Aliases

We already touched on generic type aliases with our Filter example from earlier in the chapter. And if you recall the Array and ReadonlyArray types from the last chapter (see "Read-only arrays and tuples" on page 36), those are generic type aliases too! Let's take a deeper dive into using generics in type aliases by working through a brief example.

Let's define a MyEvent type that describes a DOM event, like a click or a mousedown:

```
type MyEvent<T> = {
  target: T
  type: string
}
```

Note that this is the only valid place to declare a generic type in a type alias: right after the type alias's name, before its assignment (=).

MyEvent's `target` property points to the element the event happened on: a `<button />`, a `<div />`, and so on. For example, you might describe a button event like this:

```
type ButtonEvent = MyEvent<HTMLButtonElement>
```

When you use a generic type like MyEvent, you have to explicitly bind its type parameters when you use the type; they won't be inferred for you:

```
let myEvent: MyEvent<HTMLButtonElement | null> = {
  target: document.querySelector('#myButton'),
  type: 'click'
}
```

You can use MyEvent to build another type—say, TimedEvent. When the generic T in TimedEvent is bound, TypeScript will also bind it to MyEvent:

```
type TimedEvent<T> = {
  event: MyEvent<T>
  from: Date
  to: Date
}
```

You can use a generic type alias in a function's signature, too. When TypeScript binds a type to T, it'll also bind it to MyEvent for you:

```
function triggerEvent<T>(event: MyEvent<T>): void {
  // ...
}

triggerEvent({ // T is Element | null
  target: document.querySelector('#myButton'),
  type: 'mouseover'
})
```

Let's walk through what's happening here step by step:

1. We call `triggerEvent` with an object.

2. TypeScript sees that according to our function's signature, the argument we passed has to have the type MyEvent<T>. It also notices that we defined MyEvent<T> as {target: T, type: string}.

3. TypeScript notices that the target field of the object we passed is document.querySelector('#myButton'). That implies that T must be whatever type document.querySelector('#myButton') is: Element | null. So T is now bound to Element | null.

4. TypeScript goes through and replaces every occurrence of T with Element | null.

5. TypeScript checks that all of our types satisfy assignability. They do, so our code typechecks.

Bounded Polymorphism

 In this section I'm going to use a binary tree as an example. If you haven't worked with binary trees before, don't worry. For our purposes, the basics are:

- A binary tree is a kind of data structure.
- A binary tree consists of nodes.
- A node holds a value, and can point to up to two child nodes.
- A node can be one of two types: a *leaf node* (meaning it has no children) or an *inner node* (meaning it has at least one child).

Sometimes, saying "this thing is of some generic type T and that thing has to have the same type T" just isn't enough. Sometimes you also want to say "the type U should be *at least* T." We call this putting an *upper bound* on U.

Why might we want to do this? Let's say we're implementing a binary tree, and have three types of nodes:

1. Regular TreeNodes
2. LeafNodes, which are TreeNodes that don't have children
3. InnerNodes, which are TreeNodes that do have children

Let's start by declaring types for our nodes:

```
type TreeNode = {
  value: string
}
type LeafNode = TreeNode & {
  isLeaf: true
}
type InnerNode = TreeNode & {
  children: [TreeNode] | [TreeNode, TreeNode]
}
```

What we're saying is: a TreeNode is an object with a single property, value. The LeafNode type has all the properties TreeNode has, plus a property isLeaf that's always `true`. `InnerNode` also has all of `TreeNode`'s properties, plus a `children` property that points to either one or two children.

Next, let's write a `mapNode` function that takes a `TreeNode` and maps over its value, returning a new `TreeNode`. We want to come up with a `mapNode` function that we can use like this:

```
let a: TreeNode = {value: 'a'}
let b: LeafNode = {value: 'b', isLeaf: true}
let c: InnerNode = {value: 'c', children: [b]}

let a1 = mapNode(a, _ => _.toUpperCase()) // TreeNode
let b1 = mapNode(b, _ => _.toUpperCase()) // LeafNode
let c1 = mapNode(c, _ => _.toUpperCase()) // InnerNode
```

Now pause, and think about how you might write a `mapNode` function that takes a subtype of `TreeNode` and returns *that same subtype*. Passing in a `LeafNode` should return a `LeafNode`, an `InnerNode` should return an `InnerNode`, and a `TreeNode` should return a `TreeNode`. Consider how you'd do this before you move on. Is it possible?

Here's the answer:

```
function mapNode<T extends TreeNode>( ❶
  node: T, ❷
  f: (value: string) => string
): T { ❸
  return {
    ...node,
    value: f(node.value)
  }
}
```

❶ `mapNode` is a function that defines a single generic type parameter, `T`. `T` has an upper bound of `TreeNode`. That is, `T` can be either a `TreeNode`, or a subtype of `TreeNode`.

❷ `mapNode` takes two parameters, the first of which is a `node` of type `T`. Because in ❶ we said `node extends TreeNode`, if we passed in something that's not a `TreeNode` —say, an empty object {}, `null`, or an array of `TreeNodes`—that would be an instant red squiggly. `node` has to be either a `TreeNode` or a subtype of `TreeNode`.

❸ `mapNode` returns a value of type `T`. Remember that `T` might be a `TreeNode`, or any subtype of `TreeNode`.

Why did we have to declare `T` that way?

- If we had typed T as just T (leaving off `extends TreeNode`), then `mapNode` would have thrown a compile-time error, because you can't safely read `node.value` on an unbounded node of type T (what if a user passes in a number?).

- If we had left off the T entirely and declared `mapNode` as `(node: TreeNode, f: (value: string) => string) => TreeNode`, then we would have lost information after mapping a node: `a1`, `b1`, and `c1` would all just be `TreeNodes`.

By saying that `T extends TreeNode`, we get to preserve the input node's specific type (`TreeNode`, `LeafNode`, or `InnerNode`), even after mapping it.

Bounded polymorphism with multiple constraints

In the last example, we put a single type constraint on T: T has to be at least a `TreeNode`. But what if you want multiple type constraints?

Just extend the intersection (&) of those constraints:

```
type HasSides = {numberOfSides: number}
type SidesHaveLength = {sideLength: number}

function logPerimeter< ❶
  Shape extends HasSides & SidesHaveLength ❷
>(s: Shape): Shape { ❸
  console.log(s.numberOfSides * s.sideLength)
  return s
}

type Square = HasSides & SidesHaveLength
let square: Square = {numberOfSides: 4, sideLength: 3}
logPerimeter(square) // Square, logs "12"
```

❶ `logPerimeter` is a function that takes a single argument s of type `Shape`.

❷ `Shape` is a generic type that extends both the `HasSides` type and the `SidesHaveLength` type. In other words, a `Shape` has to at least have sides with lengths.

❸ `logPerimeter` returns a value of the exact same type you gave it.

Using bounded polymorphism to model arity

Another place where you'll find yourself using bounded polymorphism is to model variadic functions (functions that take any number of arguments). For example, let's implement our own version of JavaScript's built-in `call` function (as a reminder, `call` is a function that takes a function and a variable number of arguments, and applies those arguments to the function).[8] We'll define and use it like this, using unknown for the types we'll fill in later:

```
function call(
  f: (...args: unknown[]) => unknown,
  ...args: unknown[]
): unknown {
  return f(...args)
}

function fill(length: number, value: string): string[] {
  return Array.from({length}, () => value)
}

call(fill, 10, 'a') // evaluates to an array of 10 'a's
```

Now let's fill in the unknowns. The constraints we want to express are:

- f should be a function that takes some set of arguments T, and returns some type R. We don't know how many arguments it'll have ahead of time.
- call takes f, along with the same set of arguments T that f itself takes. Again, we don't know exactly how many arguments to expect ahead of time.
- call returns the same type R that f returns.

We'll need two type parameters: T, which is an array of arguments, and R, which is an arbitrary return value. Let's fill in the types:

```
function call<T extends unknown[], R>( ❶
  f: (...args: T) => R, ❷
  ...args: T ❸
): R { ❹
  return f(...args)
}
```

How exactly does this work? Let's walk through it step by step:

❶ call is a variadic function (as a reminder, a variadic function is a function that accepts any number of arguments) that has two type parameters: T and R. T is a subtype of unknown[]; that is, T is an array or tuple of any type.

❷ call's first parameter is a function f. f is also variadic, and its arguments share a type with args: whatever type args is, f arguments have the same exact type.

---

8 To simplify our implementation a little, we're going to design our call function to not take this into account.

❸ In addition to a function f, call has a variable number of additional parameters ...args. args is a rest parameter—that is, a parameter that describes a variable number of arguments. args's type is T, and T has to be an array type (in fact, if we forgot to say that T extends an array type, TypeScript would throw a squiggly at us), so TypeScript will infer a *tuple type* for T based on the specific arguments we passed in for args.

❹ call returns a value of type R (R is bound to whatever type f returns).

Now when we call call, TypeScript will know exactly what the return type is, and it will complain when we pass the wrong number of arguments:

```
let a = call(fill, 10, 'a')      // string[]
let b = call(fill, 10)           // Error TS2554: Expected 3 arguments; got 2.
let c = call(fill, 10, 'a', 'z') // Error TS2554: Expected 3 arguments; got 4.
```

We use a similar technique to take advantage of the way TypeScript infers tuple types for rest parameters to improve type inference for tuples in "Improving Type Inference for Tuples" on page 141.

Generic Type Defaults

Just like you can give function parameters default values, you can give generic type parameters default types. For example, let's revisit the MyEvent type from "Generic Type Aliases" on page 73. As a reminder, we used the type to model DOM events, and it looks like this:

```
type MyEvent<T> = {
  target: T
  type: string
}
```

To create a new event, we have to explicitly bind a generic type to MyEvent, representing the type of HTML element that the event was dispatched on:

```
let buttonEvent: MyEvent<HTMLButtonElement> = {
  target: myButton,
  type: string
}
```

As a convenience for when we don't know the specific element type that MyEvent will be bound to beforehand, we can add a default for MyEvent's generic:

```
type MyEvent<T = HTMLElement> = {
  target: T
  type: string
}
```

We can also use this opportunity to apply what we learned in the last few sections and add a bound to T, to make sure that T is an HTML element:

```
type MyEvent<T extends HTMLElement = HTMLElement> = {
  target: T
  type: string
}
```

Now, we can easily create an event that's not specific to a particular HTML element type, and we don't have to manually bind MyEvents T to HTMLElement when we create the event:

```
let myEvent: MyEvent = {
  target: myElement,
  type: string
}
```

Note that like optional parameters in functions, generic types with defaults have to appear after generic types without defaults:

```
// Good
type MyEvent2<
  Type extends string,
  Target extends HTMLElement = HTMLElement,
> = {
  target: Target
  type: Type
}

// Bad
type MyEvent3<
  Target extends HTMLElement = HTMLElement,
  Type extends string  // Error TS2706: Required type parameters may
> = {                  // not follow optional type parameters.
  target: Target
  type: Type
}
```

Type-Driven Development

With a powerful type system comes great power. When you write in TypeScript, you will often find yourself "leading with the types." This, of course, refers to *type-driven development*.

Type-driven development

A style of programming where you sketch out type signatures first, and fill in values later.

The point of static type systems is to constrain the types of values an expression can hold. The more expressive the type system, the more it tells you about the value contained in that expression. When you apply an expressive type system to a function, the function's type signature might end up telling you most of what you need to know about that function.

Let's look at the type signature for the map function from earlier in this chapter:

```
function map<T, U>(array: T[], f: (item: T) => U): U[] {
  // ...
}
```

Just looking at that signature—even if you've never seen map before—you should have some intuition for what map does: it takes an array of T and a function that maps from a T to a U, and returns an array of U. Notice that you didn't have to see the function's implementation to know that![9]

When you write a TypeScript program, start by defining your functions' type signatures—in other words, *lead with the types*—filling in the implementations later. By sketching out your program out at the type level first, you make sure that everything makes sense at a high level before you get down to your implementations.

You'll notice that so far, we've been doing the opposite: leading with the implementation, then deducing the types. Now that you have a grasp of writing and typing functions in TypeScript, we're going to switch modes, sketching out the types first, and filling in the details later.

Summary

In this chapter we talked about how to declare and call functions, how to type parameters, and how to express common JavaScript function features like default parameters, rest parameters, generator functions, and iterators in TypeScript. We talked about the difference between functions' call signatures and implementations, contextual typing, and the different ways to overload functions. Finally, we covered polymorphism for functions and type aliases in depth: why it's useful, how and where to declare generic types, how TypeScript infers generic types, and how to declare and add bounds and defaults to your generics. We finished off with a short note on type-driven development: what it is, and how you can use your newfound knowledge of function types to do it.

---

[9] There are a few programming languages (like the Haskell-like language Idris) that have built-in constraint solvers with the ability to *automatically* implement function bodies for you from the signatures you write!

Exercises

1. Which parts of a function's type signature does TypeScript infer: the parameters, the return type, or both?

2. Is JavaScript's `arguments` object typesafe? If not, what can you use instead?

3. You want the ability to book a vacation that starts immediately. Update the overloaded `reserve` function from earlier in this chapter ("Overloaded Function Types" on page 59) with a third call signature that takes just a destination, without an explicit start date. Update `reserve`'s implementation to support this new overloaded signature.

4. [Hard] Update our `call` implementation from earlier in the chapter ("Using bounded polymorphism to model arity" on page 77) to *only* work for functions whose second argument is a `string`. For all other functions, your implementation should fail at compile time.

5. Implement a small typesafe assertion library, `is`. Start by sketching out your types. When you're done, you should be able to use it like this:

```
// Compare a string and a string
is('string', 'otherstring') // false

// Compare a boolean and a boolean
is(true, false) // false

// Compare a number and a number
is(42, 42) // true

// Comparing two different types should give a compile-time error
is(10, 'foo') // Error TS2345: Argument of type '"foo"' is not assignable
              // to parameter of type 'number'.

// [Hard] I should be able to pass any number of arguments
is([1], [1, 2], [1, 2, 3]) // false
```

Classes and Interfaces

If you're like most programmers coming from an object-oriented programming language, classes are your bread and butter. Classes are how you organize and think about your code, and they serve as your primary unit of encapsulation. You'll be pleased to learn that TypeScript classes borrow heavily from C#, and support things like visibility modifiers, property initializers, polymorphism, decorators, and interfaces. But because TypeScript classes compile down to regular JavaScript classes, you can also express JavaScript idioms like mixins in a typesafe way.

Some of TypeScript's class features, like property initializers and decorators, are supported by JavaScript classes too,[1] and so generate runtime code. Other features, like visibility modifiers, interfaces, and generics, are TypeScript-only features that just exist at compile time, and don't generate any code when you compile your application to JavaScript.

In this chapter I'll guide you through an extended example of how we work with classes in TypeScript, so that you can gain some intuition not only for TypeScript's object-oriented language features, but for how and why we use them. Try to follow along, entering the code in your code editor as we go.

Classes and Inheritance

We're going to build a chess engine. Our engine will model a game of chess and provide an API for two players to take turns making moves.

---

1 Or are on track to soon be supported by JavaScript classes.

We'll start by sketching out the types:

```
// Represents a chess game
class Game {}

// A chess piece
class Piece {}

// A set of coordinates for a piece
class Position {}
```

There are six types of pieces:

```
// ...
class King extends Piece {}
class Queen extends Piece {}
class Bishop extends Piece {}
class Knight extends Piece {}
class Rook extends Piece {}
class Pawn extends Piece {}
```

Every piece has a color and a current position. In chess, positions are modeled as (letter, number) coordinate pairs; letters run from left to right along the x-axis, numbers from bottom to top along the y-axis (Figure 5-1).

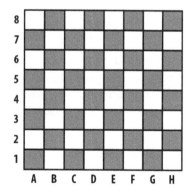

Figure 5-1. Standard algebraic notation in chess: A–H (the x-axis) are called "files" and 1–8 (the inverted y-axis) "ranks"

Let's add color and position to our Piece class:

```
type Color = 'Black' | 'White'
type File = 'A' | 'B' | 'C' | 'D' | 'E' | 'F' | 'G' | 'H'
type Rank = 1 | 2 | 3 | 4 | 5 | 6 | 7 | 8 ❶

class Position {
  constructor(
    private file: File, ❷
    private rank: Rank
  ) {}
}

class Piece {
  protected position: Position ❸
  constructor(
    private readonly color: Color, ❹
    file: File,
    rank: Rank
  ) {
    this.position = new Position(file, rank)
  }
}
```

❶ Since there are relatively few colors, ranks, and files, we can manually enumerate their possible values as type literals. This will let us squeeze out some extra safety by constraining these types' domains from all strings and all numbers to a handful of very specific strings and numbers.

❷ The `private` *access modifier* in the constructor automatically assigns the parameter to `this` (`this.file` and so on), and sets its visibility to private, meaning that code within a Position instance can read and write to it, but code outside of a Position instance can't. Different instances of Position can access each other's private members; instances of any other class—even a subclass of Position—can't.

❸ We declare the instance variable `position` as `protected`. Like `private`, `protected` assigns the property to `this`, but unlike `private`, `protected` makes the property visible both to instances of Piece and to instances of any subclass of Piece. We didn't assign `position` a value when declaring it, so we have to assign a value to it in Piece's constructor function. If we hadn't assigned it a value in the constructor, TypeScript would have told us that the variable is not *definitely assigned*, i.e., we said it's of type T, but it's actually T | undefined because it's not assigned a value in a property initializer or in the constructor—so we would need to update its signature to indicate that it's not necessarily a Position, but it might also be undefined.

❹ new `Piece` takes three parameters: `color`, `file`, and `rank`. We added two modifiers to `color`: `private`, meaning assign it to `this` and make sure it's only accessible from an instance of `Piece`, and `readonly`, meaning that after this initial assignment it can only be read and can't be written anymore.

TSC Flags: strictNullChecks and strictPropertyInitialization

To opt into definite assignment checks for class instance variables, enable `strictNullChecks` and `strictPropertyInitialization` flags in your *tsconfig.json*. If you're already using the `strict` flag, you're good to go.

TypeScript supports three access modifiers for properties and methods on a class:

`public`
> Accessible from anywhere. This is the default access level.

`protected`
> Accessible from instances of this class and its subclasses.

`private`
> Accessible from instances of this class only.

Using access modifiers, you can design classes that don't expose too much information about their implementations, and instead expose well-defined APIs for others to use.

We've defined a `Piece` class, but we don't want users to instantiate a new `Piece` directly—we want them to extend it to create a `Queen`, a `Bishop`, and so on, and instantiate *that*. We can use the type system to enforce that for us, using the `abstract` keyword:

```
// ...
abstract class Piece {
  constructor(
    // ...
```

Now if you try to instantiate a `Piece` directly, TypeScript complains:

```
new Piece('White', 'E', 1)  // Error TS2511: Cannot create an instance
                            // of an abstract class.
```

The `abstract` keyword means that you can't instantiate the class directly, but it doesn't mean you can't define some methods on it:

```
// ...
abstract class Piece {
  // ...
  moveTo(position: Position) {
```

```
      this.position = position
    }
    abstract canMoveTo(position: Position): boolean
  }
```

Our Piece class now:

- Tells its subclasses that they have to implement a method called canMoveTo that is compatible with the given signature. If a class extends Piece but forgets to implement the abstract canMoveTo method, that's a type error at compile time: when you implement an abstract class, you have to implement its abstract methods too.

- Comes with a default implementation for moveTo (which its subclasses can override if they want). We didn't put an access modifier on moveTo, so it's public by default, meaning it's readable and writable from any other code.

Let's update King to implement canMoveTo, to satisfy this new requirement. We'll also implement a distanceFrom function for convenience, so we can easily compute the distance between two pieces:

```
// ...
class Position {
  // ...
  distanceFrom(position: Position) {
    return {
      rank: Math.abs(position.rank - this.rank),
      file: Math.abs(position.file.charCodeAt(0) - this.file.charCodeAt(0))
    }
  }
}

class King extends Piece {
  canMoveTo(position: Position) {
    let distance = this.position.distanceFrom(position)
    return distance.rank < 2 && distance.file < 2
  }
}
```

When we make a new game, we'll automatically create a board and some pieces:

```
// ...
class Game {
  private pieces = Game.makePieces()

  private static makePieces() {
    return [

      // Kings
      new King('White', 'E', 1),
      new King('Black', 'E', 8),

      // Queens
      new Queen('White', 'D', 1),
```

```
      new Queen('Black', 'D', 8),

      // Bishops
      new Bishop('White', 'C', 1),
      new Bishop('White', 'F', 1),
      new Bishop('Black', 'C', 8),
      new Bishop('Black', 'F', 8),

      // ...
    ]
  }
}
```

Because of how strictly we typed `Rank` and `File`, if we had entered another letter (like `'J'`) or an out-of-range number (like `12`), TypeScript would have given us a compile-time error (Figure 5-2).

```
73      return [
74
75        // kings          [ts] Argument of type '"J"' is not assignable
76        new King('White',   to parameter of type 'File'.
77        new King('Black', 'J', 12),
78
```

Figure 5-2. TypeScript helps us stick to valid ranks and files

This is enough to show off how TypeScript classes work—I'll avoid getting into the nitty-gritty details like how to know when a knight can take a piece, how bishops move, and so on. If you're ambitious, see if you can use what we've done so far as a starting point to implement the rest of the game yourself.

To sum up:

- Declare classes with the `class` keyword. Extend them with the `extends` keyword.
- Classes can be either concrete or `abstract`. Abstract classes can have `abstract` methods and `abstract` properties.
- Methods can be `private`, `protected`, or, by default, `public`. They can be instance methods or static methods.
- Classes can have instance properties, which can also be `private`, `protected`, or, by default, `public`. You can declare them in constructor parameters or as property initializers.
- You can mark instance properties as `readonly` when declaring them.

super

Like JavaScript, TypeScript supports `super` calls. If your child class overrides a method defined on its parent class (say, if `Queen` and `Piece` both implement the `take` method), the child instance can make a `super` call to call its parent's version of the method (e.g., `super.take`). There are two kinds of `super` calls:

- Method calls, like `super.take`.
- Constructor calls, which have the special form `super()` and can only be called from a constructor function. If your child class has a constructor function, you must call `super()` from the child's constructor to correctly wire up the class (don't worry, TypeScript will warn you if you forget; it's like a cool futuristic robot elephant in that way).

Note that you can only access a parent class's methods, and not its properties, with `super`.

Using this as a Return Type

Just like you can use `this` as a value, you can also use it as a type (like we did in "Typing this" on page 50). When working with classes, the `this` type can be useful for annotating methods' return types.

For example, let's build a simplified version of ES6's `Set` data structure that supports two operations: adding a number to the set, and checking whether or not a given number is in the set. You use it like this:

```
let set = new Set
set.add(1).add(2).add(3)
set.has(2) // true
set.has(4) // false
```

Let's define the `Set` class, starting with the `has` method:

```
class Set {
  has(value: number): boolean {
    // ...
  }
}
```

How about `add`? When you call `add`, you get back an instance of `Set`. We could type that as:

```
class Set {
  has(value: number): boolean {
    // ...
  }
  add(value: number): Set {
```

```
    // ...
  }
}
```

So far, so good. What happens when we try to subclass Set?

```
class MutableSet extends Set {
  delete(value: number): boolean {
    // ...
  }
}
```

Of course, Set's add method still returns a Set, which we'll need to override with MutableSet for our subclass:

```
class MutableSet extends Set {
  delete(value: number): boolean {
    // ...
  }
  add(value: number): MutableSet {
    // ...
  }
}
```

This can get a bit tedious when working with classes that extend other classes—you have to override the signature for each method that returns this. And if you end up having to override each method to please the typechecker, what's the point of inheriting from your base class at all?

Instead, you can use this as a return type annotation to let TypeScript do the work for you:

```
class Set {
  has(value: number): boolean {
    // ...
  }
  add(value: number): this {
    // ...
  }
}
```

Now, you can remove the add override from MutableSet, since this in Set points to a Set instance, and this in MutableSet points to a MutableSet instance:

```
class MutableSet extends Set {
  delete(value: number): boolean {
    // ...
  }
}
```

This is a really convenient feature for working with chained APIs, like we do in "Builder Pattern" on page 109.

Interfaces

When you use classes, you will often find yourself using them with *interfaces*.

Like type aliases, interfaces are a way to name a type so you don't have to define it inline. Type aliases and interfaces are mostly two syntaxes for the same thing (like function expressions and function declarations), but there are a few small differences. Let's start with what they have in common. Consider the following type alias:

```
type Sushi = {
  calories: number
  salty: boolean
  tasty: boolean
}
```

It's easy to rewrite it as an interface:

```
interface Sushi {
  calories: number
  salty: boolean
  tasty: boolean
}
```

Everywhere you used your Sushi type alias, you can also use your Sushi interface. Both declarations define shapes, and those shapes are assignable to one another (in fact, they're identical!).

Things get more interesting when you start combining types. Let's model another food in addition to Sushi:

```
type Cake = {
  calories: number
  sweet: boolean
  tasty: boolean
}
```

A lot of foods have calories and are tasty—not just Sushi and Cake. Let's pull Food out into its own type, and redefine our foods in terms of it:

```
type Food = {
  calories: number
  tasty: boolean
}
type Sushi = Food & {
  salty: boolean
}
type Cake = Food & {
  sweet: boolean
}
```

Nearly equivalently, you can do that with interfaces too:

```
interface Food {
  calories: number
  tasty: boolean
}
interface Sushi extends Food {
  salty: boolean
}
interface Cake extends Food {
  sweet: boolean
}
```

 Interfaces don't have to extend other interfaces. In fact, an interface can extend any shape: an object type, a class, or another interface.

What are the differences between types and interfaces? There are three, and they're subtle.

The first is that type aliases are more general, in that their righthand side can be any type, including a type expression (a type, and maybe some type operators like & or |); for an interface, the righthand side must be a shape. For example, there is no way to rewrite the following type aliases as interfaces:

```
type A = number
type B = A | string
```

The second difference is that when you extend an interface, TypeScript will make sure that the interface you're extending is assignable to your extension. For example:

```
interface A {
  good(x: number): string
  bad(x: number): string
}

interface B extends A {
  good(x: string | number): string
  bad(x: string): string  // Error TS2430: Interface 'B' incorrectly extends
}                         // interface 'A'. Type 'number' is not assignable
                          // to type 'string'.
```

This is not the case when you use intersection types: if you turn the interfaces from the last example into type aliases and the extends into an intersection (&), TypeScript will do its best to combine your extension with the type it's extending, resulting in an overloaded signature for bad instead of a compile-time error (try it in your code editor!).

When you're modeling inheritance for object types, the assignability check that TypeScript does for interfaces can be a helpful tool to catch errors.

The third difference is that multiple interfaces with the same name in the same scope are automatically merged; multiple *type aliases* with the same name in the same scope will throw a compile-time error. This is a feature called *declaration merging*.

Declaration Merging

Declaration merging is TypeScript's way of automatically combining multiple declarations that share the same name. It came up when we introduced enums ("Enums" on page 39), and it also comes up when working with other features like `namespace` declarations (see "Namespaces" on page 222). In this section we'll briefly introduce declaration merging in the context of interfaces. For a deeper dive, head over to "Declaration Merging" on page 226.

For example, if you declare two identically named User interfaces, then TypeScript will automatically combine them for you into a single interface:

```
// User has a single field, name
interface User {
  name: string
}

// User now has two fields, name and age
interface User {
  age: number
}

let a: User = {
  name: 'Ashley',
  age: 30
}
```

Here's what happens if you repeat that example with type aliases:

```
type User = {  // Error TS2300: Duplicate identifier 'User'.
  name: string
}

type User = {  // Error TS2300: Duplicate identifier 'User'.
  age: number
}
```

Note that the two interfaces can't conflict; if one types property as a T and the other types it as a U, and T and U aren't identical, then you'll get an error:

```
interface User {
  age: string
}

interface User {
  age: number  // Error TS2717: Subsequent property declarations must have
```

```
}                        // the same type. Property 'age' must be of type 'string',
                         // but here has type 'number'.
```

And if your interface declares generics (skip ahead to "Polymorphism" on page 100 to learn more), those generics have to be declared the exact same way for two interfaces to be mergeable—down to the generic's name!

```
interface User<Age extends number> {  // Error TS2428: All declarations of 'User'
  age: Age                             // must have identical type parameters.
}

interface User<Age extends string> {
  age: Age
}
```

Interestingly, this is a rare place where TypeScript checks that two types are not only assignable, but *identical*.

Implementations

When you declare a class, you can use the `implements` keyword to say that it satisfies a particular interface. Like other explicit type annotations, this is a convenient way to add a type-level constraint that your class is implemented correctly as closely as possible to the implementation itself, so that the error from an incorrect implementation doesn't show up downstream where it's less clear why it was thrown. It's also a familiar way to implement common design patterns like adapters, factories, and strategies (see the end of this chapter for some examples).

Here's what that looks like:

```
interface Animal {
  eat(food: string): void
  sleep(hours: number): void
}

class Cat implements Animal {
  eat(food: string) {
    console.info('Ate some', food, '. Mmm!')
  }
  sleep(hours: number) {
    console.info('Slept for', hours, 'hours')
  }
}
```

`Cat` has to implement every method that `Animal` declares, and can implement more methods and properties on top if it wants.

Interfaces can declare instance properties, but they can't declare visibility modifiers (`private`, `protected`, and `public`) and they can't use the `static` keyword. You can also mark instance properties as readonly, just like we did for object types in Objects (in Chapter 3):

```
interface Animal {
  readonly name: string
  eat(food: string): void
  sleep(hours: number): void
}
```

You're not limited to implementing just one interface—you can implement as many as you want:

```
interface Animal {
  readonly name: string
  eat(food: string): void
  sleep(hours: number): void
}

interface Feline {
  meow(): void
}

class Cat implements Animal, Feline {
  name = 'Whiskers'
  eat(food: string) {
    console.info('Ate some', food, '. Mmm!')
  }
  sleep(hours: number) {
    console.info('Slept for', hours, 'hours')
  }
  meow() {
    console.info('Meow')
  }
}
```

All of these features are completely typesafe. If you forget to implement a method or a property, or implement it incorrectly, TypeScript will come to the rescue (see Figure 5-3).

```
10    [ts]
11    Class 'Cat' incorrectly implements interface
12      'Feline'.
13        Property 'meow' is missing in type 'Cat' bu
14    t required in type 'Feline'. [2420]
15
16    • index.tsx(8, 3): 'meow' is declared here.
17    class Cat
18  class Cat implements Animal, Feline {
19    name = 'Whiskers'
20    eat(food: string) {
21      console.info('Ate some', food, '. Mmm!')
22    }
23    sleep(hours: number) {
24      console.info('Slept for', hours, 'hours')
25    }
26  }
```

Figure 5-3. TypeScript throws an error when you forget to implement a required method

Implementing Interfaces Versus Extending Abstract Classes

Implementing an interface is really similar to extending an abstract class. The difference is that interfaces are more general and lightweight, and abstract classes are more special-purpose and feature-rich.

An interface is a way to model a shape. At the value level, that means an object, array, function, class, or class instance. Interfaces do not emit JavaScript code, and only exist at compile time.

An abstract class can only model, well, a class. It emits runtime code that is, you guessed it, a JavaScript class. Abstract classes can have constructors, provide default implementations, and set access modifiers for properties and methods. Interfaces can't do any of those things.

Which one you use depends on your use case. When an implementation is shared among multiple classes, use an abstract class. When you need a lightweight way to say "this class is a T," use an interface.

Classes Are Structurally Typed

Like every other type in TypeScript, TypeScript compares classes by their structure, not by their name. A class is compatible with any other type that shares its shape, including a regular old object that defines the same properties or methods as the class. This is important to keep in mind for those of you coming from C#, Java, Scala, and most other languages where classes are typed nominally. It means that if you have a function that takes a Zebra and you give it a Poodle, TypeScript might not mind:

```
class Zebra {
  trot() {
    // ...
  }
}

class Poodle {
  trot() {
    // ...
  }
}

function ambleAround(animal: Zebra) {
  animal.trot()
}

let zebra = new Zebra
let poodle = new Poodle

ambleAround(zebra)    // OK
ambleAround(poodle)   // OK
```

As the phylogeneticists among you know, a zebra is no poodle—but TypeScript doesn't mind! As long as Poodle is assignable to Zebra, TypeScript is OK with it because from our function's point of view, the two are interchangeable; all that matters is that they implement .trot. If you were using almost any other language that types classes nominally, this code would have raised an error; but TypeScript is structurally typed through and through, so this code is perfectly acceptable.

The exception to this rule is classes with private or protected fields: when checking whether or not a shape is assignable to a class, if the class has any private or protected fields and the shape is not an instance of that class or a subclass of that class, then the shape is not assignable to the class:

```
class A {
  private x = 1
}
class B extends A {}
function f(a: A) {}
```

```
f(new A)    // OK
f(new B)    // OK

f({x: 1})  // Error TS2345: Argument of type '{x: number}' is not
           // assignable to parameter of type 'A'. Property 'x' is
           // private in type 'A' but not in type '{x: number}'.
```

Classes Declare Both Values and Types

Most things that you can express in TypeScript are either values *or* types:

```
// values
let a = 1999
function b() {}

// types
type a = number
interface b {
  (): void
}
```

Types and values are namespaced separately in TypeScript. Depending on how you use a term (a or b in this example), TypeScript knows whether to resolve it to a type or to a value:

```
// ...
if (a + 1 > 3) //... // TypeScript infers from context that you mean the value a
let x: a = 3         // TypeScript infers from context that you mean the type a
```

This *contextual term resolution* is really nice, and lets us do cool things like implement companion types (see "Companion Object Pattern" on page 140).

Classes and enums are special. They are unique because they generate both a type in the type namespace and a value in the value namespace:

```
class C {}
let c: C ❶
  = new C ❷

enum E {F, G}
let e: E ❸
  = E.F ❹
```

❶   In this context, C refers to the instance type of our C class.

❷   In this context, C refers to C the value.

❸   In this context, E refers to the type of our E enum.

❹   In this context, E refers to E the value.

When we work with classes, we need a way to say "this variable should be an instance of this class" and the same goes for enums ("this variable should be a member of this enum"). Because classes and enums generate types at the type level we're able to express this "is-a" relationship easily.[2]

We also need a way to represent a class at runtime, so that we can instantiate it with new, call static methods on it, do metaprogramming with it, and operate on it with instanceof—so a class needs to generate a value too.

In the previous example C refers to an *instance of* the class C. How do you talk about the C class itself? We use the typeof keyword (a type operator provided by TypeScript, which is like JavaScript's value-level typeof but for types).

Let's create a class StringDatabase—the world's simplest database:

```
type State = {
  [key: string]: string
}

class StringDatabase {
  state: State = {}
  get(key: string): string | null {
    return key in this.state ? this.state[key] : null
  }
  set(key: string, value: string): void {
    this.state[key] = value
  }
  static from(state: State) {
    let db = new StringDatabase
    for (let key in state) {
      db.set(key, state[key])
    }
    return db
  }
}
```

What types does this class declaration generate? The instance type StringDatabase:

```
interface StringDatabase {
  state: State
  get(key: string): string | null
  set(key: string, value: string): void
}
```

And the constructor type typeof StringDatabase:

---

2 Because TypeScript is structurally typed, of course, the relationship for classes is more of a "looks-like"—any object that implements the same shape as your class will be assignable to the type of your class.

```
interface StringDatabaseConstructor {
  new(): StringDatabase
  from(state: State): StringDatabase
}
```

That is, `StringDatabaseConstructor` has a single method `.from`, and new-ing the constructor gives a `StringDatabase` instance. Combined, these two interfaces model both the constructor and instance sides of a class.

That `new()` bit is called a *constructor signature*, and is TypeScript's way of saying that a given type can be instantiated with the `new` operator. Because TypeScript is structurally typed, that's the best we can do to describe what a class is: a class is anything that can be new-ed.

In this case the constructor doesn't take any arguments, but you can use it to declare constructors that take arguments too. For example, say we update `StringDatabase` to take an optional initial state:

```
class StringDatabase {
  constructor(public state: State = {}) {}
  // ...
}
```

We could then type `StringDatabase`'s constructor signature as:

```
interface StringDatabaseConstructor {
  new(state?: State): StringDatabase
  from(state: State): StringDatabase
}
```

So, not only does a class declaration generate terms at the value and type levels, but it generates two terms at the type level: one representing an instance of the class; one representing the class constructor itself (reachable with the `typeof` type operator).

Polymorphism

Like functions and types, classes and interfaces have rich support for generic type parameters, including defaults and bounds. You can scope a generic to your whole class or interface, or to a specific method:

```
class MyMap<K, V> { ❶
  constructor(initialKey: K, initialValue: V) { ❷
    // ...
  }
  get(key: K): V { ❸
    // ...
  }
  set(key: K, value: V): void {
    // ...
  }
```

```
    merge<K1, V1>(map: MyMap<K1, V1>): MyMap<K | K1, V | V1> { ❹
      // ...
    }
    static of<K, V>(k: K, v: V): MyMap<K, V> { ❺
      // ...
    }
  }
```

❶ Bind class-scoped generic types when you declare your class. Here, K and V are available to every instance method and instance property on MyMap.

❷ Note that you cannot declare generic types in a constructor. Instead, move the declaration up to your class declaration.

❸ Use class-scoped generic types anywhere inside your class.

❹ Instance methods have access to class-level generics, and can also declare their own generics on top. .merge makes use of the K and V class-level generics, and also declares two of its own generics, K1 and V1.

❺ Static methods do not have access to their class's generics, just like at the value level they don't have access to their class's instance variables. of does not have access to the K and V declared in ❶; instead, it declares its own K and V generics.

You can bind generics to interfaces too:

```
interface MyMap<K, V> {
  get(key: K): V
  set(key: K, value: V): void
}
```

And like with functions, you can bind concrete types to generics explicitly, or let TypeScript infer the types for you:

```
let a = new MyMap<string, number>('k', 1) // MyMap<string, number>
let b = new MyMap('k', true) // MyMap<string, boolean>

a.get('k')
b.set('k', false)
```

Mixins

JavaScript and TypeScript don't have trait or mixin keywords, but it's straightforward to implement them ourselves. Both are ways to simulate *multiple inheritance* (classes that extend more than one other class) and do *role-oriented programming*, a style of programming where you don't say things like "this thing is a Shape" but instead describe properties of a thing, like "it can be measured" or "it has four sides." Instead of "is-a" relationships, you describe "can" and "has-a" relationships.

Let's build a mixin implementation.

Mixins are a pattern that allows us to *mix* behaviors and properties *into* a class. By convention, mixins:

- Can have state (i.e., instance properties)
- Can only provide concrete methods (not abstract ones)
- Can have constructors, which are called in the same order as their classes were mixed in

TypeScript doesn't have a built-in concept of mixins, but it's easy to implement them ourselves. For example, let's design a debugging library for TypeScript classes. We'll call it EZDebug. The library works by letting you log out information about whatever classes use the library, so that you can inspect them at runtime. We'll use it like this:

```
class User {
  // ...
}

User.debug() // evaluates to 'User({"id": 3, "name": "Emma Gluzman"})'
```

With a standard .debug interface, our users will be able to debug anything! Let's build it. We'll model it with a mixin, which we'll call withEZDebug. A mixin is just a function that takes a class constructor and returns a class constructor, so our mixin might look like this:

```
type ClassConstructor = new(...args: any[]) => {} ❶

function withEZDebug<C extends ClassConstructor>(Class: C) { ❷
  return class extends Class { ❸
    constructor(...args: any[]) { ❹
      super(...args) ❺
    }
  }
}
```

❶ We start by declaring a type ClassConstructor, which represents any constructor. Since TypeScript is completely structurally typed, we say that a constructor is anything that can be new-ed. We don't know what types of parameters the constructor might have, so we say it takes any number of arguments of any type.[3]

❷ We declare our withEZDebug mixin with a single type parameter, C. C has to be at least a class constructor, which we enforce with an extends clause. We let Type-

---

3 Note that TypeScript is picky here: the type of a constructor type's arguments has to be any[] (not void, unknown[], etc.) in order for us to be able to extend it.

Script infer withEZDebug's return type, which is the intersection of C and our new anonymous class.

❸ Since a mixin is a function that takes a constructor and returns a constructor, we return an anonymous class constructor.

❹ The class constructor has to take *at least* the arguments that the class you pass in might take. But remember, since we don't know what class you might pass in beforehand, I have to keep it as general as possible, which means any number of parameters of any type—just like ClassConstructor.

❺ Finally, since this anonymous class extends another class, to wire everything up correctly we need to remember to call Class's constructor too.

Like with regular JavaScript classes, if you don't have any more logic in the constructor, you can omit lines ❹ and ❺. We aren't going to put any logic into the constructor for this withEZDebug example, so we can omit them.

Now that we've set up the boilerplate, it's time to work some debugging magic. When we call .debug, we want to log out the class's constructor name and the instance's value:

```
type ClassConstructor = new(...args: any[]) => {}

function withEZDebug<C extends ClassConstructor>(Class: C) {
  return class extends Class {
    debug() {
      let Name = Class.constructor.name
      let value = this.getDebugValue()
      return Name + '(' + JSON.stringify(value) + ')'
    }
  }
}
```

But wait! How do we make sure the class implements a .getDebugValue method, so that we can call it? Think about this for a second before you move on—can you figure it out?

The answer is that instead of accepting any old class, we use a generic type to make sure the class passed into withEZDebug defines a .getDebugValue method:

```
type ClassConstructor<T> = new(...args: any[]) => T ❶

function withEZDebug<C extends ClassConstructor<{
  getDebugValue(): object ❷
}>>(Class: C) {
  // ...
}
```

❶ We add a generic type parameter to `ClassConstructor`.

❷ We bind a shape type to `ClassConstructor`, `C`, enforcing that the constructor we passed to `withEZDebug` at least defines the `.getDebugValue` method.

That's it! So, how do you use this incredible debugging utility? Like so:

```
class HardToDebugUser {
  constructor(
    private id: number,
    private firstName: string,
    private lastName: string
  ) {}
  getDebugValue() {
    return {
      id: this.id,
      name: this.firstName + ' ' + this.lastName
    }
  }
}

let User = withEZDebug(HardToDebugUser)
let user = new User(3, 'Emma', 'Gluzman')
user.debug() // evaluates to 'User({"id": 3, "name": "Emma Gluzman"})'
```

Cool, right? You can apply as many mixins to a class as you want to yield a class with richer and richer behavior, all in a typesafe way. Mixins help encapsulate behavior, and are an expressive way to specify reusable behaviors.

Decorators

Decorators are an experimental TypeScript feature that gives us a clean syntax for metaprogramming with classes, class methods, properties, and method parameters. They're just a syntax for calling a function on the thing you're decorating.

TSC Flag: experimentalDecorators

Because they're still experimental—meaning they may change in a backward-incompatible way, or may even be entirely removed in future TypeScript releases—decorators are hidden behind a TSC flag. If you're OK with that, and want to play around with the feature, set `"experimentalDecorators": true` in your *tsconfig.json* and read on.

To get a sense for how decorators work, let's start with an example:

```
@serializable
class APIPayload {
  getValue(): Payload {
```

```
    // ...
  }
}
```

The `@serializable` class decorator wraps our `APIPayload` class, and optionally returns a new class that replaces it. Without decorators, you might implement the same thing with:

```
let APIPayload = serializable(class APIPayload {
  getValue(): Payload {
    // ...
  }
})
```

For each type of decorator, TypeScript requires that you have a function in scope with the given name and the required signature for that type of decorator (see Table 5-1).

Table 5-1. Expected type signatures for the different kinds of decorator functions

What you're decorating	Expected type signature
Class	`(Constructor: {new(...any[]) => any}) => any`
Method	`(classPrototype: {}, methodName: string, descriptor: PropertyDescriptor) => any`
Static method	`(Constructor: {new(...any[]) => any}, methodName: string, descriptor: PropertyDescriptor) => any`
Method parameter	`(classPrototype: {}, paramName: string, index: number) => void`
Static method parameter	`(Constructor: {new(...any[]) => any}, paramName: string, index: number) => void`
Property	`(classPrototype: {}, propertyName: string) => any`
Static property	`(Constructor: {new(...any[]) => any}, propertyName: string) => any`
Property getter/setter	`(classPrototype: {}, propertyName: string, descriptor: PropertyDescriptor) => any`
Static property getter/setter	`(Constructor: {new(...any[]) => any}, propertyName: string, descriptor: PropertyDescriptor) => any`

TypeScript doesn't come with any built-in decorators: whatever decorators you use, you have to implement yourself (or install from NPM). The implementation for each kind of decorator—for classes, methods, properties, and function parameters—is a regular function that satisfies a specific signature, depending on what it's decorating. For example, our `@serializable` decorator might look like this:

```
type ClassConstructor<T> = new(...args: any[]) => T ❶

function serializable<
```

```
  T extends ClassConstructor<{
    getValue(): Payload ❷
  }>
>(Constructor: T) { ❸
  return class extends Constructor { ❹
    serialize() {
      return this.getValue().toString()
    }
  }
}
```

❶ Remember, new() is how we structurally type a class constructor in TypeScript.
And for a class constructor that can be extended (with extends), TypeScript
requires that we type its arguments with an any spread: new(...any[]).

❷ @serializable can decorate any class whose instances implement the
method .getValue, which returns a Payload.

❸ Class decorators are functions that take a single argument—the class. If the decorator function returns a class (as in the example) it will replace the class it's decorating at runtime; otherwise, it will return the original class.

❹ To decorate the class, we return a class that extends it and adds a .serialize
method along the way.

What happens when we try to call .serialize?

```
let payload = new APIPayload
let serialized = payload.serialize() // Error TS2339: Property 'serialize' does
                                     // not exist on type 'APIPayload'.
```

TypeScript assumes that a decorator doesn't change the shape of the thing it's decorating—meaning that you didn't add or remove methods and properties. It checks at
compile time that the class you returned is assignable to the class you passed in, but
at the time of writing, TypeScript does not keep track of extensions you make in your
decorators.

Until decorators in TypeScript become a more mature feature, I recommend you
avoid using them and stick to regular functions instead:

```
let DecoratedAPIPayload = serializable(APIPayload)
let payload = new DecoratedAPIPayload
payload.serialize()                    // string
```

We won't delve more deeply into decorators in this book. For more information,
head over to the official documentation (*http://bit.ly/2IDQd1U*).

Simulating final Classes

Though TypeScript doesn't support the `final` keyword for classes or methods, it's easy to simulate it for classes. If you haven't worked much with object-oriented languages before, `final` is the keyword some languages use to mark a class as nonextensible, or a method as nonoverridable.

To simulate `final` classes in TypeScript, we can take advantage of private constructors:

```
class MessageQueue {
  private constructor(private messages: string[]) {}
}
```

When a `constructor` is marked `private`, you can't new the class or extend it:

```
class BadQueue extends MessageQueue {}  // Error TS2675: Cannot extend a class
                                        // 'MessageQueue'. Class constructor is
                                        // marked as private.

new MessageQueue([])                    // Error TS2673: Constructor of class
                                        // 'MessageQueue' is private and only
                                        // accessible within the class
                                        // declaration.
```

As well as preventing you from extending the class—which is what we want—private constructors also prevent you from directly instantiating it. But for `final` classes we do want the ability to instantiate a class, just not to extend it. How do we keep the first restriction but get rid of the second? Easy:

```
class MessageQueue {
  private constructor(private messages: string[]) {}
  static create(messages: string[]) {
    return new MessageQueue(messages)
  }
}
```

This changes `MessageQueue`'s API a bit, but it does a great job of preventing extensions at compile time:

```
class BadQueue extends MessageQueue {}  // Error TS2675: Cannot extend a class
                                        // 'MessageQueue'. Class constructor is
                                        // marked as private.

MessageQueue.create([]) // MessageQueue
```

Design Patterns

This wouldn't be a chapter on object-oriented programming if we didn't walk through implementing a design pattern or two in TypeScript, right?

Factory Pattern

The *factory pattern* is a way to create objects of some type, leaving the decision of which concrete object to create to the specific factory that creates that object.

Let's build a shoe factory. We'll start by defining a `Shoe` type, and a few kinds of shoes:

```
type Shoe = {
  purpose: string
}

class BalletFlat implements Shoe {
  purpose = 'dancing'
}

class Boot implements Shoe {
  purpose = 'woodcutting'
}

class Sneaker implements Shoe {
  purpose = 'walking'
}
```

Note that this example uses a `type`, but we could have just as well used an `interface` instead.

Now, let's make a shoe factory:

```
let Shoe = {
  create(type: 'balletFlat' | 'boot' | 'sneaker'): Shoe { ❶
    switch (type) { ❷
      case 'balletFlat': return new BalletFlat
      case 'boot': return new Boot
      case 'sneaker': return new Sneaker
    }
  }
}
```

❶ Using a union type for `type` helps make `.create` as typesafe as possible, preventing consumers from passing in an invalid `type` at compile time.

❷ Switching on `type` makes it easy for TypeScript to enforce that we've handled every type of `Shoe`.

In this example we use the companion object pattern (see "Companion Object Pattern" on page 140) to declare a type `Shoe` and a value `Shoe` with the same name (remember that TypeScript has separate namespaces for values and for types), as a way to signal that the value provides methods for operating on the type. To use the factory, we can just call `.create`:

```
Shoe.create('boot') // Shoe
```

Voilà! We have a factory pattern. Note that we could have gone further and indicated in Shoe.create's type signature that passing in 'boot' will give a Boot, 'sneaker' will give a Sneaker, and so on, but that would break the abstraction that the factory pattern gives us (that the consumer shouldn't know what concrete class they'll get back, just that the class satisfies a particular interface).

Builder Pattern

The *builder pattern* is a way to separate the construction of an object from the way that object is actually implemented. If you've used JQuery, or ES6 data structures like Map and Set, this style of API should look familiar. Here's what it looks like:

```
new RequestBuilder()
  .setURL('/users')
  .setMethod('get')
  .setData({firstName: 'Anna'})
  .send()
```

How do we implement RequestBuilder? Easy—we'll start with a bare class:

```
class RequestBuilder {}
```

First we'll add the .setURL method:

```
class RequestBuilder {

  private url: string | null = null  ❶

  setURL(url: string): this {  ❷
    this.url = url
    return this
  }
}
```

❶ We keep track of the URL the user set in a private instance variable url, which we initialize to null.

❷ setURL's return type is this (see "Using this as a Return Type" on page 89), that is, the specific instance of RequestBuilder that the user called setURL on.

Now let's add the other methods from our example:

```
class RequestBuilder {

  private data: object | null = null
  private method: 'get' | 'post' | null = null
  private url: string | null = null

  setMethod(method: 'get' | 'post'): this {
```

```
      this.method = method
      return this
    }
    setData(data: object): this {
      this.data = data
      return this
    }
    setURL(url: string): this {
      this.url = url
      return this
    }

    send() {
      // ...
    }
  }
```

That's all there is to it.

 This traditional builder design is not completely safe: we can call .send before we set the method, URL, or data, resulting in a runtime exception (remember, that's the bad kind of exception). See Exercise 4 for some ideas about how to improve this design.

Summary

We've now explored TypeScript classes from all sides: how to declare classes; how to inherit from classes and implement interfaces; how to mark classes as abstract so they can't be instantiated; how to put a field or method on a class with static and on an instance without it; how to control access to a field or method with the private, protected, and public visibility modifiers; and how to mark a field as nonwritable using the readonly modifier. We've covered how to safely use this and super, explored what it means for classes to be both values and types at the same time, and talked about the differences between type aliases and interfaces, the basics of declaration merging, and using generic types in classes. Finally, we covered a few more advanced patterns for working with classes: mixins, decorators, and simulating final classes. And to cap the chapter off, we went through and derived a couple of common patterns for working with classes.

Exercises

1. What are the differences between a class and an interface?

2. When you mark a class's constructor as private, that means you can't instantiate or extend the class. What happens when you mark it as protected instead? Play around with this in your code editor, and see if you can figure it out.

3. Extend the implementation we developed "Factory Pattern" on page 108 to make it safer, at the expense of breaking the abstraction a bit. Update the implementation so that a consumer knows at compile time that calling `Shoe.create('boot')` returns a `Boot` and calling `Shoe.create('balletFlat')` returns a `BalletFlat` (rather than both returning a `Shoe`). Hint: think back to "Overloaded Function Types" on page 59.

4. [Hard] As an exercise, think about how you might design a typesafe builder pattern. Extend the Builder pattern "Builder Pattern" on page 109 to:

   a. Guarantee at compile time that someone can't call `.send` before setting at least a URL and a method. Would it be easier to make this guarantee if you also force the user to call methods in a specific order? (Hint: what can you return instead of `this`?)

   b. [Harder] How would you change your design if you wanted to make this guarantee, but still let people call methods in any order? (Hint: what TypeScript feature can you use to make each method's return type "add" to the `this` type after each method call?)

Advanced Types

TypeScript has a world-class type system that supports powerful type-level programming features that might make even the crotchetiest Haskell programmer jealous. As you by now know, that type system isn't just incredibly expressive, but also easy to use, and makes declaring type constraints and relationships simple, terse, and most of the time, inferred.

We need such an expressive and unusual type system because JavaScript is so dynamic. Modeling things like prototypes, dynamically bound this, function overloads, and always-changing objects requires a rich type system and a utility belt of type operators that would make Batman do a double-take.

I'll start this chapter with a deep dive into subtyping, assignability, variance, and widening in TypeScript, giving more definition to the intuitions you've been developing over the last several chapters. I'll then cover TypeScript's control-flow-based type-checking features in more detail, including refinement and totality, and continue with some advanced type-level programming features: keying into and mapping over object types, using conditional types, defining your own type guards, and escape hatches like type assertions and definite assignment assertions. Finally, I'll cover advanced patterns for squeezing more safety out of your types: the companion object pattern, improving inference for tuple types, simulating nominal types, and safely extending the prototype.

Relationships Between Types

Let's begin by taking a closer look at type relations in TypeScript.

Subtypes and Supertypes

We talked a little about assignability in "Talking About Types" on page 18. Now that you've seen most of the types TypeScript has to offer we can dive deeper, starting from the top: what's a subtype?

Subtype

If you have two types A and B, and B is a subtype of A, then you can safely use a B anywhere an A is required (Figure 6-1).

Figure 6-1. B is a subtype of A

If you look back at Figure 3-1 at the very beginning of Chapter 3, you'll see what the subtype relations built into TypeScript are. For example:

- Array is a subtype of Object.
- Tuple is a subtype of Array.
- Everything is a subtype of any.
- never is a subtype of everything.
- If you have a class Bird that extends Animal, then Bird is a subtype of Animal.

From the definition I just gave for subtype, that means:

- Anywhere you need an Object you can also use an Array.
- Anywhere you need an Array you can also use a Tuple.
- Anywhere you need an any you can also use an Object.
- You can use a never anywhere.
- Anywhere you need an Animal you can also use a Bird.

As you might have guessed, a supertype is the opposite of a subtype.

Supertype

If you have two types A and B, and B is a supertype of A, then
you can safely use an A anywhere a B is required
(Figure 6-2).

Figure 6-2. B is a supertype of A

Again from the flowchart in Figure 3-1:

- Array is a supertype of Tuple.
- Object is a supertype of Array.
- Any is a supertype of everything.
- Never is a supertype of nothing.
- Animal is a supertype of Bird.

This is just the opposite of how subtypes work, and nothing more.

Variance

For most types it's pretty easy to intuit whether or not some type A is a subtype of
another type B. For simple types like number, string, and so on, you can just look
them up in the flowchart in Figure 3-1, or reason through it ("number is contained in
the union number | string, so it must be a subtype of it").

But for parameterized (generic) types and other more complex types, it gets more
complicated. Consider these cases:

- When is Array<A> a subtype of Array<B>?
- When is a shape A a subtype of another shape B?
- When is a function (a: A) => B a subtype of another function (c: C) => D?

Subtyping rules for types that contain other types (i.e., things with type parameters
like Array<A>, shapes with fields like {a: number}, or functions like (a: A) => B)
are harder to reason about, and the answers aren't as clear-cut. In fact, subtyping

rules for these kinds of complex types are a big point of disagreement among programming languages—almost no two languages are alike!

To make the following rules easier to read, I'm going to introduce a few pieces of syntax that let us talk about types a little more precisely and tersely. This syntax is not valid TypeScript; it's just a way for you and me to share a common language when we talk about types. And don't worry, I swear the syntax isn't math:

- A <: B means "A is a subtype of or the same as the type B."
- A >: B means "A is a supertype of or the same as the type B."

Shape and array variance

To get some intuition for why exactly languages disagree on subtyping rules for complex types, let me take you through an example complex type: shapes. Say you have a shape describing a user in your application. You might represent it with a pair of types that look something like this:

```
// An existing user that we got from the server
type ExistingUser = {
  id: number
  name: string
}

// A new user that hasn't been saved to the server yet
type NewUser = {
  name: string
}
```

Now suppose an intern at your company is tasked with writing some code to delete a user. They start it like this:

```
function deleteUser(user: {id?: number, name: string}) {
  delete user.id
}

let existingUser: ExistingUser = {
  id: 123456,
  name: 'Ima User'
}

deleteUser(existingUser)
```

deleteUser takes an object of type {id?: number, name: string}, and it's passed an existingUser of type {id: number, name: string}. Notice that the type of the id property (number) is a *subtype* of the expected type (number | undefined). Therefore the entire object {id: number, name: string} is a subtype of {id?: number, name: string}, so TypeScript lets it fly.

Do you see the safety issue here? It's a subtle one: after passing an `ExistingUser` to `deleteUser`, TypeScript doesn't know that the user's `id` has been deleted, so if we read `existingUser.id` after deleting it with `deleteUser(existingUser)`, TypeScript still thinks `existingUser.id` is of type `number`!

Clearly, using an object type in a place where something expects its supertype can be unsafe. So why does TypeScript allow it? In general, TypeScript is not designed to be perfectly safe; instead, its type system tries to strike a balance between catching real mistakes and being easy to use, without you needing to get a degree in programming language theory to understand why something is an error. This specific case of unsafety is a practical one: since destructive updates (like deleting a property) are relatively rare in practice, TypeScript is lax and lets you assign an object to a place where its supertype is expected.

What about the opposite direction—can you assign an object to a place where its subtype is expected?

Let's add a new type for a legacy user, then delete a user of that type (imagine you're adding types to code your coworker wrote before you started using TypeScript):

```typescript
type LegacyUser = {
  id?: number | string
  name: string
}

let legacyUser: LegacyUser = {
  id: '793331',
  name: 'Xin Yang'
}

deleteUser(legacyUser) // Error TS2345: Argument of type 'LegacyUser' is not
                       // assignable to parameter of type '{id?: number |
                       // undefined, name: string}'. Type 'string' is not
                       // assignable to type 'number | undefined'.
```

When we pass a shape with a property whose type is a supertype of the expected type, TypeScript complains. That's because `id` is a `string | number | undefined`, and `deleteUser` only handles the case of an `id` that's a `number | undefined`.

TypeScript's behavior is as follows: if you expect a shape, you can also pass a type with property types that are `<:` their expected types, but you cannot pass a shape with property types that are supertypes of their expected types. When talking about types, we say that TypeScript shapes (objects and classes) are *covariant* in their property types. That is, for an object A to be assignable to an object B, each of its properties must be `<:` its corresponding property in B.

More generally, covariance is just one of four sorts of variance:

Invariance
> You want exactly a T.

Covariance
> You want a <: T.

Contravariance
> You want a >: T.

Bivariance
> You're OK with either <: T or >: T.

In TypeScript, every complex type is covariant in its members—objects, classes, arrays, and function return types—with one exception: function parameter types, which are *contravariant*.

Not all languages make this same design decision. In some languages objects are *invariant* in their property types, because as we saw, covariant property types can lead to unsafe behavior. Some languages have different rules for mutable and immutable objects (try to reason through it yourself!). Some languages—like Scala, Kotlin, and Flow—even have explicit syntax for programmers to specify variance for their own data types.

When designing TypeScript, its authors opted for a balance between ease of use and safety. When you make objects invariant in their property types, even though it's safer, it can make a type system tedious to use because you end up banning things that are safe in practice (e.g., if we didn't `delete` the `id` in `deleteUser`, then it would have been perfectly safe to pass in an object that's a supertype of the expected type).

Function variance

Let's start with a few examples.

A function A is a subtype of function B if A has the same or lower arity (number of parameters) than B and:

1. A's `this` type either isn't specified, or is >: B's `this` type.

2. Each of A's parameters is >: its corresponding parameter in B.

3. A's return type is <: B's return type.

Read that over a few times, and make sure you understand what each rule means. You might have noticed that for a function A to be a subtype of function B, we say that its `this` type and parameters must be >: their counterparts in B, while its return type has to be <:! Why does the direction flip like that? Why isn't it simply <: for each component (this type, parameter types, and return type), like it is for objects, arrays, unions, and so on?

To answer this question, let's derive it ourselves. We'll start by defining three types (we're going to use a class for clarity, but this works for any choice of types where A <: B <: C):

```
class Animal {}
class Bird extends Animal {
  chirp() {}
}
class Crow extends Bird {
  caw() {}
}
```

In this example, Crow is a subtype of Bird, which is a subtype of Animal. That is, Crow <: Bird <: Animal.

Now, let's define a function that takes a Bird, and makes it chirp:

```
function chirp(bird: Bird): Bird {
  bird.chirp()
  return bird
}
```

So far, so good. What kinds of things does TypeScript let you pass into chirp?

```
chirp(new Animal) // Error TS2345: Argument of type 'Animal' is not assignable
chirp(new Bird)   // to parameter of type 'Bird'.
chirp(new Crow)
```

You can pass an instance of Bird (because that's what chirp's parameter bird's type is) or an instance of Crow (because it's a subtype of Bird). Great: passing in a subtype works as expected.

Let's make a new function. This time, its parameter will be a *function*:

```
function clone(f: (b: Bird) => Bird): void {
  // ...
}
```

clone needs a function f that takes a Bird and returns a Bird. What types of functions can you safely pass for f? Clearly you can pass a function that takes a Bird and returns a Bird:

```
function birdToBird(b: Bird): Bird {
  // ...
}
clone(birdToBird) // OK
```

What about a function that takes a Bird and returns a Crow, or an Animal?

```
function birdToCrow(d: Bird): Crow {
  // ...
}
clone(birdToCrow) // OK

function birdToAnimal(d: Bird): Animal {
  // ...
}
clone(birdToAnimal) // Error TS2345: Argument of type '(d: Bird) => Animal' is
                    // not assignable to parameter of type '(b: Bird) => Bird'.
                    // Type 'Animal' is not assignable to type 'Bird'.
```

birdToCrow works as expected, but birdToAnimal gives us an error. Why? Imagine
that clone's implementation looks like this:

```
function clone(f: (b: Bird) => Bird): void {
  let parent = new Bird
  let babyBird = f(parent)
  babyBird.chirp()
}
```

If we passed to our clone function an f that returned an Animal, then we couldn't
call .chirp on it! So TypeScript has to make sure, at compile time, that the function
we passed in returns *at least* a Bird.

We say that functions are *covariant* in their return types, which is a fancy way of saying that for a function to be a subtype of another function, its return type has to be <:
the other function's return type.

OK, what about parameter types?

```
function animalToBird(a: Animal): Bird {
  // ...
}
clone(animalToBird) // OK

function crowToBird(c: Crow): Bird {
  // ...
}
clone(crowToBird) // Error TS2345: Argument of type '(c: Crow) => Bird' is not
                  // assignable to parameter of type '(b: Bird) => Bird'.
```

For a function to be assignable to another function, its parameter types (including
this) all have to be >: their corresponding parameter types in the other function. To
see why, think about how a user might have implemented crowToBird before passing
it into clone. What if they did this?

```
function crowToBird(c: Crow): Bird {
  c.caw()
  return new Bird
}
```

Now if `clone` called `crowToBird` with a new `Bird`, we'd get an exception because `.caw` is only defined on `Crow`s, not on all `Bird`s.

This means functions are *contravariant* in their parameter and `this` types. That is, for a function to be a subtype of another function, each of its parameters and its `this` type must be `>:` its corresponding parameter in the other function.

Thankfully, you don't have to memorize and recite these rules. Just have them in the back of your mind when your code editor gives you a red squiggly when you pass an incorrectly typed function somewhere, so you know why TypeScript is giving you the error it does.

TSC Flag: strictFunctionTypes

For legacy reasons, functions in TypeScript are actually covariant in their parameter and `this` types by default. To opt into the safer, contravariant behavior we just explored, be sure to enable the `{"strictFunctionTypes": true}` flag in your *tsconfig.json*.

`strict` mode includes `strictFunctionTypes`, so if you're already using `{"strict": true}`, you're good to go.

Assignability

Subtype and supertype relations are core concepts in any statically typed language. They're also important to understanding how *assignability* works (as a reminder, assignability refers to TypeScript's rules for whether or not you can use a type A where another type B is required).

When TypeScript wants to answer the question "Is type A assignable to type B?" it follows a few simple rules. For *non-enum types*—like arrays, booleans, numbers, objects, functions, classes, class instances, and strings, including literal types—A is assignable to B if either of the following is true:

1. A `<:` B.
2. A is `any`.

Rule 1 is just the definition of what a subtype is: if A is a subtype of B, then wherever you need a B you can also use an A.

Rule 2 is the exception to rule 1, and is a convenience for interoperating with JavaScript code.

For *enum types* created with the `enum` or `const enum` keywords, a type A is assignable to an enum B if either of these is true:

1. A is a member of enum B.

2. B has at least one member that's a `number`, and A is a `number`.

Rule 1 is exactly the same as for simple types (if A is a member of enum B, then A's type is B, so all we're saying is B <: B).

Rule 2 is a convenience for working with enums. As we talked about in "Enums" on page 39, rule 2 is a big source of unsafety in TypeScript, and this is one reason I suggest throwing the baby out with the bathwater and avoiding enums entirely.

Type Widening

Type widening is key to understanding how TypeScript's type inference works. In general, TypeScript will be lenient when inferring your types, and will err on the side of inferring a more general type rather than the most specific type possible. This makes your life as a programmer easier, and means less time spent quelling the type-checker's complaints.

In Chapter 3, you already saw a few instances of type widening in action. Let's look at a few more examples.

When you declare a variable in a way that allows it to be mutated later (e.g., with `let` or `var`), its type is widened from its literal value to the base type that literal belongs to:

```
let a = 'x'            // string
let b = 3              // number
var c = true           // boolean
const d = {x: 3}       // {x: number}

enum E {X, Y, Z}
let e = E.X            // E
```

Not so for immutable declarations:

```
const a = 'x'          // 'x'
const b = 3            // 3
const c = true         // true

enum E {X, Y, Z}
const e = E.X          // E.X
```

You can use an explicit type annotation to prevent your type from being widened:

```
let a: 'x' = 'x'           // 'x'
let b: 3 = 3               // 3
var c: true = true         // true
const d: {x: 3} = {x: 3}   // {x: 3}
```

When you reassign a nonwidened type using `let` or `var`, TypeScript widens it for you. To tell TypeScript to keep it narrow, add an explicit type annotation to your original declaration:

```
const a = 'x'            // 'x'
let b = a               // string

const c: 'x' = 'x'      // 'x'
let d = c               // 'x'
```

Variables initialized to `null` or `undefined` are widened to any:

```
let a = null            // any
a = 3                   // any
a = 'b'                 // any
```

But when a variable initialized to `null` or `undefined` leaves the scope it was declared in, TypeScript assigns it a definite type:

```
function x() {
  let a = null          // any
  a = 3                 // any
  a = 'b'               // any
  return a
}

x()                     // string
```

The const type

TypeScript comes with a special `const` type that you can use to opt out of type widening a declaration at a time. Use it as a type assertion (read ahead to "Type Assertions" on page 148):

```
let a = {x: 3}              // {x: number}
let b: {x: 3}              // {x: 3}
let c = {x: 3} as const    // {readonly x: 3}
```

`const` opts your type out of widening and recursively marks its members as `readonly`, even for deeply nested data structures:

```
let d = [1, {x: 2}]              // (number | {x: number})[]
let e = [1, {x: 2}] as const    // readonly [1, {readonly x: 2}]
```

Use `as const` when you want TypeScript to infer your type as narrowly as possible.

Excess property checking

Type widening also comes into the picture when TypeScript checks whether or not one object type is assignable to another object type.

Recall from "Shape and array variance" on page 116 that object types are covariant in their members. But if TypeScript stuck to this rule without doing any additional checks, it could lead to a problem.

For example, consider an `Options` object you might pass into a class to configure it:

```
type Options = {
  baseURL: string
  cacheSize?: number
  tier?: 'prod' | 'dev'
}

class API {
  constructor(private options: Options) {}
}

new API({
  baseURL: 'https://api.mysite.com',
  tier: 'prod'
})
```

Now, what happens if you misspell an option?

```
new API({
  baseURL: 'https://api.mysite.com',
  tierr: 'prod'       // Error TS2345: Argument of type '{tierr: string}'
})                    // is not assignable to parameter of type 'Options'.
                      // Object literal may only specify known properties,
                      // but 'tierr' does not exist in type 'Options'.
                      // Did you mean to write 'tier'?
```

This is a common bug when working with JavaScript, so it's really helpful that Type-Script helps us catch it. But if object types are covariant in their members, how is it that TypeScript catches this?

That is:

- We expected the type {baseURL: string, cacheSize?: number, tier?: 'prod' | 'dev'}.

- We passed in the type {baseURL: string, tierr: string}.

- The type we passed in is a subtype of the type we expected, but somehow, Type-Script knew to report an error.

TypeScript was able to catch this due to its *excess property checking*, which works like this: when you try to assign a fresh object literal type T to another type U, and T has properties that aren't present in U, TypeScript reports an error.

A *fresh object literal type* is the type TypeScript infers from an object literal. If that object literal either uses a type assertion (see "Type Assertions" on page 148) or is

---

assigned to a variable, then the fresh object literal type is *widened* to a regular object type, and its freshness disappears.

This definition is dense, so let's walk through our example again, trying a few more variations on the theme this time:

```
type Options = {
  baseURL: string
  cacheSize?: number
  tier?: 'prod' | 'dev'
}

class API {
  constructor(private options: Options) {}
}

new API({ ❶
  baseURL: 'https://api.mysite.com',
  tier: 'prod'
})

new API({ ❷
  baseURL: 'https://api.mysite.com',
  badTier: 'prod'    // Error TS2345: Argument of type '{baseURL: string; badTier:
})                   // string}' is not assignable to parameter of type 'Options'.

new API({ ❸
  baseURL: 'https://api.mysite.com',
  badTier: 'prod'
} as Options)

let badOptions = { ❹
  baseURL: 'https://api.mysite.com',
  badTier: 'prod'
}
new API(badOptions)

let options: Options = { ❺
  baseURL: 'https://api.mysite.com',
  badTier: 'prod'    // Error TS2322: Type '{baseURL: string; badTier: string}'
}                    // is not assignable to type 'Options'.
new API(options)
```

❶ We instantiate `API` with a `baseURL` and one of our two optional properties, `tier`. This works as expected.

❷ Here, we misspell `tier` as `badTier`. The options object we pass to `new API` is fresh (because its type is inferred, it isn't assigned to a variable, and we don't make a type assertion about its type), so TypeScript runs an excess property check on it, revealing the excess `badTier` property (which is defined in our options object but not on the `Options` type).

❸ We assert that our invalid options object is of type `Options`. TypeScript no longer considers it fresh, and bails out of excess property checking: no error. If you're not familiar with the `as T` syntax, read ahead to "Type Assertions" on page 148.

❹ We assign our options object to a variable, `badOptions`. TypeScript no longer considers it to be fresh, and bails out of excess property checking: no error.

❺ When we explicitly type `options` as `Options`, the object we assign to `options` is fresh, so TypeScript performs excess property checking, catching our bug. Note that in this case the excess property check doesn't happen when we pass `options` to `new API`; rather, it happens when we try to assign our options object to the variable `options`.

Don't worry—you don't need to memorize these rules. They are TypeScript's internal heuristics for catching the most bugs possible in a practical way, so as not to be a burden on you, the programmer. Just keep them in mind when you're wondering how TypeScript knew to complain about that one bug that even Ivan, the battle-weathered gatekeeper of your company's codebase and master code reviewer, didn't notice.

Refinement

TypeScript performs flow-based type inference, which is a kind of symbolic execution where the typechecker uses control flow statements like `if`, `?`, `||`, and `switch`, as well as type queries like `typeof`, `instanceof`, and `in`, to *refine* types as it goes, just like a programmer reading through the code would.[1] It's an incredibly convenient feature for a typechecker to have, but is another one of those things that remarkably few languages support.[2]

---

1 Symbolic execution is a form of program analysis where you use a special program called a symbolic evaluator to run your program the same way a runtime would, but without assigning definite values to variables; instead, each variable is modelled as a *symbol* whose value gets constrained as the program runs. Symbolic execution lets you say things like "this variable is never used," or "this function never returns," or "in the positive branch of the `if` statement on line 102, variable x is guaranteed not to be `null`."

2 Flow-based type inference is supported by a handful of languages, including TypeScript, Flow, Kotlin, and Ceylon. It's a way to refine types within a block of code, and is an alternative to C/Java-style explicit type annotations and Haskell/OCaml/Scala-style pattern matching. The idea is to take a symbolic execution engine and embed it right in the typechecker, in order to give feedback to the typechecker and reason through a program in a way that is closer to how a human programmer might do it.

Let's walk through an example. Say we've built an API for defining CSS rules in Type-Script, and a coworker wants to use it to set an HTML element's width. They pass in the width, which we then want to parse and validate.

We'll first implement a function to parse a CSS string into a value and a unit:

```
// We use a union of string literals to describe
// the possible values a CSS unit can have
type Unit = 'cm' | 'px' | '%'

// Enumerate the units
let units: Unit[] = ['cm', 'px', '%']

// Check each unit, and return null if there is no match
function parseUnit(value: string): Unit | null {
  for (let i = 0; i < units.length; i++) {
    if (value.endsWith(units[i])) {
      return units[i]
    }
  }
  return null
}
```

We can then use parseUnit to parse a width value passed to us by a user. width might be a number (which we assume is in pixels), or a string with units attached, or it might be null or undefined.

We take advantage of type refinement a few times in this example:

```
type Width = {
  unit: Unit,
  value: number
}

function parseWidth(width: number | string | null | undefined): Width | null {
  // If width is null or undefined, return early
  if (width == null) { ❶
    return null
  }

  // If width is a number, default to pixels
  if (typeof width === 'number') { ❷
    return {unit: 'px', value: width}
  }

  // Try to parse a unit from width
  let unit = parseUnit(width)
  if (unit) { ❸
    return {unit, value: parseFloat(width)}
  }

  // Otherwise, return null
```

```
    return null ❹
  }
```

❶ TypeScript is smart enough to know that doing a loose equality check against
    null will return true for both null and undefined in JavaScript. It knows that if
    this check passes then we will return, and if we didn't return that means the
    check didn't pass, so from then on width's type is number | string (it can't be
    null or undefined anymore). We say that the type was refined from number |
    string | null | undefined to number | string.

❷ A typeof check queries a value at runtime to see what its type is. TypeScript
    takes advantage of typeof at compile time too: in the if branch where the check
    passes, TypeScript knows that width is a number; otherwise (since that branch
    returns) width must be a string—it's the only type left.

❸ Because calling parseUnit might return null, we check if it did by testing
    whether its result is truthy.[3] TypeScript knows that if unit is truthy then it must
    be of type Unit in the if branch—otherwise, unit must be falsy, meaning it must
    be of type null (refined from Unit | null).

❹ Finally, we return null. This can only happen if the user passed a string for
    width, but that string contained a unit that we don't support.

I've spelled out exactly what TypeScript was thinking for each of the type refinements
it performed here, but I hope this was already intuitive and obvious for you, the programmer reading that code. TypeScript does a superb job of taking what's going
through your mind as you read and write code, and crystallizing it in the form of
typechecking and inference rules.

Discriminated union types

As we just learned, TypeScript has a deep understanding of how JavaScript works,
and is able to follow along as you refine your types, just like you would when you
trace through your program in your head.

For example, say we're building a custom event system for an application. We start by
defining a couple of event types, along with a function to handle events that come in.
Imagine that UserTextEvent models a keyboard event (e.g., the user typed something
in a text <input />) and UserMouseEvent models a mouse event (e.g., the user moved
their mouse to the coordinates [100, 200]):

---

3 JavaScript has seven falsy values: null, undefined, NaN, 0, -0, "", and of course, false. Everything else is
  truthy.

```
type UserTextEvent = {value: string}
type UserMouseEvent = {value: [number, number]}

type UserEvent = UserTextEvent | UserMouseEvent

function handle(event: UserEvent) {
  if (typeof event.value === 'string') {
    event.value  // string
    // ...
    return
  }
  event.value     // [number, number]
}
```

Inside the `if` block, TypeScript knows that `event.value` has to be a `string` (because of the `typeof` check), which implies that after the `if` block `event.value` has to be a tuple of `[number, number]` (because of the `return` in the `if` block).

What happens if we make this a little more complicated? Let's add some more information to our event types, and see how TypeScript fares when we refine our types:

```
type UserTextEvent = {value: string, target: HTMLInputElement}
type UserMouseEvent = {value: [number, number], target: HTMLElement}

type UserEvent = UserTextEvent | UserMouseEvent

function handle(event: UserEvent) {
  if (typeof event.value === 'string') {
    event.value  // string
    event.target // HTMLInputElement | HTMLElement (!!!)
    // ...
    return
  }
  event.value     // [number, number]
  event.target    // HTMLInputElement | HTMLElement (!!!)
}
```

While the refinement worked for `event.value`, it didn't carry over to `event.target`. Why? When `handle` takes a parameter of type `UserEvent`, that doesn't mean we have to pass a `UserTextEvent` or `UserMouseEvent`—in fact, we could pass an argument of type `UserMouseEvent | UserTextEvent`. And since members of a union might overlap, TypeScript needs a more reliable way to know when we're in one case of a union type versus another case.

The way to do this is to use a literal type to *tag* each case of your union type. A good tag is:

- On the same place in each case of your union type. That means the same object field if it's a union of object types, or the same index if it's a union of tuple types. In practice, tagged unions usually use object types.

- Typed as a literal type (a literal string, number, boolean, etc.). You can mix and match different types of literals, but it's good practice to stick to a single type; typically, that's a string literal type.

- Not generic. Tags should not take any generic type arguments.

- Mutually exclusive (i.e., unique within the union type).

With that in mind, let's update our event types again:

```
type UserTextEvent = {type: 'TextEvent', value: string, target: HTMLInputElement}
type UserMouseEvent = {type: 'MouseEvent', value: [number, number],
                       target: HTMLElement}

type UserEvent = UserTextEvent | UserMouseEvent

function handle(event: UserEvent) {
  if (event.type === 'TextEvent') {
    event.value  // string
    event.target // HTMLInputElement
    // ...
    return
  }
  event.value    // [number, number]
  event.target   // HTMLElement
}
```

Now when we refine `event` based on the value of its tagged field (`event.type`), TypeScript knows that in the `if` branch `event` has to be a `UserTextEvent`, and after the `if` branch it has to be a `UserMouseEvent`. Since the tag is unique per union type, TypeScript knows that the two are mutually exclusive.

Use tagged unions when writing a function that has to handle the different cases of a union type. For example, they're invaluable when working with Flux actions, Redux reducers, or React's `useReducer`.

Totality

> A programmer puts two glasses on her bedside table before going to sleep: a full one, in case she gets thirsty, and an empty one, in case she doesn't.
>
> —Anonymous

Totality, also called *exhaustiveness checking*, is what allows the typechecker to make sure you've covered all your cases. It comes to us from Haskell, OCaml, and other languages that are based around pattern matching.

TypeScript will check for totality in a variety of cases, and give you helpful warnings when you've missed a case. This is an incredibly helpful feature for preventing real bugs. For example:

```
type Weekday = 'Mon' | 'Tue'| 'Wed' | 'Thu' | 'Fri'
type Day = Weekday | 'Sat' | 'Sun'

function getNextDay(w: Weekday): Day {
  switch (w) {
    case 'Mon': return 'Tue'
  }
}
```

We clearly missed a few days (it's been a long week). TypeScript comes to the rescue:

```
Error TS2366: Function lacks ending return statement and
return type does not include 'undefined'.
```

TSC Flag: noImplicitReturns

To ask TypeScript to check that all of your functions' code paths return a value (and throw the preceding warning if you missed a spot), enable the noImplicitReturns flag in your *tsconfig.json*. Whether you enable this flag or not is up to you: some people prefer a code style with fewer explicit returns, and some people are fine with a few extra returns in the name of better type safety and more bugs caught by the typechecker.

This error message is telling us that either we missed some cases and should cover them with a catchall return statement at the end that returns something like 'Sat' (that'd be nice, huh), or we should adjust getNextDay's return type to Day | undefined. After we add a case for each Day, the error goes away (try it!). Because we annotated getNextDay's return type, and not all branches are guaranteed to return a value of that type, TypeScript warns us.

The implementation details in this example aren't important: no matter what kind of control structure you use—switch, if, throw, and so on—TypeScript will watch your back to make sure you have every case covered.

Here's another example:

```
function isBig(n: number) {
  if (n >= 100) {
    return true
  }
}
```

Maybe a client's continued voicemails about that missed deadline have you jittery, and you forgot to handle numbers under 100 in your business-critical isBig function. Again, never fear—TypeScript is watching out for you:

```
Error TS7030: Not all code paths return a value.
```

Or maybe the weekend gave you a chance to clear your mind, and you realized that you should rewrite that getNextDay example from earlier to be more efficient. Instead of using a switch, why not a constant-time lookup in an object?

```
let nextDay = {
  Mon: 'Tue'
}

nextDay.Mon // 'Tue'
```

With your Bichon Frise yapping away in the other room (something about the neighbor's dog?), you absentmindedly forgot to fill in the other days in your new nextDay object before you committed your code and moved on to other things.

While TypeScript will give you an error the next time you try to access nextDay.Tue, you could have been more proactive about it when declaring nextDay in the first place. There are two ways to do that, as you'll learn in "The Record Type" on page 137 and "Mapped Types" on page 137; but before we get there, let's take a slight detour into type operators for object types.

Advanced Object Types

Objects are central to JavaScript, and TypeScript gives you a whole bunch of ways to express and manipulate them safely.

Type Operators for Object Types

Remember union (|) and intersection (&), the two type operators I introduced in "Union and intersection types" on page 32? It turns out they're not the only type operators TypeScript gives you! Let's run through a few more type operators that come in handy for working with shapes.

The keying-in operator

Say you have a complex nested type to model the GraphQL API response you got back from your social media API of choice:

```
type APIResponse = {
  user: {
    userId: string
    friendList: {
      count: number
      friends: {
        firstName: string
        lastName: string
      }[]
    }
```

```
    }
  }
```

You might fetch that response from the API, then render it:

```
function getAPIResponse(): Promise<APIResponse> {
  // ...
}

function renderFriendList(friendList: unknown) {
  // ...
}

let response = await getAPIResponse()
renderFriendList(response.user.friendList)
```

What should the type of friendList be? (It's stubbed out as unknown for now.) You could type it out and reimplement your top-level APIResponse type in terms of it:

```
type FriendList = {
  count: number
  friends: {
    firstName: string
    lastName: string
  }[]
}

type APIResponse = {
  user: {
    userId: string
    friendList: FriendList
  }
}

function renderFriendList(friendList: FriendList) {
  // ...
}
```

But then you'd have to come up with names for each of your top-level types, which you don't always want (e.g., if you used a build tool to generate TypeScript types from your GraphQL schema). Instead, you can *key in* to your type:

```
type APIResponse = {
  user: {
    userId: string
    friendList: {
      count: number
      friends: {
        firstName: string
        lastName: string
      }[]
    }
  }
}
```

```
}
type FriendList = APIResponse['user']['friendList']

function renderFriendList(friendList: FriendList) {
  // ...
}
```

You can key in to any shape (object, class constructor, or class instance), and any array. For example, to get the type of an individual friend:

```
type Friend = FriendList['friends'][number]
```

number is a way to key in to an array type; for tuples, use 0, 1, or another number literal type to represent the index you want to key in to.

The syntax for keying in is intentionally similar to how you look up fields in regular JavaScript objects—just as you might look up a value in an object, so you can look up a type in a shape. Note that you have to use bracket notation, not dot notation, to look up property types when keying in.

The keyof operator

Use keyof to get all of an object's keys as a union of string literal types. Using the previous APIResponse example:

```
type ResponseKeys = keyof APIResponse // 'user'
type UserKeys = keyof APIResponse['user'] // 'userId' | 'friendList'
type FriendListKeys =
  keyof APIResponse['user']['friendList'] // 'count' | 'friends'
```

Combining the keying-in and keyof operators, you can implement a typesafe getter function that looks up the value at the given key in an object:

```
function get< ❶
  O extends object,
  K extends keyof O ❷
>(
  o: O,
  k: K
): O[K] { ❸
  return o[k]
}
```

❶ get is a function that takes an object o and a key k.

❷ keyof O is a union of string literal types, representing all of o's keys. The generic type K extends—and is a subtype of—that union. For example, if o has the type {a: number, b: string, c: boolean}, then keyof o is the type 'a' | 'b' |

'c', and K (which extends keyof o) could be the type 'a', 'b', 'a' | 'c', or any other subtype of keyof o.

❸ O[K] is the type you get when you look up K in O. Continuing the example from ❷, if K is 'a', then we know at compile time that get returns a number. Or, if K is 'b' | 'c', then we know get returns string | boolean.

What's cool about these type operators is how precisely and safely they let you describe shape types:

```
type ActivityLog = {
  lastEvent: Date
  events: {
    id: string
    timestamp: Date
    type: 'Read' | 'Write'
  }[]
}

let activityLog: ActivityLog = // ...
let lastEvent = get(activityLog, 'lastEvent') // Date
```

TypeScript goes to work for you, verifying *at compile time* that the type of lastEvent is Date. Of course, you could extend this in order to key in to an object more deeply too. Let's overload get to accept up to three keys:

```
type Get = { ❶
  <
    O extends object,
    K1 extends keyof O
  >(o: O, k1: K1): O[K1] ❷
  <
    O extends object,
    K1 extends keyof O,
    K2 extends keyof O[K1] ❸
  >(o: O, k1: K1, k2: K2): O[K1][K2] ❹
  <
    O extends object,
    K1 extends keyof O,
    K2 extends keyof O[K1],
    K3 extends keyof O[K1][K2]
  >(o: O, k1: K1, k2: K2, k3: K3): O[K1][K2][K3] ❺
}

let get: Get = (object: any, ...keys: string[]) => {
  let result = object
  keys.forEach(k => result = result[k])
  return result
}

get(activityLog, 'events', 0, 'type') // 'Read' | 'Write'
```

As you saw, mapped types have their own special syntax. And like index signatures, you can have at most one mapped type per object:

```
type MyMappedType = {
  [Key in UnionType]: ValueType
}
```

As the name implies, it's a way to map over an object's key and value types. In fact, TypeScript uses mapped types to implement its built-in `Record` type we used earlier:

```
type Record<K extends keyof any, T> = {
  [P in K]: T
}
```

Mapped types give you more power than a mere `Record` because in addition to letting you give types to an object's keys and values, when you combine them with keyed-in types, they let you put constraints on which value type corresponds to which key name.

Let's quickly run through some of the things you can do with mapped types.

```
type Account = {
  id: number
  isEmployee: boolean
  notes: string[]
}

// Make all fields optional
type OptionalAccount = {
  [K in keyof Account]?: Account[K] ❶
}

// Make all fields nullable
type NullableAccount = {
  [K in keyof Account]: Account[K] | null ❷
}

// Make all fields read-only
type ReadonlyAccount = {
  readonly [K in keyof Account]: Account[K] ❸
}

// Make all fields writable again (equivalent to Account)
type Account2 = {
  -readonly [K in keyof ReadonlyAccount]: Account[K] ❹
}

// Make all fields required again (equivalent to Account)
type Account3 = {
  [K in keyof OptionalAccount]-?: Account[K] ❺
}
```

❶ We create a new object type `OptionalAccount` by mapping over `Account`, marking each field as optional along the way.

❷ We create a new object type `NullableAccount` by mapping over `Account`, adding `null` as a possible value for each field along the way.

❸ We create a new object type `ReadonlyAccount` by taking `Account` and making each of its fields read-only (that is, readable but not writable).

❹ We can mark fields as optional (?) or `readonly`, and we can also unmark them. With the minus (-) operator—a special type operator only available with mapped types—we can undo ? and `readonly`, making fields required and writable again, respectively. Here we create a new object type `Account2`, equivalent to our `Account` type, by mapping over `ReadonlyAccount` and removing the `readonly` modifier with the minus (-) operator.

❺ We create a new object type `Account3`, equivalent to our original `Account` type, by mapping over `OptionalAccount` and removing the optional (?) operator with the minus (-) operator.

 Minus (-) has a corresponding plus (+) type operator. You will probably never use this operator directly, because it's implied: within a mapped type, `readonly` is equivalent to `+readonly`, and ? is equivalent to +?. + is just there for completeness.

Built-in mapped types

The mapped types we derived in the last section are so useful that TypeScript ships with many of them built in:

`Record<Keys, Values>`
    An object with keys of type `Keys` and values of type `Values`

`Partial<Object>`
    Marks every field in `Object` as optional

`Required<Object>`
    Marks every field in `Object` as nonoptional

`Readonly<Object>`
    Marks every field in `Object` as read-only

`Pick<Object, Keys>`
    Returns a subtype of `Object`, with just the given `Keys`

Companion Object Pattern

The companion object pattern comes to us from Scala (*http://bit.ly/2I9Nqg2*), and is a way to pair together objects and classes that share the same name. In TypeScript, there's a similar pattern that's similarly useful—we'll also call it the companion object pattern—that we can use to pair together a type and an object.

It looks like this:

```
type Currency = {
  unit: 'EUR' | 'GBP' | 'JPY' | 'USD'
  value: number
}

let Currency = {
  DEFAULT: 'USD',
  from(value: number, unit = Currency.DEFAULT): Currency {
    return {unit, value}
  }
}
```

Remember that in TypeScript, types and values live in separate namespaces; you'll read a little more about this in "Declaration Merging" on page 226. That means in the same scope, you can have the same name (in this example, Currency) bound to both a type and a value. With the companion object pattern, we exploit this separate namespacing to declare a name twice: first as a type, then as a value.

This pattern has a few nice properties. It lets you group type and value information that's semantically part of a single name (like Currency) together. It also lets consumers import both at once:

```
import {Currency} from './Currency'

let amountDue: Currency = { ❶
  unit: 'JPY',
  value: 83733.10
}

let otherAmountDue = Currency.from(330, 'EUR') ❷
```

❶ Using Currency as a type

❷ Using Currency as a value

Use the companion object pattern when a type and an object are semantically related, with the object providing utility methods that operate on the type.

Advanced Function Types

Let's take a look at a few more advanced techniques that are often used with function types.

Improving Type Inference for Tuples

When you declare a tuple in TypeScript, TypeScript will be lenient about inferring that tuple's type. It will infer the most general possible type based on what you gave it, ignoring the length of your tuple and which position holds which type:

```
let a = [1, true] // (number | boolean)[]
```

But sometimes you want inference that's stricter, that would treat a as a fixed-length tuple and not as an array. You could, of course, use a type assertion to cast your tuple to a tuple type (more on this in "Type Assertions" on page 148). Or, you could use an as const assertion ("The const type" on page 123) to infer the tuple's type as narrowly as possible, marking it as read-only.

What if you want to type your tuple as a tuple, but avoid a type assertion, and avoid the narrow inference and read-only modifier that as const gives you? To do that, you can take advantage of the way TypeScript infers types for rest parameters (jump back to "Using bounded polymorphism to model arity" on page 77 for more about that):

```
function tuple< ❶
  T extends unknown[] ❷
>(
  ...ts: T ❸
): T { ❹
  return ts ❺
}

let a = tuple(1, true) // [number, boolean]
```

❶ We declare a tuple function that we'll use to construct tuple types (instead of using the built-in [] syntax).

❷ We declare a single type parameter T that's a subtype of unknown[] (meaning T is an array of any kind of type).

❸ tuple takes a variable number of parameters, ts. Because T describes a rest parameter, TypeScript will infer a tuple type for it.

❹ tuple returns a value of the same tuple type that it inferred ts as.

❺ Our function returns the same argument that we passed it. The magic is all in the types.

Take advantage of this technique in order to avoid type assertions when your code uses lots of tuple types.

User-Defined Type Guards

For some kinds of `boolean`-returning functions, simply saying that your function returns a `boolean` may not be enough. For example, let's write a function that tells you if you passed it a `string` or not:

```
function isString(a: unknown): boolean {
  return typeof a === 'string'
}

isString('a') // evaluates to true
isString([7]) // evaluates to false
```

So far so good. What happens if you try to use `isString` in some real-world code?

```
function parseInput(input: string | number) {
  let formattedInput: string
  if (isString(input)) {
    formattedInput = input.toUpperCase() // Error TS2339: Property 'toUpperCase'
  }                                       // does not exist on type 'number'.
}
```

What gives? If `typeof` works for regular type refinement (see "Refinement" on page 126), why doesn't it work here?

The thing about type refinement is it's only powerful enough to refine the type of a variable in the scope you're in. As soon as you leave that scope, the refinement doesn't carry over to whatever new scope you're in. In our `isString` implementation, we refined the input parameter's type to `string` using `typeof`, but because type refinement doesn't carry over to new scopes, it got lost—all TypeScript knows is that `isString` returned a `boolean`.

What we can do is tell the typechecker that not only does `isString` return a `boolean`, but whenever that `boolean` is `true`, the argument we passed to `isString` is a `string`. To do that, we use something called a *user-defined type guard*:

```
function isString(a: unknown): a is string {
  return typeof a === 'string'
}
```

Type guards are a built-in TypeScript feature, and are what lets you refine types with `typeof` and `instanceof`. But sometimes, you need the ability to declare type guards yourself—that's what the `is` operator is for. When you have a function that refines its parameters' types and returns a `boolean`, you can use a user-defined type guard to make sure that refinement is flowed whenever you use that function.

User-defined type guards are limited to a single parameter, but they aren't limited to simple types:

```
type LegacyDialog = // ...
type Dialog = // ...

function isLegacyDialog(
  dialog: LegacyDialog | Dialog
): dialog is LegacyDialog {
  // ...
}
```

You won't use user-defined type guards often, but when you do, they're awesome for writing clean, reusable code. Without them, you'd have to inline all your `typeof` and `instanceof` type guards instead of building functions like `isLegacyDialog` and `isString` to perform those same checks in a better-encapsulated, more readable way.

Conditional Types

Conditional types might be the single most unique feature in all of TypeScript. At a high level, conditional types let you say, "Declare a type T that depends on types U and V; if U <: V, then assign T to A, and otherwise, assign T to B."

In code it might look like this:

```
type IsString<T> = T extends string   ❶
  ? true   ❷
  : false  ❸

type A = IsString<string> // true
type B = IsString<number> // false
```

Let's break that down line by line.

❶ We declare a new conditional type `IsString` that takes a generic type T. The "condition" part of this conditional type is `T extends string`; that is, "Is T a subtype of `string`?"

❷ If T is a subtype of `string`, we resolve to the type `true`.

❸ Otherwise, we resolve to the type `false`.

Note how the syntax looks just like a regular value-level ternary expression, but at the type level. And like regular ternary expressions, you can nest them too.

Conditional types aren't limited to type aliases. You can use them almost anywhere you can use a type: in type aliases, interfaces, classes, parameter types, and generic defaults in functions and methods.

Distributive Conditionals

While you can express simple conditions like the examples we just looked at in a variety of ways in TypeScript—with conditional types, overloaded function signatures, and mapped types—conditional types let you do more. The reason for this is that they follow the *distributive law* (remember, from algebra class?). That means if you have a conditional type, then the expressions on the right are equivalent to those on the left in Table 6-1.

Table 6-1. Distributing conditional types

This...	Is equivalent to
string extends T ? A : B	string extends T ? A : B
(string | number) extends T ? A : B	(string extends T ? A : B) | (number extends T ? A : B)
(string | number | boolean) extends T ? A : B	(string extends T ? A : B) | (number extends T ? A : B) | (boolean extends T ? A : B)

I know, I know, you didn't shell out for this book to learn about math—you're here for the types. So let's get more concrete. Let's say we have a function that takes some variable of type T, and lifts it to an array of type T[]. What happens if we pass in a union type for T?

```
type ToArray<T> = T[]
type A = ToArray<number>          // number[]
type B = ToArray<number | string> // (number | string)[]
```

Pretty straightforward. Now what happens if we add a conditional type? (Note that the conditional doesn't actually do anything here because both its branches resolve to the same type T[]; it's just here to tell TypeScript to *distribute* T over the tuple type.) Take a look:

```
type ToArray2<T> = T extends unknown ? T[] : T[]
type A = ToArray2<number> // number[]
type B = ToArray2<number | string> // number[] | string[]
```

Did you catch that? When you use a conditional type, TypeScript will distribute union types over the conditional's branches. It's like taking the conditional type and mapping (er, *distributing*) it over each element in the union.

Why does any of this matter? Well, it lets you safely express a bunch of common operations.

For example, TypeScript comes with & for computing what two types have in common and | for taking a union of two types. Let's build `Without<T, U>`, which computes the types that are in T but not in U.

```
type Without<T, U> = T extends U ? never : T
```

You use `Without` like so:

```
type A = Without<
  boolean | number | string,
  boolean
> // number | string
```

Let's walk through how TypeScript computes this type:

1. Start with the inputs:

   ```
   type A = Without<boolean | number | string, boolean>
   ```

2. Distribute the condition over the union:

   ```
   type A = Without<boolean, boolean>
           | Without<number, boolean>
           | Without<string, boolean>
   ```

3. Substitute in `Without`'s definition and apply T and U:

   ```
   type A = (boolean extends boolean ? never : boolean)
           | (number extends boolean ? never : number)
           | (string extends boolean ? never : string)
   ```

4. Evaluate the conditions:

   ```
   type A = never
           | number
           | string
   ```

5. Simplify:

   ```
   type A = number | string
   ```

If it wasn't for the distributive property of conditional types, we would have ended up with `never` (if you're not sure why, walk through what would happen for yourself!).

The infer Keyword

The final feature of conditional types is the ability to declare generic types as part of a condition. As a refresher, so far we've seen just one way to declare generic type parameters: using angle brackets (`<T>`). Conditional types have their own syntax for declaring generic types inline: the `infer` keyword.

Let's declare a conditional type `ElementType`, which gets the type of an array's elements:

```
type ElementType<T> = T extends unknown[] ? T[number] : T
type A = ElementType<number[]> // number
```

Now, let's rewrite it using `infer`:

```
type ElementType2<T> = T extends (infer U)[] ? U : T
type B = ElementType2<number[]> // number
```

In this simple example `ElementType` is equivalent to `ElementType2`. Notice how the `infer` clause declares a new type variable, U—TypeScript will infer the type of U from context, based on what T you passed to `ElementType2`.

Also notice why we declared U inline instead of declaring it up front, alongside T. What would have happened if we did declare it up front?

```
type ElementUgly<T, U> = T extends U[] ? U : T
type C = ElementUgly<number[]> // Error TS2314: Generic type 'ElementUgly'
                               // requires 2 type argument(s).
```

Uh-oh. Because `ElementUgly` defines two generic types, T and U, we have to pass both of them in when instantiating `ElementUgly`. But if we do that, that defeats the point of having an `ElementUgly` type in the first place; it puts the burden of computing U on the caller, when we wanted `ElementUgly` to compute the type itself.

Honestly, this was a bit of a silly example because we already have the keying-in operator (`[]`) to look up the type of an array's elements. What about a more complicated example?

```
type SecondArg<F> = F extends (a: any, b: infer B) => any ? B : never

// Get the type of Array.slice
type F = typeof Array['prototype']['slice']

type A = SecondArg<F> // number | undefined
```

So, `[].slice`'s second argument is a `number | undefined`. And we know this at compile time—try doing *that* in Java.

Built-in Conditional Types

Conditional types let you express some really powerful operations at the type level. That's why TypeScript ships with a few globally available conditional types out of the box:

Exclude<T, U>

Like our `Without` type from before, computes those types in T that are not in U:

```
type A = number | string
type B = string
type C = Exclude<A, B>  // number
```

Extract<T, U>

Computes the types in T that you can assign to U:

```
type A = number | string
type B = string
type C = Extract<A, B>  // string
```

NonNullable<T>

Computes a version of T that excludes null and undefined:

```
type A = {a?: number | null}
type B = NonNullable<A['a']>  // number
```

ReturnType<F>

Computes a function's return type (note that this doesn't work as you'd expect for generic and overloaded functions):

```
type F = (a: number) => string
type R = ReturnType<F>  // string
```

InstanceType<C>

Computes the instance type of a class constructor:

```
type A = {new(): B}
type B = {b: number}
type I = InstanceType<A>  // {b: number}
```

Escape Hatches

Sometimes you don't have time to type something perfectly, and you just want Type-Script to trust that what you're doing is safe. Maybe a type declaration for a third party module you're using is wrong and you want to test your code before contributing the fix back to DefinitelyTyped,[4] or maybe you're getting data from an API and you haven't regenerated type declarations with Apollo yet.

Luckily, TypeScript knows that we're only human, and gives us a few escape hatches for when we just want to do something and don't have time to prove to TypeScript that it's safe.

 In case it's not obvious, you should use the following TypeScript features as little as possible. If you find yourself relying on them, you might be doing something wrong.

---

4 DefinitelyTyped (*https://github.com/DefinitelyTyped/DefinitelyTyped*) is the open source repository for type declarations for third-party JavaScript. To learn more, jump ahead to "JavaScript That Has Type Declarations on DefinitelyTyped" on page 245.

Type Assertions

If you have a type B and A <: B <: C, then you can assert to the typechecker that B is actually an A or a C. Notably, you can only assert that a type is a supertype or a subtype of itself—you can't, for example, assert that a number is a string, because those types aren't related.

TypeScript gives us two syntaxes for type assertions:

```
function formatInput(input: string) {
  // ...
}

function getUserInput(): string | number {
  // ...
}

let input = getUserInput()

// Assert that input is a string
formatInput(input as string) ❶

// This is equivalent to
formatInput(<string>input) ❷
```

❶ We use a type assertion (as) to tell TypeScript that input is a string, not a string | number as the types would have us believe. You might do this, for example, if you want to quickly test out your formatInput function and you know for sure that getUserInput returns a string for your test.

❷ The legacy syntax for type assertions uses angle brackets. The two syntaxes are functionally equivalent.

 Prefer as syntax for type assertions over angle bracket (<>) syntax. The former is unambiguous, but the latter can clash with TSX syntax (see "TSX = JSX + TypeScript" on page 202). Use TSLint's no-angle-bracket-type-assertion (*http://bit.ly/2WEGGKe*) rule to automatically enforce this for your codebase.

Sometimes, two types might not be sufficiently related, so you can't assert that one is the other. To get around this, simply assert as any (remember from "Assignability" on page 121 that any is assignable to anything), then spend a few minutes in the corner thinking about what you've done:

```
function addToList(list: string[], item: string) {
  // ...
}
```

```
addToList('this is really,' as any, 'really unsafe')
```

Clearly, type assertions are unsafe, and you should avoid using them when possible.

Nonnull Assertions

For the special case of nullable types—that is, a type that's T | null or T | null | undefined—TypeScript has special syntax for asserting that a value of that type is a T, and not null or undefined. This comes up in a few places.

For example, say we've written a framework for showing and hiding dialogs in a web app. Each dialog gets a unique ID, which we use to get a reference to the dialog's DOM node. Once a dialog is removed from the DOM, we delete its ID, indicating that it's no longer live in the DOM:

```
type Dialog = {
  id?: string
}

function closeDialog(dialog: Dialog) {
  if (!dialog.id) {                    ❶
    return
  }
  setTimeout(() =>                     ❷
    removeFromDOM(
      dialog,
      document.getElementById(dialog.id) // Error TS2345: Argument of type
                                         // 'string | undefined' is not assignable
                                         // to parameter of type 'string'.  ❸
    )
  )
}

function removeFromDOM(dialog: Dialog, element: Element) {
  element.parentNode.removeChild(element) // Error TS2531: Object is possibly
                                          //'null'.  ❹
  delete dialog.id
}
```

❶ If the dialog is already deleted (so it has no id), we return early.

❷ We remove the dialog from the DOM on the next turn of the event loop, so that any other code that depends on dialog has a chance to finish running.

❸ Because we're inside the arrow function, we're now in a new scope. TypeScript doesn't know if some code mutated dialog between ❶ and ❸, so it invalidates the refinement we made in ❶. On top of that, while we know that if dialog.id is defined then an element with that ID definitely exists in the DOM (because we

designed our framework that way), all TypeScript knows is that calling docu
ment.getElementById returns an HTMLElement | null. We know it'll always be
a nonnullable HTMLElement, but TypeScript doesn't know that—it only knows
about the types we gave it.

❹ Similarly, while we know that the dialog is definitely in the DOM and it definitely
has a parent DOM node, all TypeScript knows is that the type of ele
ment.parentNode is Node | null.

One way to fix this is to add a bunch of if (_ === null) checks everywhere. While
that's the right way to do it if you're unsure if something is null or not, TypeScript
comes with special syntax for when you're sure it's not null | undefined:

```
type Dialog = {
  id?: string
}

function closeDialog(dialog: Dialog) {
  if (!dialog.id) {
    return
  }
  setTimeout(() =>
    removeFromDOM(
      dialog,
      document.getElementById(dialog.id!)!
    )
  )
}

function removeFromDOM(dialog: Dialog, element: Element) {
  element.parentNode!.removeChild(element)
  delete dialog.id
}
```

Notice the sprinkling of nonnull assertion operators (!) that tell TypeScript that
we're sure dialog.id, the result of our document.getElementById call, and ele
ment.parentNode are defined. When a nonnull assertion follows a type that might be
null or undefined, TypeScript will assume that the type is defined: T | null | unde
fined becomes a T, number | string | null becomes number | string, and so on.

When you find yourself using nonnull assertions a lot, it's often a sign that you
should refactor your code. For example, we could get rid of an assertion by splitting
Dialog into a union of two types:

```
type VisibleDialog = {id: string}
type DestroyedDialog = {}
type Dialog = VisibleDialog | DestroyedDialog
```

We can then update closeDialog to take advantage of the union:

```
function closeDialog(dialog: Dialog) {
  if (!('id' in dialog)) {
    return
  }
  setTimeout(() =>
    removeFromDOM(
      dialog,
      document.getElementById(dialog.id)!
    )
  )
}

function removeFromDOM(dialog: VisibleDialog, element: Element) {
  element.parentNode!.removeChild(element)
  delete dialog.id
}
```

After we check that `dialog` has an `id` property defined—implying that it's a `VisibleDialog`—even inside the arrow function TypeScript knows that the reference to `dialog` hasn't changed: the `dialog` inside the arrow function is the same `dialog` outside the function, so the refinement carries over instead of being invalidated like it was in the last example.

Definite Assignment Assertions

TypeScript has special syntax for the special case of nonnull assertions for definite assignment checks (as a reminder, a definite assignment check is TypeScript's way of making sure that by the time you use a variable, that variable has been assigned a value). For example:

```
let userId: string

userId.toUpperCase() // Error TS2454: Variable 'userId' is used
                     // before being assigned.
```

Clearly, TypeScript just did us a great service by catching this error. We declared the variable `userId`, but forgot to assign a value to it before we tried to convert it to uppercase. This would have been a runtime error if TypeScript hadn't noticed it!

But, what if our code looks more like this?

```
let userId: string
fetchUser()

userId.toUpperCase() // Error TS2454: Variable 'userId' is used
                     // before being assigned.

function fetchUser() {
  userId = globalCache.get('userId')
}
```

We happen to have the world's greatest cache, and when we query this cache we get a cache hit 100% of of the time. So after the call to `fetchUser`, `userId` is guaranteed to be defined. But TypeScript isn't able to statically detect that, so it still throws the same error as before. We can use a definite assignment assertion to tell TypeScript that `userId` will definitely be assigned by the time we read it (notice the exclamation mark):

```
let userId!: string
fetchUser()

userId.toUpperCase() // OK

function fetchUser() {
  userId = globalCache.get('userId')
}
```

As with type assertions and nonnull assertions, if you find yourself using definite assignment assertions often, you might be doing something wrong.

Simulating Nominal Types

By this point in the book, if I were to shake you awake at three in the morning and yell "IS TYPESCRIPT'S TYPE SYSTEM STRUCTURAL OR NOMINAL?!" you'd yell back "OF COURSE IT'S STRUCTURAL! NOW GET OUT OF MY HOUSE OR I'LL CALL THE POLICE!" That would be a fair response to me breaking in for early morning type system questions.

Laws aside, the reality is that sometimes nominal types really are useful. For example, let's say you have a few `ID` types in your application, representing unique ways of addressing the different types of objects in your system:

```
type CompanyID = string
type OrderID = string
type UserID = string
type ID = CompanyID | OrderID | UserID
```

A value of type `UserID` might be a simple hash that looks like `"d21b1dbf"`. So while you might alias it as `UserID`, under the hood it's of course just a regular `string`. A function that takes a `UserID` might look like this:

```
function queryForUser(id: UserID) {
  // ...
}
```

This is great documentation, and it helps other engineers on your team know for sure which type of `ID` they should pass in. But since `UserID` is just an alias for `string`, this approach does little to prevent bugs. An engineer might accidentally pass in the wrong type of `ID`, and the types system will be none the wiser!

```
let id: CompanyID = 'b4843361'
queryForUser(id) // OK (!!!)
```

This is where *nominal types* come in handy.[5] While TypeScript doesn't support nominal types out of the box, we can simulate them with a technique called *type branding*. Type branding takes a little work to set up, and using it in TypeScript is not as smooth an experience as it is in languages that have built-in support for nominal type aliases. That said, branded types can make your program significantly safer.

 Depending on your application and the size of your engineering team (the larger your team, the more likely this technique will come in handy for preventing mistakes), you may not need to do this.

Start by creating a synthetic *type brand* for each of your nominal types:

```
type CompanyID = string & {readonly brand: unique symbol}
type OrderID = string & {readonly brand: unique symbol}
type UserID = string & {readonly brand: unique symbol}
type ID = CompanyID | OrderID | UserID
```

An intersection of `string` and `{readonly brand: unique symbol}` is, of course, gibberish. I chose it because it's impossible to naturally construct that type, and the only way to create a value of that type is with an assertion. That's the crucial property of branded types: they make it hard to accidentally use a wrong type in their place. I used `unique symbol` as the "brand" because it's one of two truly nominal kinds of types in TypeScript (the other is `enum`); I took an intersection of that brand with `string` so that we can assert that a given `string` is a given branded type.

We now need a way to create values of type `CompanyID`, `OrderID`, and `UserID`. To do that, we'll use the companion object pattern (introduced in "Companion Object Pattern" on page 140). We'll make a constructor for each branded type, using a type assertion to construct a value of each of our gibberish types:

```
function CompanyID(id: string) {
  return id as CompanyID
}

function OrderID(id: string) {
  return id as OrderID
}

function UserID(id: string) {
  return id as UserID
}
```

---

5 In some languages, these are also called *opaque types*.

Finally, let's see what it feels like to use these types:

```
function queryForUser(id: UserID) {
  // ...
}

let companyId = CompanyID('8a6076cf')
let orderId = OrderID('9994acc1')
let userId = UserID('d21b1dbf')

queryForUser(userId)    // OK
queryForUser(companyId) // Error TS2345: Argument of type 'CompanyID' is not
                        // assignable to parameter of type 'UserID'.
```

What's nice about this approach is how little runtime overhead it has: just one function call per ID construction, which will probably be inlined by your JavaScript VM anyway. At runtime, each ID is simply a string—the brand is purely a compile-time construct.

Again, for most applications this approach is overkill. But for large applications, and when working with easily confused types like different kinds of IDs, branded types can be a killer safety feature.

Safely Extending the Prototype

When building JavaScript applications, tradition holds that it's unsafe to extend prototypes for built-in types. This rule of thumb goes back to before the days of jQuery, when wise JavaScript mages built libraries like MooTools (*https://mootools.net*) that extended and overwrote built-in prototype methods directly. But when too many mages augmented prototypes at once, conflicts arose. And without static type systems, you'd only find out about these conflicts from angry users at runtime.

If you're not coming from JavaScript, you may be surprised to learn that in JavaScript, you can modify any built-in method (like [].push, 'abc'.toUpperCase, or Object.assign) at runtime. Because it's such a dynamic language, JavaScript gives you direct access to prototypes for every built-in object—Array.prototype, Function.prototype, Object.prototype, and so on.

While back in the day extending these prototypes was unsafe, if your code is covered by a static type system like TypeScript, then you can now do it safely.[6]

---

6 There are other reasons why you might want to avoid extending the prototype, like code portability, making your dependency graphs more explicit, or improving performance by only loading those methods that you actually use. However, safety is no longer one of those reasons.

For example, we'll add a zip method to the Array prototype. It takes two things to safely extend the prototype. First, in a *.ts* file (say, *zip.ts*), we extend the type of Array's prototype; then, we augment the prototype with our new zip method:

```
// Tell TypeScript about .zip
interface Array<T> { ❶
  zip<U>(list: U[]): [T, U][]
}

// Implement .zip
Array.prototype.zip = function<T, U>(
  this: T[], ❷
  list: U[]
): [T, U][] {
  return this.map((v, k) =>
    tuple(v, list[k]) ❸
  )
}
```

❶ We start by telling TypeScript that we're adding zip to Array. We take advantage of interface merging ("Declaration Merging" on page 93) to augment the global Array<T> interface, adding our own zip method to the already globally defined interface.

Since our file doesn't have any explicit imports or exports—meaning it's in script mode, as described in "Module Mode Versus Script Mode" on page 222—we were able to augment the global Array interface directly by declaring an interface with the exact same name as the existing Array<T> interface, and letting TypeScript take care of merging the two for us. If our file were in module mode (which might be the case if, for example, we needed to import something for our zip implementation), we'd have to wrap our global extension in a declare global type declaration (see "Type Declarations" on page 230):

```
declare global {
  interface Array<T> {
    zip<U>(list: U[]): [T, U][]
  }
}
```

global is a special namespace containing all the globally defined values (anything that you can use in a module-mode file without importing it first; see Chapter 10) that lets you augment names in the global scope from a file in module mode.

❷ We then implement the zip method on Array's prototype. We use a this type so that TypeScript correctly infers the T type of the array we're calling .zip on.

❸ Because TypeScript infers the mapping function's return type as `(T | U)[]` (TypeScript isn't smart enough to realize that it's in fact always a tuple with `T` in the zeroth index and `U` in the first), we use our `tuple` utility (from "Improving Type Inference for Tuples" on page 141) to create a tuple type without resorting to a type assertion.

Notice that when we declare `interface Array<T>` we augment the global `Array` namespace for our whole TypeScript project—meaning even if we don't import *zip.ts* from our file, TypeScript will think that `[].zip` is available. But in order to augment `Array.prototype`, we have to be sure that whatever file uses `zip` loads *zip.ts* first, in order to install the `zip` method on `Array.prototype`. How do we make sure that any file that uses `zip` loads *zip.ts* first?

Easy: we update our *tsconfig.json* to explicitly exclude *zip.ts* from our project, so that consumers have to explicitly `import` it first:

```
{
  *exclude*: [
    "./zip.ts"
  ]
}
```

Now we can use `zip` as we please, with total safety:

```
import './zip'

[1, 2, 3]
  .map(n => n * 2)        // number[]
  .zip(['a', 'b', 'c'])  // [number, string][]
```

Running this gives us the result of first mapping, then zipping the array:

```
[
  [2, 'a'],
  [4, 'b'],
  [6, 'c']
]
```

Summary

In this chapter we covered the most advanced features of TypeScript's type system: from the ins and outs of variance to flow-based type inference, refinement, type widening, totality, and mapped and conditional types. We then derived a few advanced patterns for working with types: type branding to simulate nominal types, taking advantage of the distributive property of conditional types to operate on types at the type level, and safely extending prototypes.

If you didn't understand or don't remember everything, that's OK—come back to this chapter later, and use it as a reference when you're struggling with how to express something more safely.

Exercises

1. For each of the following pairs of types, decide if the first type is assignable to the second type, and why or why not. Think about these in terms of subtyping and variance, and refer to the rules at the start of the chapter if you're unsure (if you're still unsure, just type it into your code editor to check!):

   a. `1` and `number`

   b. `number` and `1`

   c. `string` and `number | string`

   d. `boolean` and `number`

   e. `number[]` and `(number | string)[]`

   f. `(number | string)[]` and `number[]`

   g. `{a: true}` and `{a: boolean}`

   h. `{a: {b: [string]}}` and `{a: {b: [number | string]}}`

   i. `(a: number) => string` and `(b: number) => string`

   j. `(a: number) => string` and `(a: string) => string`

   k. `(a: number | string) => string` and `(a: string) => string`

   l. `E.X` (defined in an enum `enum E {X = 'X'}`) and `F.X` (defined in an enum `enum F {X = 'X'}`)

2. If you have an object type `type O = {a: {b: {c: string}}}`, what's the type of `keyof O`? What about `O['a']['b']`?

3. Write an `Exclusive<T, U>` type that computes the types that are in either `T` or `U`, but not both. For example, `Exclusive<1 | 2 | 3, 2 | 3 | 4>` should resolve to `1 | 4`. Write out step by step how the typechecker evaluates `Exclusive<1 | 2, 2 | 4>`.

4. Rewrite the example (from "Definite Assignment Assertions" on page 151) to avoid the definite assignment assertion.

Handling Errors

A physicist, a structural engineer, and a programmer were in a car driving over a steep alpine pass when the brakes failed. The car went faster and faster, they were struggling to get around the corners, and once or twice the flimsy crash barrier saved them from tumbling down the side of the mountain. They were sure they were all going to die, when suddenly they spotted an escape lane. They pulled into the escape lane, and came safely to a halt.

The physicist said, "We need to model the friction in the brake pads and the resultant temperature rise, and see if we can work out why they failed."

The structural engineer said, "I think I've got a few spanners in the back. I'll take a look and see if I can work out what's wrong."

The programmer said, "Why don't we see if it's reproducible?"

—Anonymous

TypeScript does everything it can to move runtime exceptions to compile time: from the rich type system it provides to the powerful static and symbolic analyses it performs, it works hard so you don't have to spend your Friday nights debugging misspelled variables and null pointer exceptions (and so your on-call coworker doesn't have to be late to their great aunt's birthday party because of it).

Unfortunately, regardless of what language you write in, sometimes runtime exceptions do sneak through. TypeScript is really good about preventing them, but even it can't prevent things like network and filesystem failures, errors parsing user input, stack overflows, and out of memory errors. What it does do—thanks to its lush type system—is give you lots of ways to deal with the runtime errors that end up making it through.

In this chapter I'll walk you through the most common patterns for representing and handling errors in TypeScript:

- Returning null
- Throwing exceptions
- Returning exceptions
- The Option type

Which mechanism you use is up to you, and depends on your application. As I cover each error-handling mechanism, I'll talk about its pros and cons so you can make the right choice for yourself.

Returning null

We're going to write a program that asks a user for their birthday, which we will then parse into a Date object:

```
function ask() {
  return prompt('When is your birthday?')
}

function parse(birthday: string): Date {
  return new Date(birthday)
}

let date = parse(ask())
console.info('Date is', date.toISOString())
```

We should probably validate the date the user entered—it's just a text prompt, after all:

```
// ...
function parse(birthday: string): Date | null {
  let date = new Date(birthday)
  if (!isValid(date)) {
    return null
  }
  return date
}

// Checks if the given date is valid
function isValid(date: Date) {
  return Object.prototype.toString.call(date) === '[object Date]'
    && !Number.isNaN(date.getTime())
}
```

When we consume this, we're forced to first check if the result is null before we can use it:

```
// ...
let date = parse(ask())
if (date) {
  console.info('Date is', date.toISOString())
} else {
  console.error('Error parsing date for some reason')
}
```

Returning `null` is the most lightweight way to handle errors in a typesafe way. Valid user input results in a `Date`, invalid user input in a `null`, and the type system checks for us that we handled both.

However, we lose some information doing it this way `parse` doesn't tell us why exactly the operation failed, which stinks for whatever engineer has to comb through our logs to debug this, as well as the user who gets a pop up saying that there was an "Error parsing date for some reason" rather than a specific, actionable error like "Enter a date in the form YYYY/MM/DD."

Returning `null` is also difficult to compose: having to check for `null` after every operation can become verbose as you start to nest and chain operations.

Throwing Exceptions

Let's throw an exception instead of returning `null`, so that we can handle specific failure modes and have some metadata about the failure so we can debug it more easily.

```
// ...
function parse(birthday: string): Date {
  let date = new Date(birthday)
  if (!isValid(date)) {
    throw new RangeError('Enter a date in the form YYYY/MM/DD')
  }
  return date
}
```

Now when we consume this code, we need to be careful to catch the exception so that we can handle it gracefully without crashing our whole application:

```
// ...
try {
  let date = parse(ask())
  console.info('Date is', date.toISOString())
} catch (e) {
  console.error(e.message)
}
```

We probably want to be careful to rethrow other exceptions, so we don't silently swallow every possible error:

```
// ...
try {
```

```
    let date = parse(ask())
    console.info('Date is', date.toISOString())
  } catch (e) {
    if (e instanceof RangeError) {
      console.error(e.message)
    } else {
      throw e
    }
  }
}
```

We might want to subclass the error for something more specific, so that when
another engineer changes parse or ask to throw other RangeErrors, we can differentiate between our error and the one they added:

```
// ...

// Custom error types
class InvalidDateFormatError extends RangeError {}
class DateIsInTheFutureError extends RangeError {}

function parse(birthday: string): Date {
  let date = new Date(birthday)
  if (!isValid(date)) {
    throw new InvalidDateFormatError('Enter a date in the form YYYY/MM/DD')
  }
  if (date.getTime() > Date.now()) {
    throw new DateIsInTheFutureError('Are you a timelord?')
  }
  return date
}

try {
  let date = parse(ask())
  console.info('Date is', date.toISOString())
} catch (e) {
  if (e instanceof InvalidDateFormatError) {
    console.error(e.message)
  } else if (e instanceof DateIsInTheFutureError) {
    console.info(e.message)
  } else {
    throw e
  }
}
```

Looking good. We can now do more than just signal that something failed: we can
use a custom error to indicate *why* it failed. These errors might come in handy when
combing through our server logs to debug an issue, or we can map them to specific
error dialogs to give our users actionable feedback about what they did wrong and
how they can fix it. We can also effectively chain and nest operations by wrapping

any number of operations in a single `try`/`catch` (we don't have to check each operation for failure, like we did when returning `null`).

What does it feel like to use this code? Say the big `try`/`catch` is in one file, and the rest of the code is in a library being imported from somewhere else. How would an engineer know to catch those specific types of errors (`InvalidDateFormatError` and `DateIsInTheFutureError`), or to even just check for a regular old `RangeError`? (Remember that TypeScript doesn't encode exceptions as part of a function's signature.) We could indicate it in our function's name (`parseThrows`), or include it in a docblock:

```
/**
 * @throws {InvalidDateFormatError} The user entered their birthday incorrectly.
 * @throws {DateIsInTheFutureError} The user entered a birthday in the future.
 */
function parse(birthday: string): Date {
  // ...
```

But in practice, an engineer probably wouldn't wrap this code in a `try`/`catch` and check for exceptions at all, because engineers are lazy (at least, I am), and the type system isn't telling them that they missed a case and should handle it. Sometimes, though—like in this example—errors are so expected that downstream code really should handle them, lest they cause the program to crash.

How else can we indicate to consumers that they should handle both the success and the error cases?

Returning Exceptions

TypeScript isn't Java, and doesn't support `throws` clauses.[1] But we can achieve something similar with union types:

```
// ...
function parse(
  birthday: string
): Date | InvalidDateFormatError | DateIsInTheFutureError {
  let date = new Date(birthday)
  if (!isValid(date)) {
    return new InvalidDateFormatError('Enter a date in the form YYYY/MM/DD')
  }
  if (date.getTime() > Date.now()) {
    return new DateIsInTheFutureError('Are you a timelord?')
  }
```

---

1 If you haven't worked with Java before, a `throws` clause indicates which types of runtime exceptions a method might throw, so a consumer has to handle those exceptions.

```
  return date
}
```

Now a consumer is forced to handle all three cases—InvalidDateFormatError, DateIsInTheFutureError, and successful parse—or they'll get a TypeError at compile time:

```
// ...
let result = parse(ask()) // Either a date or an error
if (result instanceof InvalidDateFormatError) {
  console.error(result.message)
} else if (result instanceof DateIsInTheFutureError) {
  console.info(result.message)
} else {
  console.info('Date is', result.toISOString())
}
```

Here, we successfully took advantage of TypeScript's type system to:

- Encode likely exceptions in parse's signature.
- Communicate to consumers which specific exceptions might be thrown.
- Force consumers to handle (or rethrow) each of the exceptions.

A lazy consumer can avoid handling each error individually. But they have to do so explicitly:

```
// ...
let result = parse(ask()) // Either a date or an error
if (result instanceof Error) {
  console.error(result.message)
} else {
  console.info('Date is', result.toISOString())
}
```

Of course, your program might still crash due to an out of memory error or a stack overflow exception, but there's not much we can do to recover from those.

This approach is lightweight and doesn't require fancy data structures, but it's also informative enough that consumers will know what type of failure an error represents and what to search for to find more information.

A downside is that chaining and nesting error-giving operations can quickly get verbose. If a function returns T | Error1, then any function that consumes that function has two options:

1. Explicitly handle Error1.
2. Handle T (the success case) and pass Error1 through to its consumers to handle. If you do this enough, the list of possible errors that a consumer has to handle grows quickly:

```
function x(): T | Error1 {
  // ...
}
function y(): U | Error1 | Error2 {
  let a = x()
  if (a instanceof Error) {
    return a
  }
  // Do something with a
}
function z(): U | Error1 | Error2 | Error3 {
  let a = y()
  if (a instanceof Error) {
    return a
  }
  // Do something with a
}
```

This approach is verbose, but gives us excellent safety.

The Option Type

You can also describe exceptions using special-purpose data types. This approach has some downsides compared to returning unions of values and errors (notably, interoperability with code that doesn't use these data types), but it does give you the ability to chain operations over possibly errored computations. Three of the most popular options (heh!) are the Try, Option,[2] and Either types. In this chapter, we'll just cover the Option type;[3] the other two are similar in spirit.

 Note that the Try, Option, and Either data types don't come built into JavaScript environments the same way that Array, Error, Map, or Promise are. If you want to use these types, you'll have to find implementations on NPM, or write them yourself.

The Option type comes to us from languages like Haskell, OCaml, Scala, and Rust. The idea is that instead of returning a value, you return a *container* that may or may not have a value in it. The container has a few methods defined on it, which lets you chain operations even though there may not actually be a value inside. The container can be pretty much any data structure, so long as it can hold a value. For example, you could use an array as the container:

---

2 Also called the Maybe type.

3 Google "try type" or "either type" for more information on those types.

```
// ...
function parse(birthday: string): Date[] {
  let date = new Date(birthday)
  if (!isValid(date)) {
    return []
  }
  return [date]
}

let date = parse(ask())
date
  .map(_ => _.toISOString())
  .forEach(_ => console.info('Date is', _))
```

 As you may have noticed, a downside of Option is that, much like our original null-returning approach, it doesn't tell the consumer why the error happened; it just signals that something went wrong.

Where Option really shines is when you need to do multiple operations in a row, each of which might fail.

For example, before we assumed that prompt always succeeds, and parse might fail. But what if prompt can fail too? That might happen if the user cancelled out of the birthday prompt—that's an error and we shouldn't continue our computation. We can model that with... another Option!

```
function ask() {
  let result = prompt('When is your birthday?')
  if (result === null) {
    return []
  }
  return [result]
}
// ...
ask()
  .map(parse)
  .map(date => date.toISOString())
    // Error TS2339: Property 'toISOString' does not exist on type 'Date[]'.
  .forEach(date => console.info('Date is', date))
```

Yikes—that didn't work. Since we mapped an array of Dates (Date[]) to an array of arrays of Dates (Date[][]), we need to flatten it back to an array of Dates before we can keep going:

```
flatten(ask()
  .map(parse))
  .map(date => date.toISOString())
  .forEach(date => console.info('Date is', date))
```

```
// Flattens an array of arrays into an array
function flatten<T>(array: T[][]): T[] {
  return Array.prototype.concat.apply([], array)
}
```

This is all getting a bit unwieldy. Because the types don't tell you much (everything is a regular array), it's hard to understand what's going on in that code at a glance. To fix this, let's wrap what we're doing—putting a value in a container, exposing a way to operate on that value, and exposing a way to get a result back from the container—in a special data type that helps document our approach. Once we're done implementing it, you'll be able to use the data type like this:

```
ask()
  .flatMap(parse)
  .flatMap(date => new Some(date.toISOString()))
  .flatMap(date => new Some('Date is ' + date))
  .getOrElse('Error parsing date for some reason')
```

We'll define our Option type like this:

- Option is an interface that's implemented by two classes: Some<T> and None (see Figure 7-1). They are the two kinds of Options. Some<T> is an Option that contains a value of type T, and None is an Option without a value, which represents a failure.

- Option is both a type and a function. Its type is an interface that simply serves as the supertype of Some and None. Its function is the way to create a new value of type Option.

Option <T>

Some <T>   None

Figure 7-1. Option<T> has two cases: Some<T> and None

Let's start by sketching out the types:

```
interface Option<T> {} ❶
class Some<T> implements Option<T> { ❷
  constructor(private value: T) {}
}
class None implements Option<never> {} ❸
```

❶ Option<T> is an interface that we'll share between Some<T> and None.

❷ Some<T> represents a successful operation that resulted in a value. Like the array we used before, Some<T> is a container for that value.

❸ None represents an operation that failed, and does not contain a value.

These types are equivalent to the following in our array-based Option implementation:

- Option<T> is [T] | [].
- Some<T> is [T].
- None is [].

What can you do with an Option? For our bare-bones implementation, we'll define just two operations:

flatMap
:   A way to chain operations on a possibly empty Option

getOrElse
:   A way to retrieve a value from an Option

We'll start by defining these operations on our Option interface, meaning that Some<T> and None will need to provide concrete implementations for them:

```
interface Option<T> {
  flatMap<U>(f: (value: T) => Option<U>): Option<U>
  getOrElse(value: T): T
}
class Some<T> extends Option<T> {
  constructor(private value: T) {}
}
class None extends Option<never> {}
```

That is:

- flatMap takes a function f that takes a value of type T (the type of the value the Option contains) and returns an Option of U. flatMap calls f with the Option's value, and returns a new Option<U>.

- getOrElse takes a default value of the same type T as the value that the Option contains, and returns either that default value (if the Option is an empty None) or the Option's value (if the Option is a Some<T>).

Guided by the types, let's implement these methods for Some<T> and None:

```
interface Option<T> {
  flatMap<U>(f: (value: T) => Option<U>): Option<U>
  getOrElse(value: T): T
}
class Some<T> implements Option<T> {
  constructor(private value: T) {}
```

```
  flatMap<U>(f: (value: T) => Option<U>): Option<U> {  ❶
    return f(this.value)
  }
  getOrElse(): T {  ❷
    return this.value
  }
}
class None implements Option<never> {
  flatMap<U>(): Option<U> {  ❸
    return this
  }
  getOrElse<U>(value: U): U {  ❹
    return value
  }
}
```

❶ When we call flatMap on a Some<T>, we pass in a function f, which flatMap calls
   with the Some<T>'s value to yield a new Option of a new type.

❷ Calling getOrElse on a Some<T> just returns the Some<T>'s value.

❸ Since a None represents a failed computation, calling flatMap on it always returns
   a None: once a computation fails, we can't recover from that failure (at least not
   with our particular Option implementation).

❹ Calling getOrElse on a None always returns the value we passed into getOrElse.

We can actually go a step beyond this naive implementation, and specify our types
better. If all you know is that you have an Option and a function from T to
Option<U>, then an Option<T> always flatMaps to an Option<U>. But when you
know you have a Some<T> or a None, you can be more specific.

Table 7-1 shows the result types we want when calling flatMap on the two types of
Options.

Table 7-1. Result of calling .flatMap(f) on Some<T> and None

	From Some<T>	From None
To Some<U>	Some<U>	None
To None	None	None

That is, we know that mapping over a None always results in a None, and mapping
over a Some<T> results in either a Some<T> or a None, depending on what calling f
returns. We'll exploit this and use overloaded signatures to give flatMap more specific types:

```
interface Option<T> {
  flatMap<U>(f: (value: T) => None): None
  flatMap<U>(f: (value: T) => Option<U>): Option<U>
  getOrElse(value: T): T
}
class Some<T> implements Option<T> {
  constructor(private value: T) {}
  flatMap<U>(f: (value: T) => None): None
  flatMap<U>(f: (value: T) => Some<U>): Some<U>
  flatMap<U>(f: (value: T) => Option<U>): Option<U> {
    return f(this.value)
  }
  getOrElse(): T {
    return this.value
  }
}
class None implements Option<never> {
  flatMap(): None {
    return this
  }
  getOrElse<U>(value: U): U {
    return value
  }
}
```

We're almost done. All that's left to do is implement the Option function, which we'll use to create new Options. We already implemented the Option *type* as an interface; now we're going to implement a function with the same name (remember that TypeScript has two separate namespaces for types and for values) as a way to create a new Option, similar to what we did in "Companion Object Pattern" on page 140. If a user passes in null or undefined, we'll give them back a None; otherwise, we'll return a Some. Once again, we'll overload the signature to do that:

```
function Option<T>(value: null | undefined): None ❶
function Option<T>(value: T): Some<T> ❷
function Option<T>(value: T): Option<T> { ❸
  if (value == null) {
    return new None
  }
  return new Some(value)
}
```

❶ If the consumer calls Option with null or undefined, we return a None.

❷ Otherwise, we return a Some<T>, where T is the type of value the user passed in.

❸ Finally, we manually calculate an upper bound for the two overloaded signatures. The upper bound of null | undefined and T is T | null | undefined, which simplifies to T. The upper bound of None and Some<T> is None | Some<T>, which we already have a name for: Option<T>.

That's it. We've derived a fully working, minimal Option type that lets us safely perform operations over maybe-null values. We use it like this:

```
let result = Option(6)                // Some<number>
  .flatMap(n => Option(n * 3))        // Some<number>
  .flatMap(n => new None)             // None
  .getOrElse(7)                       // 7
```

Getting back to our birthday prompt example, our code now works as we'd expect:

```
ask()                                              // Option<string>
  .flatMap(parse)                                  // Option<Date>
  .flatMap(date => new Some(date.toISOString()))   // Option<string>
  .flatMap(date => new Some('Date is ' + date))    // Option<string>
  .getOrElse('Error parsing date for some reason') // string
```

Options are a powerful way to work with series of operations that may or may not succeed. They give you excellent type safety, and signal to consumers via the type system that a given operation might fail.

However, Options aren't without their downsides. They signal failure with a None, so you don't get more details about what failed and why. They also don't interoperate with code that doesn't use Options (you'll have to explicitly wrap those APIs to return Options).

Still, what you did there was pretty neat. The overloads you added let you do something that you can't express in most languages, even those that rely on the Option type for working with nullable values. By restricting Option to just Some or None where possible via overloaded call signatures, you made your code a whole lot safer, and a whole lot of Haskell programmers very jealous. Now go grab yourself a cold one—you deserve it.

Summary

In this chapter we covered the different ways to signal and recover from errors in TypeScript: returning null, throwing exceptions, returning exceptions, and the Option type. You now have an arsenal of approaches for safely working with things that might fail. Which approach you choose is up to you, and depends on:

- Whether you want to simply signal that something failed (null, Option), or give more information about why it failed (throwing and returning exceptions).

- Whether you want to force consumers to explicitly handle every possible exception (returning exceptions), or write less error-handling boilerplate (throwing exceptions).

- Whether you need a way to compose errors (Option), or simply handle them when they come up (null, exceptions).

Exercises

1. Design a way to handle errors for the following API, using one of the patterns from this chapter. In this API, every operation might fail—feel free to update the API's method signatures to allow for failures (or don't, if you prefer). Think about how you might perform a sequence of actions while handling errors that come up (e.g., getting the logged-in user's ID, then getting their list of friends, then getting each friend's name):

```
class API {
  getLoggedInUserID(): UserID
  getFriendIDs(userID: UserID): UserID[]
  getUserName(userID: UserID): string
}
```

Asynchronous Programming, Concurrency, and Parallelism

So far in this book, we've dealt mostly with synchronous programs—programs that take some input, do some stuff, and run to completion in a single pass. But the really interesting programs—the building blocks of real-world applications that make network requests, interact with databases and filesystems, respond to user interaction, offload CPU-intensive work to separate threads—all make use of asynchronous APIs like callbacks, promises, and streams.

These asynchronous tasks are where JavaScript really shines and sets itself apart from other mainstream multithreaded languages like Java and C++. Popular JavaScript engines like V8 and SpiderMonkey do with one thread what traditionally required many threads, by being clever and multiplexing tasks over a single thread while other tasks are idling. This *event loop* is the standard threading model for JavaScript engines, and the one that we'll assume you're using. From an end user's perspective, it usually doesn't matter whether your engine uses an event looped model or a multi-threaded one, but it does affect the explanations I'll be giving for how things work and why we design things the way we do.

This event-looped concurrency model is how JavaScript avoids all the common footguns endemic to multithreaded programming, along with the overhead of synchronized data types, mutexes, semaphores, and all the other bits of multithreading jargon. And when you do run JavaScript over multiple threads, it's rare to use shared memory; the typical pattern is to use message passing and to serialize data when sending it between threads. It's a design reminiscent of Erlang, actor systems, and other purely functional concurrency models, and is what makes multithreaded programming in JavaScript foolproof.

That said, asynchronous programming does make programs harder to reason about, because you can no longer mentally trace through a program line by line; you have to know when to pause and move execution elsewhere, and when to resume again.

TypeScript gives us the tools to reason about asynchronous programs: types let us trace through asynchronous work, and built-in support for async/await let us apply familiar synchronous thinking to asynchronous programs. We can also use Type-Script to specify strict message-passing protocols for multithreaded programs (it's a lot simpler than it sounds). If all else fails, TypeScript can give you a back rub when your coworker's asynchronous code gets too complicated and you have to stay late debugging it (behind a compiler flag, of course).

But before we get to working with asynchronous programs, let's talk a bit more about how asynchronicity actually works in modern JavaScript engines—how is it that we can suspend and resume execution on what seems to be a single thread?

JavaScript's Event Loop

Let's start with an example. We'll set a couple of timers, one that fires after one millisecond, and the other after two:

```
setTimeout(() => console.info('A'), 1)
setTimeout(() => console.info('B'), 2)
console.info('C')
```

Now, what will get logged to the console? Is it A, B, C?

If you're a JavaScript programmer, you know intuitively the answer is no—the actual firing order is C, A, then B. If you haven't worked with JavaScript or TypeScript before, this behavior might seem mysterious and unintuitive. In reality, it's pretty straightforward; it just doesn't follow the same concurrency model as a sleep would in C, or scheduling work in another thread would in Java.

At a high level, the JavaScript VM simulates concurrency like this (see Figure 8-1):

- The main JavaScript thread calls into native asynchronous APIs like XMLHTTPRequest (for AJAX requests), setTimeout (for sleeping), readFile (for reading a file from disk), and so on. These APIs are provided by the JavaScript platform—you can't create them yourself.[1]
- Once you call into a native asynchronous API, control returns to the main thread and execution continues as if the API was never called.

---

[1] Well, you can if you fork your browser platform, or build a C++ NodeJS extension.

- Once the asynchronous operation is done, the platform puts a *task* in its *event queue*. Each thread has its own queue, used for relaying the results of asynchronous operations back to the main thread. A task includes some metainformation about the call, and a reference to a callback function from the main thread.
- Whenever the main thread's call stack is emptied, the platform will check its event queue for pending tasks. If there's a task waiting, the platform runs it; that triggers a function call, and control returns to that main thread function. When the call stack resulting from that function call is once again empty, the platform again checks the event queue for tasks that are ready to go. This loop repeats until both the call stack and the event queue are empty, and all asynchronous native API calls have completed.

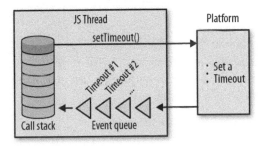

Figure 8-1. JavaScript's event loop: what happens when you call an asynchronous API

Armed with this information, it's time to go back to our setTimeout example. Here's what happens:

1. We call setTimeout, which calls a native timeout API with a reference to the callback we passed in and the argument 1.
2. We call setTimeout again, which calls the native timeout API again with a reference to the second callback we passed in and the argument 2.
3. We log C to the console.
4. In the background, after at least one millisecond, our JavaScript platform adds a task to its event queue indicating that the timeout for the first setTimeout has elapsed, and that its callback is now ready to be called.
5. After another millisecond, the platform adds a second task to the event queue for the second setTimeout's callback.
6. Since the call stack is empty, after step 3 is done the platform looks at its event queue to see if there are any tasks in it. If steps 4 and/or 5 are done, then it will find some tasks. For each task, it will call the corresponding callback function.

7. Once both timers have elapsed and the event queue and call stack are empty, the program exits.

That's why we logged C, A, B, and not A, B, C. With this baseline out of the way, we can start talking about how to type asynchronous code safely.

Working with Callbacks

The basic unit of the asynchronous JavaScript program is the *callback*. A callback is a plain old function that you pass as an argument to another function. As in a synchronous program, that other function invokes your function when it's done doing whatever it does (making a network request, etc.). Callbacks invoked by asynchronous code are just functions, and there's no giveaway in their type signatures that they are invoked asynchronously.

For NodeJS native APIs like `fs.readFile` (used to asynchronously read the contents of a file from disk) and `dns.resolveCname` (used to asynchronously resolve `CNAME` records), the convention for callbacks is that the first parameter is an error or `null`, and the second parameter is a result or `null`.

Here's what `readFile`'s type signature looks like:

```
function readFile(
  path: string,
  options: {encoding: string, flag?: string},
  callback: (err: Error | null, data: string | null) => void
): void
```

Notice that there's nothing special about either `readFile`'s type or `callback`'s type: both are regular JavaScript functions. Looking at the signature, there's no indication that `readFile` is asynchronous and that control will be passed to the next line right after `readFile` is called (not waiting for its result).

To run the following example yourself, be sure to first install type declarations for NodeJS:

```
npm install @types/node --save-dev
```

To learn more about third-party type declarations, jump ahead to "JavaScript That Has Type Declarations on DefinitelyTyped" on page 245.

For example, let's write a NodeJS program that reads and writes to your Apache access log:

```
import * as fs from 'fs'

// Read data from an Apache server's access log
fs.readFile(
  '/var/log/apache2/access_log',
  {encoding: 'utf8'},
  (error, data) => {
    if (error) {
      console.error('error reading!', error)
      return
    }
    console.info('success reading!', data)
  }
)

// Concurrently, write data to the same access log
fs.appendFile(
  '/var/log/apache2/access_log',
  'New access log entry',
  error => {
    if (error) {
      console.error('error writing!', error)
    }
  })
```

Unless you're a TypeScript or JavaScript engineer and are familiar with how NodeJS's built-in APIs work, and know that they're asynchronous and you can't rely on the order in which API calls appear in your code to dictate in which order filesystem operations actually happen, you wouldn't know that we just introduced a subtle bug where the first readFile call may or may not return the access log with our new line appended, depending on how busy the filesystem is at the time this code runs.

You might know that readFile is asynchronous from experience, or because you saw it in NodeJS's documentation, or because you know that NodeJS generally sticks to the convention that if a function's last argument is a function that takes two arguments—an Error | null and a T | null, in that order—then the function is usually asynchronous, or because you ran across the hall to your neighbor for a cup of sugar and ended up staying for a while to chit-chat, then you somehow got on the topic of asynchronous programming in NodeJS and they told you about that time they had a similar issue a couple of months ago and how they fixed it.

Whatever it was, the types certainly didn't help you get there.

Besides the fact that you can't use types to help guide your intuition about the nature of a function's synchronicity, callbacks are also difficult to sequence—which can lead to what some people call "callback pyramids":

```
async1((err1, res1) => {
  if (res1) {
    async2(res1, (err2, res2) => {
      if (res2) {
        async3(res2, (err3, res3) => {
          // ...
        })
      }
    })
  }
})
```

When sequencing operations, you usually want to continue down the chain when an operation succeeds, bailing out as soon as you hit an error. With callbacks, you have to do this manually; when you start accounting for synchronous errors too (e.g., the NodeJS convention is to throw when you give it a badly typed argument, rather than calling your provided callback with an Error object), properly sequencing callbacks can get error-prone.

And sequencing is just one kind of operation you might want to run over asynchronous tasks—you might also want to run functions in parallel to know when they're all done, race them to get the result of the first one that finishes, and so on.

This is a limitation of plain old callbacks. Without more sophisticated abstractions for operating on asynchronous tasks, working with multiple callbacks that depend on each other in some way can get messy fast.

To recap:

- Use callbacks to do simple asynchronous tasks.
- While callbacks are great for modeling simple tasks, they quickly get hairy as you try to do things with *lots* of asynchronous tasks.

Regaining Sanity with Promises

Luckily, we're not the first programmers to run into these limitations. In this section we'll develop the concept of *promises*, which are a way to abstract over asynchronous work so that we can compose it, sequence it, and so on. Even if you've worked with promises or futures before, this will be a helpful exercise to understand how they work.

Most modern JavaScript platforms include built-in support for promises. In this section we'll develop our own partial `Promise` implementation as an exercise, but in practice, you should use a built-in or off-the-shelf implementation instead. Check whether or not your favorite platform supports promises here (*http://bit.ly/ 2uMxkk5*), or jump ahead to "lib" on page 254 to learn more about polyfilling promises on platforms they're not natively supported on.

We'll start with an example of how we want to use `Promise` to first append to a file, then read back the result:

```
function appendAndReadPromise(path: string, data: string): Promise<string> {
  return appendPromise(path, data)
    .then(() => readPromise(path))
    .catch(error => console.error(error))
}
```

Notice how there's no callback pyramid here—we've effectively linearized what we want to do into a single, easy-to-understand chain of asynchronous tasks. When one succeeds, the next one runs; if it fails, we skip to the `catch` clause. With a callback-based API, this might have looked more like:

```
function appendAndRead(
  path: string,
  data: string
  cb: (error: Error | null, result: string | null) => void
) {
  appendFile(path, data, error => {
    if (error) {
      return cb(error, null)
    }
    readFile(path, (error, result) => {
      if (error) {
        return cb(error, null)
      }
      cb(null, result)
    })
  })
}
```

Let's design a `Promise` API that lets us do this.

`Promise` starts from humble beginnings:

```
class Promise {
}
```

A new `Promise` takes a function we call an *executor*, which the `Promise` implementation will call with two arguments, a `resolve` function and a `reject` function:

```
type Executor = (
  resolve: Function,
  reject: Function
) => void

class Promise {
  constructor(f: Executor) {}
}
```

How do `resolve` and `reject` work? Let's demonstrate it by thinking about how we would manually wrap a callback-based NodeJS API like `fs.readFile` in a `Promise`-based API. We use NodeJS's built-in `fs.readFile` API like this:

```
import {readFile} from 'fs'

readFile(path, (error, result) => {
  // ...
})
```

Wrapping that API in our `Promise` implementation, it now looks like this:

```
import {readFile} from 'fs'

function readFilePromise(path: string): Promise<string> {
  return new Promise((resolve, reject) => {
    readFile(path, (error, result) => {
      if (error) {
        reject(error)
      } else {
        resolve(result)
      }
    })
  })
}
```

So, the type of `resolve`'s parameter depends on which specific API we're using (in this case, its parameter's type would be whatever `result`'s type is), and the type of `reject`'s parameter is always some type of `Error`. Back to our implementation, let's update our code by replacing our unsafe `Function` types with more specific types:

```
type Executor<T, E extends Error> = (
  resolve: (result: T) => void,
  reject: (error: E) => void
) => void
// ...
```

Because we want to be able to get a sense for what type a `Promise` will resolve to just by looking at the `Promise` (for example, `Promise<number>` represents an asynchronous task that results in a `number`), we'll make `Promise` generic, and pass its type parameters down to the `Executor` type in its constructor:

```
// ...
class Promise<T, E extends Error> {
  constructor(f: Executor<T, E>) {}
}
```

So far, so good. We defined Promise's constructor API and understand what the types at play are. Now, let's think about chaining—what are the operations we want to expose to run a sequence of Promises, propagate their results, and catch their exceptions? If you look back to the initial code example at the start of this section, that's what then and catch are for. Let's add them to our Promise type:

```
// ...
class Promise<T, E extends Error> {
  constructor(f: Executor<T, E>) {}
  then<U, F extends Error>(g: (result: T) => Promise<U, F>): Promise<U, F>
  catch<U, F extends Error>(g: (error: E) => Promise<U, F>): Promise<U, F>
}
```

then and catch are two ways to sequence Promises: then maps a successful result of a Promise to a new Promise,[2] and catch recovers from a rejection by mapping an error to a new Promise.

Using then looks like this:

```
let a: () => Promise<string, TypeError> = // ...
let b: (s: string) => Promise<number, never> = // ...
let c: () => Promise<boolean, RangeError> = // ...

a()
  .then(b)
  .catch(e => c()) // b won't error, so this is if a errors
  .then(result => console.info('Done', result))
  .catch(e => console.error('Error', e))
```

Because the type of b's second type argument is never (meaning b will never throw an error), the first catch clause will only get called if a errors. But notice that when we use a Promise, we don't have to care about the fact that a might throw but b won't —if a succeeds then we map the Promise to b, and otherwise we jump to the first catch clause and map the Promise to c. If c succeeds then we log Done, and if it rejects then we catch again. This mimics how regular old try/catch statements work, and does for asynchronous tasks what try/catch does for synchronous ones (see Figure 8-2).

---

2 Eagle-eyed readers will notice how similar this API is to the flatMap API we developed in "The Option Type" on page 165. That similarity is no accident! Both Promise and Option are inspired by the Monad design pattern popularized by the functional programming language Haskell.

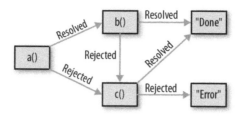

Figure 8-2. The Promise state machine

We also have to handle the case of Promises that throw actual exceptions (as in, throw Error('foo')). When we implement then and catch, we'll do this by wrapping code in try/catches and rejecting in the catch clause. This does have a few implications, though. It means that:

1. Every Promise has the potential to reject, and we can't statically check for this (because TypeScript doesn't support indicating in a function's signature which exceptions the function might throw).

2. A Promise won't always be rejected with an Error. Because TypeScript has no choice but to inherit JavaScript's behavior, and in JavaScript when you throw you can throw anything—a string, a function, an array, a Promise, and not necessarily an Error—we can't assume that a rejection will be a subtype of Error. It's unfortunate, but this is a sacrifice we'll make in the name of not having to force consumers to try/catch every promise chain (which might be spread across multiple files or modules!).

Taking that into account, let's loosen our Promise type a bit by not typing errors:

```
type Executor<T> = (
  resolve: (result: T) => void,
  reject: (error: unknown) => void
) => void

class Promise<T> {
  constructor(f: Executor<T>) {}
  then<U>(g: (result: T) => Promise<U>): Promise<U> {
    // ...
  }
  catch<U>(g: (error: unknown) => Promise<U>): Promise<U> {
    // ...
  }
}
```

We now have a fully baked Promise interface.

I'll leave it as an exercise for you to hook it all together with implementations for then and catch. The implementation for Promise is notoriously tricky to write correctly—if you're ambitious and have a couple of hours free, head over to the ES2015 specification (*http://bit.ly/2JT3KUh*) for a walkthrough of how Promise's state machine should work under the hood.

async and await

Promises are a really powerful abstraction for working with asynchronous code. They're such a popular pattern that they even have their own JavaScript (and therefore, TypeScript) syntax: async and await. This syntax lets you interact with asynchronous operations the same way you do with synchronous ones.

 Think of await as language-level syntax sugar for .then. When you await a Promise, you have to do so in an async block. And instead of .catch, you can wrap your await in a regular try/catch block.

Let's say you have the following promise (we didn't cover finally in the previous section, but it behaves the way you think it would, firing after both then and catch have a chance to fire):

```
function getUser() {
  getUserID(18)
    .then(user => getLocation(user))
    .then(location => console.info('got location', location))
    .catch(error => console.error(error))
    .finally(() => console.info('done getting location'))
}
```

To convert this code to async and await, first put it in an async function, then await the promise's result:

```
async function getUser() {
  try {
    let user = await getUserID(18)
    let location = await getLocation(user)
    console.info('got location', user)
  } catch(error) {
    console.error(error)
  } finally {
    console.info('done getting location')
  }
}
```

Since async and await are JavaScript features, we won't go into them in depth here—suffice it to say that TypeScript has full support for them, and they are completely typesafe. Use them whenever you work with promises, to make it easier to reason about chained operations and avoid lots of thens. To learn more about `async` and `await`, head over to their documentation on MDN (*https://mzl.la/2TJLFYt*).

Async Streams

While promises are fantastic for modeling, sequencing, and composing future values, what if you have multiple values, which will become available at multiple points in the future? This is less exotic than it sounds—think bits of a file being read from the filesystem, pixels of a video streaming over the internet from the Netflix server to your laptop, a bunch of keystrokes as you fill out a form, some friends coming over to your house for a dinner party, or votes being deposited into a ballot box throughout the course of Super Tuesday. While these things may sound pretty different on the surface, you can look at them all as asynchronous streams; they are all lists of things where each thing comes in at some point in the future.

There are a few ways to model this, the most common being with an event emitter (like NodeJS's `EventEmitter`) or with a reactive programming library like RxJS (*https://www.npmjs.com/package/@reactivex/rxjs*).[3] The difference between the two is like the difference between callbacks and promises: events are quick and lightweight, while reactive programming libraries are more powerful, and give you the ability to compose and sequence streams of events.

We'll go over event emitters in the following section. To learn more about reactive programming, head over to the documentation for your favorite reactive programming library—for example, RxJS (*https://www.npmjs.com/package/@reactivex/rxjs*), MostJS (*https://github.com/mostjs/core*), or xstream (*https://www.npmjs.com/package/xstream*).

Event Emitters

At a high level, event emitters offer APIs that support emitting events on a channel and listening for events on that channel:

```
interface Emitter {

  // Send an event
  emit(channel: string, value: unknown): void

  // Do something when an event is sent
```

---

3 Observables are the basic building block of reactive programming's approach to doing things to values over time. There's an in-progress proposal to standardize `Observables` in the `Observable` proposal (*https://tc39.github.io/proposal-observable/*). Look forward to a deeper dive into `Observables` in a future edition of this book, once the proposal is more broadly adopted by JavaScript engines.

```
  on(channel: string, f: (value: unknown) => void): void

}
```

Event emitters are a popular design pattern in JavaScript. You might have encountered them when using DOM events, JQuery events, or NodeJS's `EventEmitter` module.

In most languages, event emitters like this one are unsafe. That's because the type of `value` depends on the specific `channel`, and in most languages you can't use types to represent that relationship. Unless your language supports both overloaded function signatures and literal types, you're going to have trouble saying "this is the type of event emitted on this channel." Macros that generate methods to emit events and listen on each channel are a common workaround to this problem, but in TypeScript, you can express this naturally and safely using the type system.

For example, say we're using the NodeRedis client (*https://github.com/NodeRedis/ node_redis*), a Node API for the popular Redis in-memory datastore. It works like this:

```
import Redis from 'redis'

// Create a new instance of a Redis client
let client = redis.createClient()

// Listen for a few events emitted by the client
client.on('ready', () => console.info('Client is ready'))
client.on('error', e => console.error('An error occurred!', e))
client.on('reconnecting', params => console.info('Reconnecting...', params))
```

As programmers using the Redis library, we want to know what types of arguments to expect in our callbacks when we use the on API. But because the type of each argument depends on the channel that Redis emits on, a single type won't cut it. If we were the authors of this library, the simplest way to achieve safety would be with an overloaded type:

```
type RedisClient = {
  on(event: 'ready', f: () => void): void
  on(event: 'error', f: (e: Error) => void): void
  on(event: 'reconnecting',
     f: (params: {attempt: number, delay: number}) => void): void
}
```

This works pretty well, but it's a bit wordy. Let's express it in terms of a mapped type (see "Mapped Types" on page 137), pulling out the event definitions into their own type, `Events`:

```
type Events = {  ❶
  ready: void
  error: Error
  reconnecting: {attempt: number, delay: number}
```

```
  }

type RedisClient = { ❷
  on<E extends keyof Events>(
    event: E,
    f: (arg: Events[E]) => void
  ): void
}
```

❶ We start by defining a single object type that enumerates every event the Redis client might emit, along with the arguments for that event.

❷ We map over our Events type, telling TypeScript that on can be called with any of the events we defined.

We can then use this type to make the Node–Redis library safer, by typing both of its methods—emit and on—as safely as possible:

```
// ...
type RedisClient = {
  on<E extends keyof Events>(
    event: E,
    f: (arg: Events[E]) => void
  ): void
  emit<E extends keyof Events>(
    event: E,
    arg: Events[E]
  ): void
}
```

This pattern of pulling out event names and arguments into a shape and mapping over that shape to generate listeners and emitters is common in real-world Type-Script code. It's also terse, and very safe. When an emitter is typed this way you can't misspell a key, mistype an argument, or forget to pass in an argument. It also serves as documentation for engineers using your code, as their code editors will suggest to them the possible events they might listen on and the types of parameters in those events' callbacks.

Emitters in the Wild

Using mapped types to build typesafe event emitters is a popular pattern. For example, it's how DOM events are typed in TypeScript's standard library. WindowEventMap is a mapping from event name to event type, which the .addEventListener and .removeEventListener APIs map over to produce better, more specific event types than the default Event type:

```
// lib.dom.ts
interface WindowEventMap extends GlobalEventHandlersEventMap {
  // ...
```

```
      contextmenu: PointerEvent
      dblclick: MouseEvent
      devicelight: DeviceLightEvent
      devicemotion: DeviceMotionEvent
      deviceorientation: DeviceOrientationEvent
      drag: DragEvent
      // ...
    }

    interface Window extends EventTarget, WindowTimers, WindowSessionStorage,
      WindowLocalStorage, WindowConsole, GlobalEventHandlers, IDBEnvironment,
      WindowBase64, GlobalFetch {
      // ...
      addEventListener<K extends keyof WindowEventMap>(
        type: K,
        listener: (this: Window, ev: WindowEventMap[K]) => any,
        options?: boolean | AddEventListenerOptions
      ): void
      removeEventListener<K extends keyof WindowEventMap>(
        type: K,
        listener: (this: Window, ev: WindowEventMap[K]) => any,
        options?: boolean | EventListenerOptions
      ): void
    }
```

Typesafe Multithreading

So far, we've been talking about asynchronous programs that you might run on a single CPU thread, a class of programs that most JavaScript and TypeScript programs you'll write will likely fall into. But sometimes, when doing CPU-intensive tasks, you might opt for true parallelism: the ability to split out work across multiple threads, in order to do it faster or to keep your main thread idle and responsive. In this section, we'll explore a few patterns for writing safe, parallel programs in the browser and on the server.

In the Browser: With Web Workers

Web Workers are a widely supported way to do multithreading in the browser. You spin up some workers—special restricted background threads—from the main JavaScript thread, and use them to do things that would have otherwise blocked the main thread and made the UI unresponsive (i.e., CPU-bound tasks). Web Workers are a way to run code in the browser in a truly parallel way; while asynchronous APIs like Promise and setTimeout run code concurrently, Workers give you the ability to run code in parallel, on another CPU thread. Web Workers can send network requests, write to the filesystem, and so on, with a few minor restrictions.

Because Web Workers are a browser-provided API, its designers put a lot of emphasis on safety—not type safety like we know and love, but *memory safety*. Anyone that's written C, C++, Objective C, or multithreaded Java or Scala knows the pitfalls of concurrently manipulating shared memory. When you have multiple threads reading from and writing to the same piece of memory, it's really easy to run into all sorts of concurrency issues like nondeterminism, deadlocks, and so on.

Because browser code must be particularly safe, and minimize the chances of crashing the browser and causing a poor user experience, the primary way to communicate between the main thread and Web Workers, and between Web Workers and other Web Workers, is with *message passing*.

To follow along with the examples in this section, be sure to tell TSC that you're planning to run this code in a browser by enabling the dom lib in your *tsconfig.json*:

```
{
  "compilerOptions": {
    "lib": ["dom", "es2015"]
  }
}
```

And for the code that you're running in a Web Worker, use the webworker lib:

```
{
  "compilerOptions": {
    "lib": ["webworker", "es2015"]
  }
}
```

If you're using a single *tsconfig.json* for both your Web Worker script and your main thread, enable both at once.

The message passing API works like this. You first spawn a web worker from a thread:

```
// MainThread.ts
let worker = new Worker('WorkerScript.js')
```

Then, you pass messages to that worker:

```
// MainThread.ts
let worker = new Worker('WorkerScript.js')

worker.postMessage('some data')
```

You can pass almost any kind of data to another thread with the postMessage API.[4]

The main thread will clone the data you pass before handing it off to the worker thread.[5] On the Web Worker side, you listen to incoming events with the globally available onmessage API:

```
// WorkerScript.ts
onmessage = e => {
  console.log(e.data) // Logs out 'some data'
}
```

To communicate in the opposite direction—from the worker back to the main thread —you use the globally available postMessage to send a message to the main thread, and the .onmessage method in the main thread to listen for incoming messages. To put it all together:

```
// MainThread.ts
let worker = new Worker('WorkerScript.js')
worker.onmessage = e => {
  console.log(e.data) // Logs out 'Ack: "some data"'
}
worker.postMessage('some data')

// WorkerScript.ts
onmessage = e => {
  console.log(e.data) // Logs out 'some data'
  postMessage(Ack: "${e.data}")
}
```

This API is a lot like the event emitter API we looked at in "Event Emitters" on page 184. It's a simple way to pass messages around, but without types, we don't know that we've correctly handled all the possible types of messages that might be sent.

Since this API is really just an event emitter, we can apply the same techniques as for regular event emitters to type it. For example, let's build a simple messaging layer for a chat client, which we'll run in a worker thread. The messaging layer will push updates to the main thread, and we won't worry about things like error handling, permissions, and so on. We'll start by defining some incoming and outgoing message types (the main thread sends Commands to the worker thread, and the worker thread send Events back to the main thread):

---

4 Except for functions, errors, DOM nodes, property descriptors, getters and setters, and prototype methods and properties. For more information, head over to the HTML5 specification (*http://w3c.github.io/html/ infrastructure.html#safe-passing-of-structured-data*).

5 You can also use the Transferable API to pass certain types of data (like ArrayBuffer) between threads by reference. In this section we won't be using Transferable to explicitly transfer object ownership across threads, but that's an implementation detail. If you use Transferable for your use case, the approach is identical from a type safety point of view.

```
// MainThread.ts
type Message = string
type ThreadID = number
type UserID = number
type Participants = UserID[]

type Commands = {
  sendMessageToThread: [ThreadID, Message]
  createThread: [Participants]
  addUserToThread: [ThreadID, UserID]
  removeUserFromThread: [ThreadID, UserID]
}

type Events = {
  receivedMessage: [ThreadID, UserID, Message]
  createdThread: [ThreadID, Participants]
  addedUserToThread: [ThreadID, UserID]
  removedUserFromThread: [ThreadID, UserID]
}
```

How could we apply these types to the Web Worker messaging API? The simplest way might be to define a union of all possible message types, then switch on the Message type. But this can get pretty tedious. For our Command type, it might look something like this:

```
// WorkerScript.ts
type Command =                                              ❶
  | {type: 'sendMessageToThread', data: [ThreadID, Message]} ❷
  | {type: 'createThread', data: [Participants]}
  | {type: 'addUserToThread', data: [ThreadID, UserID]}
  | {type: 'removeUserFromThread', data: [ThreadID, UserID]}

onmessage = e =>                                            ❸
  processCommandFromMainThread(e.data)

function processCommandFromMainThread(                      ❹
  command: Command
) {
  switch (command.type) {                                  ❺
    case 'sendMessageToThread':
      let [threadID, message] = command.data
      console.log(message)
    // ...
  }
}
```

❶ We define a union of all possible commands that the main thread might send to a worker thread, along with the arguments for each command.

❷ This is just a regular union type. When defining long union types, leading with pipes (|) can make those types easier to read.

---

❸ We take messages sent over the untyped onmessage API, and delegate handling them to our typed processCommandFromMainThread API.

❹ processCommandFromMainThread takes care of handling all incoming messages from the main thread. It's a safe, typed wrapper for the untyped onmessage API.

❺ Since the Command type is a discriminated union type (see "Discriminated union types" on page 128), we use a switch to exhaustively handle every possible type of message the main thread might send our way.

Let's abstract Web Workers' snowflake API behind a familiar EventEmitter-based API. That way we can cut down on the verbosity of our incoming and outgoing message types.

We'll start by constructing a typesafe wrapper for NodeJS's EventEmitter API (which is available for the browser under the events package (*https:// www.npmjs.com/package/events*) on NPM):

```
import EventEmitter from 'events'

class SafeEmitter<
  Events extends Record<PropertyKey, unknown[]>   ❶
> {
  private emitter = new EventEmitter   ❷
  emit<K extends keyof Events>(   ❸
    channel: K,
    ...data: Events[K]
  ) {
    return this.emitter.emit(channel, ...data)
  }
  on<K extends keyof Events>(   ❹
    channel: K,
    listener: (...data: Events[K]) => void
  ) {
    return this.emitter.on(channel, listener)
  }
}
```

❶ SafeEmitter declares a generic type Events, a Record mapping from Property Key (TypeScript's built-in type for valid object keys: string, number, or Symbol) to a list of parameters.

❷ We declare emitter as a private member on SafeEmitter. We do this instead of extending SafeEmitter because our signatures for emit and on are more restrictive than their overloaded counterparts in EventEmitter, and since functions are contravariant in their parameters (remember, for a function a to be assignable to another function b its parameters have to be supertypes of their counterparts in b) TypeScript won't let us declare these overloads.

❸ emit takes a channel plus arguments corresponding to the list of parameters we defined in the Events type.

❹ Similarly, on takes a channel and a listener. listener takes a variable number of arguments corresponding to the list of parameters we defined in the Events type.

We can use SafeEmitter to dramatically cut down on the boilerplate it takes to safely implement a listening layer. On the worker side, we delegate all onmessage calls to our emitter and expose a convenient and safe listener API to consumers:

```typescript
// WorkerScript.ts
type Commands = {
  sendMessageToThread: [ThreadID, Message]
  createThread: [Participants]
  addUserToThread: [ThreadID, UserID]
  removeUserFromThread: [ThreadID, UserID]
}

type Events = {
  receivedMessage: [ThreadID, UserID, Message]
  createdThread: [ThreadID, Participants]
  addedUserToThread: [ThreadID, UserID]
  removedUserFromThread: [ThreadID, UserID]
}

// Listen for events coming from the main thread
let commandEmitter = new SafeEmitter    <Commands>()

// Emit events back to the main thread
let eventEmitter = new SafeEmitter      <Events>()

// Wrap incoming commands from the main thread
// using our typesafe event emitter
onmessage = command =>
  commandEmitter.emit(
    command.data.type,
    ...command.data.data
  )

// Listen for events issued by the worker, and send them to the main thread
eventEmitter.on('receivedMessage', data =>
  postMessage({type: 'receivedMessage', data})
)
eventEmitter.on('createdThread', data =>
  postMessage({type: 'createdThread', data})
)
// etc.

// Respond to a sendMessageToThread command from the main thread
```

```
commandEmitter.on('sendMessageToThread', (threadID, message) =>
  console.log(OK, I will send a message to threadID ${threadID})
)

// Send an event back to the main thread
eventEmitter.emit('createdThread', 123, [456, 789])
```

On the flip side, we can also use an `EventEmitter`-based API to send commands back from the main thread to the worker thread. Note that if you use this pattern in your own code, you might consider using a more full-featured emitter (like Paolo Fragomeni's excellent `EventEmitter2` (*https://www.npmjs.com/package/eventemitter2*)) that supports wildcard listeners, so you don't have to manually add a listener for each type of event:

```
// MainThread.ts
type Commands = {
  sendMessageToThread: [ThreadID, Message]
  createThread: [Participants]
  addUserToThread: [ThreadID, UserID]
  removeUserFromThread: [ThreadID, UserID]
}

type Events = {
  receivedMessage: [ThreadID, UserID, Message]
  createdThread: [ThreadID, Participants]
  addedUserToThread: [ThreadID, UserID]
  removedUserFromThread: [ThreadID, UserID]
}

let commandEmitter = new SafeEmitter    <Commands>()
let eventEmitter = new SafeEmitter    <Events>()

let worker = new Worker('WorkerScript.js')

// Listen for events coming from our worker,
// and re-emit them using our typesafe event emitter
worker.onmessage = event =>
  eventEmitter.emit(
    event.data.type,
    ...event.data.data
  )

// Listen for commands issues by this thread, and send them to our worker
commandEmitter.on('sendMessageToThread', data =>
  worker.postMessage({type: 'sendMessageToThread', data})
)
commandEmitter.on('createThread', data =>
  worker.postMessage({type: 'createThread', data})
)
// etc.

// Do something when the worker tells us a new thread was created
eventEmitter.on('createdThread', (threadID, participants) =>
  console.log('Created a new chat thread!', threadID, participants)
)
```

```
// Send a command to our worker
commandEmitter.emit('createThread', [123, 456])
```

That's it! We've created a simple typesafe wrapper for the familiar event emitter abstraction that we can use in a variety of settings, from cursor events in a browser to communication across threads, making passing messages between threads safe. This is a common pattern in TypeScript: even if something is unsafe, you can usually wrap it in a typesafe API.

Typesafe protocols

So far, we've looked at passing messages back and forth between two threads. What would it take to extend the technique to say that a particular command always receives a specific event as a response?

Let's build a simple call-response protocol, which we can use to move function evaluation across threads. We can't easily pass functions between threads, but we can define functions in a worker thread and send arguments to them, then send results back. For example, let's say we're building a matrix math engine that supports three operations: finding the determinant of a matrix, computing the dot product of two matrices, and inverting a matrix.

You know the drill—let's start by sketching out the types for these three operations:

```
type Matrix = number[][]

type MatrixProtocol = {
  determinant: {
    in: [Matrix]
    out: number
  }
  'dot-product': {
    in: [Matrix, Matrix]
    out: Matrix
  }
  invert: {
    in: [Matrix]
    out: Matrix
  }
}
```

We define matrices in our main thread, and run all computations in workers. Once again, the idea is to wrap an unsafe operation (sending and receiving untyped messages from a worker) with a safe one, exposing a well-defined, typed API for consumers to use. In this naive implementation, we start by defining a simple request-response protocol Protocol, which lists out the operations a worker can perform along with their expected input and output types.[6] We then define a generic `createProtocol` function that takes a `Protocol` and a file path to a Worker, and returns a function that takes a `command` in that protocol and returns a final function that we can call to actually evaluate that `command` for a specific set of arguments. OK, here we go:

```
type Protocol = { ❶
  [command: string]: {
    in: unknown[]
    out: unknown
  }
}

function createProtocol<P extends Protocol>(script: string) { ❷
 return <K extends keyof P>(command: K) => ❸
   (...args: P[K]['in']) => ❹
   new Promise<P[K]['out']>((resolve, reject) => { ❺
     let worker = new Worker(script)
     worker.onerror = reject
     worker.onmessage = event => resolve(event.data.data)
     worker.postMessage({command, args})
   })
}
```

❶ We start by defining a general-purpose `Protocol` type that is not specific to our `MatrixProtocol`.

❷ When we call `createProtocol`, we pass in a file path to a worker `script`, along with a specific `Protocol`.

❸ `createProtocol` returns an anonymous function that we can then invoke with a `command`, which is a key in the `Protocol` we bound in ❷.

❹ We then call that function with whatever the specific `in` type is for the command we passed in in ❸.

❺ This gives us back a `Promise` for the specific `out` type for that command, as defined in our particular protocol. Note that we have to explicitly bind a type parameter to `Promise`, otherwise it defaults to `{}`.

Now let's apply our `MatrixProtocol` type plus the path to our Web Worker script to `createProtocol` (we won't get into the nitty-gritty of how to compute a determinant,

---

6 This implementation is naive because it spawns a new worker every time we issue a command; in the real world, you probably want to have a pooling mechanism that keeps a warm pool of workers around, and recycles freed workers.

and I'll assume that you've implemented it in *MatrixWorkerScript.ts*). We'll get back a function that we can use to run a specific command in that protocol:

```
let runWithMatrixProtocol = createProtocol<MatrixProtocol>(
  'MatrixWorkerScript.js'
)
let parallelDeterminant = runWithMatrixProtocol('determinant')

parallelDeterminant([[1, 2], [3, 4]])
  .then(determinant =>
    console.log(determinant) // -2
  )
```

Cool, huh? We've taken something totally unsafe—untyped message passing between threads—and abstracted over it with a fully typesafe request-response protocol. All the commands you can run using that protocol live in one place (`MatrixProtocol`), and our core logic (`createProtocol`) lives separately from our concrete protocol implementation (`runWithMatrixProtocol`).

Anytime you need to communicate between two processes—whether on the same machine or between multiple computers on a network—typesafe protocols are a great tool to make that communication safe. While this section helped develop some intuition for what problems protocols solve, for a real-world application you'll likely want to reach for an existing tool like Swagger, gRPC, Thrift, or GraphQL—for an overview, head over to "Typesafe APIs" on page 210.

In NodeJS: With Child Processes

To follow along with the examples in this section, be sure to install type declarations for NodeJS from NPM:

```
npm install @types/node --save-dev
```

To learn more about using type declarations, jump ahead to "JavaScript That Has Type Declarations on DefinitelyTyped" on page 245.

Typesafe parallelism in NodeJS works the same way as it does for Web Worker threads in the browser (see "Typesafe protocols" on page 194). While the message-passing layer itself is unsafe, it's easy to build a typesafe API over it. NodeJS's child process API looks like this:

```
// MainThread.ts
import {fork} from 'child_process'

let child = fork('./ChildThread.js') ❶

child.on('message', data => ❷
  console.info('Child process sent a message', data)
)
```

```
child.send({type: 'syn', data: [3]}) ❸
```

❶ We use NodeJS's `fork` API to spawn a new child process.

❷ We listen to incoming messages from a child process using the on API. There are a few messages that a NodeJS child process might send to its parent; here, we just care about the `'message'` message.

❸ We use the `send` API to send messages to a child process.

In our child thread, we listen to messages coming in from the main thread using the `process.on` API and send messages back with `process.send`:

```
// ChildThread.ts
process.on('message', data => ❶
  console.info('Parent process sent a message', data)
)

process.send({type: 'ack', data: [3]}) ❷
```

❶ We use the on API on the globally defined `process` to listen for incoming messages from a parent thread.

❷ We use the `send` API on `process` to send messages to the parent process.

Because the mechanics are so similar to Web Workers, I'll leave it as an exercise to implement a typesafe protocol to abstract over interprocess communication in NodeJS.

Summary

In this chapter we started with the basics of JavaScript's event loop, and continued on to a discussion of the building blocks of asynchronous code in JavaScript and how to safely express them in TypeScript: callbacks, promises, `async`/`await`, and event emitters. We then covered multithreading, exploring passing messages between threads (in the browser and on the server) and building full protocols for communicating between threads.

As with Chapter 7, which technique you use is up to you:

- For simple asynchronous tasks, callbacks are as straightforward as it gets.
- For more complex tasks that need to be sequenced and parallelized, promises and `async`/`await` are your friend.
- When a promise doesn't cut it (e.g., if you're firing an event multiple times), reach for event emitters or a reactive streams library like RxJS.

- To extend these techniques to multiple threads, use event emitters, typesafe protocols, or typesafe APIs (see "Typesafe APIs" on page 210).

Exercises

1. Implement a general-purpose `promisify` function, which takes any function that takes exactly one argument and a callback and wraps it in a function that returns a promise. When you're done, you should be able to use `promisify` like this (install type declarations for NodeJS first, with `npm install @types/node --save-dev`):

```
import {readFile} from 'fs'

let readFilePromise = promisify(readFile)
readFilePromise('./myfile.ts')
  .then(result => console.log('success reading file', result.toString()))
  .catch(error => console.error('error reading file', error))
```

2. In the section on "Typesafe protocols" on page 194 we derived one half of a protocol for typesafe matrix math. Given this half of the protocol that runs in the main thread, implement the other half that runs in a Web Worker thread.

3. Use a mapped type (as in "In the Browser: With Web Workers" on page 187) to implement a typesafe message-passing protocol for NodeJS's `child_process`.

Frontend and Backend Frameworks

While you could build every part of your application yourself from the ground up—the networking and database layers on the server, a user interface framework and state management solution on the frontend—you probably shouldn't. It's hard to get the details right, and luckily for us, lots of these hard problems on the frontend and backend have already been solved by other engineers. By taking advantage of existing tools, libraries, and frameworks to build things both on the frontend and the backend, we can iterate quickly and on stable ground when building our own applications.

In this chapter, we'll go through some of the most popular tools and frameworks that solve common problems on both the client and the server. We'll talk about what you might use each framework for, and how to safely integrate it into your TypeScript application.

Frontend Frameworks

TypeScript is a natural fit for the world of frontend applications. With its rich support for JSX and its ability to safely model mutability, TypeScript lends structure and safety to your application and makes it easier to write correct, maintainable code in the fast-paced environment that is frontend development.

Of course, all of the built-in DOM APIs are typesafe. To use them from TypeScript, just include their type declarations in your project's *tsconfig.json*:

```
{
  "compilerOptions": {
    "lib": ["dom", "es2015"]
  }
}
```

That will tell TypeScript to include *lib.dom.d.ts*—its built-in browser and DOM type declarations—when typechecking your code.

 The lib *tsconfig.json* option just tells TypeScript to include a set of specific type declarations when processing the code in your project; it won't emit any extra code, or generate any JavaScript that will exist at runtime. It won't, for example, make the DOM magically work in a NodeJS environment (your code will compile, but it will fail at runtime)—it's on you to make sure that your type declarations match up to what your JavaScript environment actually supports at runtime. Jump ahead to "Building Your TypeScript Project" on page 249 to learn more.

With DOM type declarations enabled, you'll be able to safely consume DOM and browser APIs to do things like:

```
// Read properties from the global window object
let model = {
  url: window.location.href
}

// Create an <input /> element
let input = document.createElement('input')

// Give it some CSS classes
input.classList.add('Input', 'URLInput')

// When the user types, update the model
input.addEventListener('change', () =>
  model.url = input.value.toUpperCase()
)

// Inject the <input /> into the DOM
document.body.appendChild(input)
```

Of course, all of that code is typechecked and comes with the normal goodies like in-editor autocompletion. For example, consider something like this:

```
document.querySelector('.Element').innerHTML // Error TS2531: Object is
                                             // possibly 'null'.
```

TypeScript will throw an error because the return type of `querySelector` is nullable.

While for simple frontend applications these low-level DOM APIs are enough and will give you what you need to do safe, type-guided programming for the browser, most real-world frontend applications use a framework to abstract away how DOM rendering and rerendering, data binding, and events work. The following sections will give some pointers on how to effectively use TypeScript with a few of the most popular browser frameworks.

React

React is among the most popular frontend frameworks today, and is a great choice when it comes to type safety.

The reason React is so safe is because React components—the basic building blocks of React applications—are both defined and consumed in TypeScript. This property is hard to find among frontend frameworks, and means that both component definitions and consumers are typechecked. You can use types to say things like "this component takes a user ID and a color" or "this component can only have list items as children." These constraints are then enforced by TypeScript, verifying that your components do what they say they do.

This safety around component definitions and consumers—the *view layer* of a frontend application—is killer. The view is traditionally the place where typos, missed attributes, mistyped parameters, and improperly nested elements cause programmers to collectively spend thousands of hours tearing their hair out and indignantly refreshing their browsers. The day you start typing your views with TypeScript and React is the day you double your and your team's productivity on the frontend.

A JSX primer

When using React, you define your views using a special DSL called *JavaScript XML* (JSX) that you embed straight into your JavaScript code. It sort of looks like HTML in your JavaScript. You then run your JavaScript through a JSX compiler that rewrites that funky JSX syntax into regular JavaScript function calls.

The process looks something like this. Say you're building a menu app for your friend's restaurant, and you list out a few items on the brunch menu with the following JSX:

```
<ul class='list'>
  <li>Homemade granola with yogurt</li>
  <li>Fantastic french toast with fruit</li>
  <li>Tortilla Española with salad</li>
</ul>
```

After running that code through a JSX compiler like Babel's `transform-react-jsx` plugin (*http://bit.ly/2uENY4M*), you'll get the following output:

```
React.createElement(
  'ul',
  {'class': 'list'},
  React.createElement(
    'li',
    null,
    'Homemade granola with yogurt'
  ),
  React.createElement(
    'li',
```

```
    null,
    'Fantastic French toast with fruit'
  ),
  React.createElement(
    'li',
    null,
    'Tortilla Española with salad'
  )
);
```

TSC Flag: esModuleInterop

Because JSX compiles to a call to `React.createElement`, be sure to import the React library into each file where you use JSX so that you have a variable named `React` in scope:

```
import React from 'react'
```

Don't worry—if you forget, TypeScript will warn you:

```
<ul /> // Error TS2304: Cannot find name 'React'.
```

Also note that I've set `{"esModuleInterop": true}` in my *tsconfig.json* to support importing `React` without a wildcard (*) import. If you're following along, either enable `esModuleInterop` in your own *tsconfig.json*, or use a wildcard import instead:

```
import * as React from 'react'
```

The nice thing about JSX is you can write what looks a lot like normal HTML, then compile it automatically to a JavaScript engine–friendly format. As an engineer you only use a familiar, high-level, declarative DSL, and you don't have to deal with the implementation details.

You don't need JSX to work with React (you can write that compiled code directly and it'll work fine), and you can use JSX without React (the specific function call that JSX tags compile to—`React.createElement` in the previous example—is configurable), but the combination of React with JSX is magical, and makes writing views really fun, and really, really safe.

TSX = JSX + TypeScript

Files that contain JSX use the file extension *.jsx*. And TypeScript files that contain JSX use the *.tsx* extension. TSX is to JSX what TypeScript is to JavaScript—a compile-time safety and assistance layer to help you be more productive and produce code with fewer mistakes. To enable TSX support for your project, add the following line to your *tsconfig.json*:

```
{
  "compilerOptions": {
    "jsx": "react"
```

```
    }
  }
```

The `jsx` directive has three modes at the time of writing:

`react`

Compile JSX to a *.js* file using the JSX pragma (by default, `React.createEle`
`ment`).

`react-native`

Preserve JSX without compiling it, but do emit a file with a *.js* extension.

`preserve`

Typecheck JSX but don't compile it away, and emit a file with a *.jsx* extension.

Under the hood, TypeScript exposes a few hooks for typing TSX in a pluggable way. These are special types on the `global.JSX` namespace that TypeScript looks at as the source of truth for TSX types throughout your program. If you're just using React, you don't need to go that low-level; but if you're building your own TypeScript library that uses TSX (and doesn't use React)—or if you're curious how the React type declarations do it—head over to Appendix G.

Using TSX with React

React lets us declare two kinds of components: function components and class components. Both kinds of components take some properties and render some TSX. From a consumer's point of view, they are identical.

Declaring and rendering a function component looks like this:

```
import React from 'react' ❶

type Props = { ❷
  isDisabled?: boolean
  size: 'Big' | 'Small'
  text: string
  onClick(event: React.MouseEvent<HTMLButtonElement>): void ❸
}

export function FancyButton(props: Props) { ❹
  const [toggled, setToggled] = React.useState(false) ❺
  return <button
    className={'Size-' + props.size}
    disabled={props.isDisabled || false}
    onClick={event => {
      setToggled(!toggled)
      props.onClick(event)
    }}
  >{props.text}</button>
}
```

```
let button = <FancyButton ❻
  size='Big'
  text='Sign Up Now'
  onClick={() => console.log('Clicked!')}
/>
```

❶ We have to bring the `React` variable into the current scope in order to use TSX with React. Since TSX is compiled to `React.createElement` function calls, that means we need to import `React` so that it's defined at runtime.

❷ We start by declaring the specific set of props we can pass to our `FancyButton` component. `Props` is always an object type, and is named `Props` by convention. For our `FancyButton` component, `isDisabled` is optional, while the rest of our props are required.

❸ React has its own set of wrapper types for DOM events. When using React events, be sure to use React's event types rather than regular DOM event types.

❹ A function component is just a regular function that has up to one parameter (the `props` object) and returns a React-renderable type. React is permissive and can render a wide range of types: TSX, strings, numbers, booleans, `null`, and `undefined`.

❺ We use React's `useState` hook to declare local state for a function component. `useState` is one of a handful of hooks available in React, which you can combine to create your own custom hooks. Note that because we passed the initial value `false` to `useState`, TypeScript was able to infer that the piece of state is a `boolean`; if we'd instead used a type that TypeScript wasn't able to infer—for example, an array—we would have bound the type explicitly (e.g., with `useS tate<number[]>([])`).

❻ We use TSX syntax to create an instance of `FancyButton`. The `<FancyButton />` syntax is almost identical to calling `FancyButton`, but it lets React manage the lifecycle of `FancyButton` for us.

That's it. TypeScript enforces that:

- JSX is well formed. Tags are closed and properly nested, and tag names aren't misspelled.

- When we instantiate a `<FancyButton />` we pass all required—plus any optional —props to `FancyButton` (`size`, `text`, and `onClick`), and that the props are all correctly typed.

- We don't pass any extraneous props to FancyButton, just the ones that are required.

A class component is similar:

```
import React from 'react' ❶
import {FancyButton} from './FancyButton'

type Props = { ❷
  firstName: string
  userId: string
}

type State = { ❸
  isLoading: boolean
}

class SignupForm extends React.Component<Props, State> { ❹
  state = { ❺
    isLoading: false
  }
  render() { ❻
    return <> ❼
      <h2>Sign up for a 7-day supply of our tasty
          toothpaste now, {this.props.firstName}.</h2>
      <FancyButton
        isDisabled={this.state.isLoading}
        size='Big'
        text='Sign Up Now'
        onClick={this.signUp}
      />
    </>
  }
  private signUp = async () => { ❽
    this.setState({isLoading: true})
    try {
      await fetch('/api/signup?userId=' + this.props.userId)
    } finally {
      this.setState({isLoading: false})
    }
  }
}

let form = <SignupForm firstName='Albert' userId='13ab9g3' /> ❾
```

❶ Like before, we import React to bring it into scope.

❷ Like before, we declare a Props type to define what data we need to pass in when creating an instance of <SignupForm />.

❸ We declare a State type to model our component's local state.

❹ To declare a class component, we extend the React.Component base class.

❺ We use a property initializer to declare default values for local state.

❻ Like with function components, a class component's render method returns something renderable by React: TSX, a string, a number, a boolean, null, or undefined.

❼ TSX supports fragments using the special <>...</> syntax. A fragment is a nameless TSX element that wraps other TSX, and is a way to avoid rendering extra DOM elements in places where you need to return a single TSX element. For example, a React component's render method needs to return a single TSX element; to do that, we could have wrapped our code with a <div> or any other element, but that would have incurred unnecessary overhead during rendering.

❽ We define signUp using an arrow function, to make sure that this in the function doesn't get re-bound.

❾ Finally, we instantiate our SignupForm. Like when instantiating function components, we could have directly new-ed it with new SignupForm({firstName: 'Albert', userId: '13ab9g3'}) instead, but that would mean that React couldn't manage the SignupForm instance's lifecycle for us.

Notice how we mix and match value-based (FancyButton, SignupForm) and intrinsic (section, h2) components in this example. We put TypeScript to work to verify things like:

- That all required state fields were defined either in the state initializer, or in the constructor
- That whatever we access on props and state actually exists, and is of the type we think it is
- That we don't write to this.state directly, because in React, state updates have to go through the setState API
- That calling render really returns some JSX

With TypeScript you can make your React code safer, and become a better, happier person as a result.

We didn't use React's `PropTypes` feature, which is a way to declare and check props' types at runtime. Since TypeScript is already checking types for us at compile time, we don't need to do it again.

Angular

Contributed by Shyam Seshadri

Angular is a more fully featured frontend framework than React, and comes with support not just for rendering views but also for sending and managing network requests, routing, and dependency injection. It's built from the ground up to work with TypeScript (in fact, the framework itself is written in TypeScript!).

Central to the way Angular works is the Ahead-of-Time (AoT) compiler built into Angular CLI, Angular's command-line utility, that grabs the type information you gave it with your TypeScript annotations and uses that information to compile your code down to regular JavaScript. Instead of calling TypeScript directly, Angular applies a whole bunch of optimizations and transformations to your code before ultimately delegating to TypeScript and compiling it down to JavaScript.

Let's see how Angular uses TypeScript and its AoT compiler to make writing frontend applications safe.

Scaffolding

To initialize a new Angular project, start by globally installing Angular CLI using NPM:

```
npm install @angular/cli --global
```

Then, use Angular CLI to initialize a new Angular application:

```
ng new my-angular-app
```

Follow the prompts, and Angular CLI will set up a bare-bones Angular application for you.

In this book we won't go into depth on how an Angular application is structured, or how to configure and run it. For detailed information, head over to the official Angular documentation (*https://angular.io/docs*).

Components

Let's build an Angular component. Angular components are like React components, and include a way to describe a component's DOM structure, styling, and controller. With Angular, you generate component boilerplate with Angular CLI, then fill in the details by hand. An Angular component consists of a few different files:

- A template, which describes the DOM a component renders
- A set of CSS styles
- A component class, which is a TypeScript class that dictates your components' business logic

Let's start with the component class:

```
import {Component, OnInit} from '@angular/core'

@Component({
  selector: 'simple-message',
  styleUrls: ['./simple-message.component.css'],
  templateUrl: './simple-message.component.html'
})
export class SimpleMessageComponent implements OnInit {
  message: string
  ngOnInit() {
    this.message = 'No messages, yet'
  }
}
```

For the most part, this is a pretty standard TypeScript class, with just a few differences that bring out how Angular leverages TypeScript. Namely:

- Angular's lifecycle hooks are available as TypeScript interfaces—just declare which ones you implement (ngOnChanges, ngOnInit, etc.). TypeScript then enforces that you implement methods that comply with the lifecycle hooks you want. In this example we implemented the OnInit interface, which requires that we implement the ngOnInit method.

- Angular makes heavy use of TypeScript decorators (see "Decorators" on page 104) to declare metadata related to your Angular components, services, and modules. In this example, we used a selector to declare how people can consume our component, and we used templateUrls and styleUrl to link an HTML template and CSS stylesheet to our component.

TSC Flag: fullTemplateTypeCheck

To enable typechecking for your Angular templates (you should!), be sure to enable `fullTemplateTypeCheck` in your *tsconfig.json*:

```
{
  "angularCompilerOptions": {
    "fullTemplateTypeCheck": true
  }
}
```

Note that `angularCompilerOptions` isn't specifying options for TSC. Rather, it defines compiler flags specific to Angular's AoT compiler.

Services

Angular comes with a built-in dependency injector (DI), which is a way for the framework to take care of instantiating services and passing them in as arguments to components and services that depend on them. This can make it easier to instantiate and test services and components.

Let's update `SimpleMessageComponent` to inject a dependency, `MessageService`, responsible for fetching messages from the server:

```
import {Component, OnInit} from '@angular/core'
import {MessageService} from '../services/message.service'

@Component({
  selector: 'simple-message',
  templateUrl: './simple-message.component.html',
  styleUrls: ['./simple-message.component.css']
})
export class SimpleMessageComponent implements OnInit {
  message: string
  constructor(
    private messageService: MessageService
  ) {}
  ngOnInit() {
    this.messageService.getMessage().subscribe(response =>
      this.message = response.message
    )
  }
}
```

Angular's AoT compiler looks at the parameters that your component's `constructor` takes, plucks out their types (e.g., `MessageService`), and searches the relevant dependency injector's dependency map for a dependency of that specific type. It then instantiates that dependency (new-ing it) if it hasn't been instantiated yet, and passes it into the `SimpleMessageComponent` instance's constructor. All of this DI stuff is pretty complicated, but it can be convenient as your application grows and you have multiple dependencies you might use depending on how the app is configured (e.g., `ProductionAPIService` versus `DevelopmentAPIService`) or when testing it (`MockAPI Service`).

Now let's take a quick look at how to define a service:

```
import {Injectable} from '@angular/core'
import {HttpClient} from '@angular/common/http'

@Injectable({
  providedIn: 'root'
})
export class MessageService {
  constructor(private http: HttpClient) {}
  getMessage() {
    return this.http.get('/api/message')
  }
}
```

Whenever we create a service in Angular, we again use TypeScript decorators to register it as something that is `Injectable`, and we define whether it is provided at the root level of the application or in a submodule. Here, we registered the service `MessageService`, allowing us to inject it anywhere in our application. In the constructor of any component or service, we can just ask for a `MessageService` and Angular will magically take care of passing it in.

With how to safely use these two popular frontend frameworks out of the way, let's move on to typing the interface between your frontend and your backend.

Typesafe APIs

Contributed by Nick Nance

Regardless of which frontend and backend frameworks you decide to use, you'll want a way to safely communicate across machines—from client to server, server to client, server to server, and client to client.

There are a few competing tools and standards in this space. But before we explore what they are and how they work, let's think about how we might build our own solution, and what benefits and drawbacks it might have (we are engineers, after all).

The problem we want to solve is this: though our clients and servers might be 100% typesafe—bastions of safety—at some point they'll need to talk to each other over untyped network protocols like HTTP, TCP, or some other socket-based protocols. How might we make this communication typesafe?

A good starting point could be a typesafe protocol like the one we developed in "Typesafe protocols" on page 194. It might look something like this:

```
type Request =
  | {entity: 'user', data: User}
  | {entity: 'location', data: Location}

// client.ts
async function get<R extends Request>(entity: R['entity']): Promise<R['data']> {
  let res = await fetch(/api/${entity})
  let json = await res.json()
  if (!json) {
    throw ReferenceError('Empty response')
  }
  return json
}

// app.ts
async function startApp() {
  let user = await get('user')  // User
}
```

You could build corresponding post and put functions to write back to your REST API, and add a type for each entity your server supports. On the backend, you'd then implement a corresponding set of handlers for each type of entity, reading from your database to return to the client whatever entity it asked for.

But what happens if your server isn't written in TypeScript, or if you aren't able to share your Request type between the client and server (leading to the two getting out of sync over time), or if you don't use REST (maybe you use GraphQL instead)? Or what if you have other clients to support, like Swift clients on iOS or Java clients on Android?

That's where typed, code-generated APIs come in. They come in a lot of flavors, each with libraries available in a bunch of languages (including TypeScript)—for example:

- Swagger (*https://github.com/swagger-api/swagger-codegen*) for RESTful APIs
- Apollo (*https://www.npmjs.com/package/apollo*) and Relay (*https://facebook.github.io/relay/*) for GraphQL
- gRPC (*https://grpc.io/*) and Apache Thrift (*https://thrift.apache.org/*) for RPC

These tools rely on a common source of truth for both server and clients—data models for Swagger, GraphQL schemas for Apollo, Protocol Buffers for gRPC—which are then compiled into language-specific bindings for whatever language you might be using (in our case, that's TypeScript).

This code generation is what prevents your client and server (or multiple clients) from getting out of sync with each other; since every platform shares a common schema, you won't run into the case where you updated your iOS app to support a field, but forgot to press Merge on your pull request to add server support for it.

Diving into the details of each framework is out of scope for this book. Pick one for your project, and head over to its documentation to learn more.

Backend Frameworks

When you build an application that interacts with a database, you might start with raw SQL or API calls, which are inherently untyped:

```
// PostgreSQL, using node-postgres
let client = new Client
let res = await client.query(
  'SELECT name FROM users where id = $1',
  [739311]
) // any

// MongoDB, using node-mongodb-native
db.collection('users')
  .find({id: 739311})
  .toArray((err, user) =>
    // user is any
  )
```

With a bit of manual typing you can make these APIs safer and get rid of most of your anys:

```
db.collection('users')
  .find({id: 739311})
  .toArray((err, user: User) =>
    // user is any
  )
```

However, raw SQL APIs are still fairly low-level, and it's still easy to use the wrong type, or forget a type and accidentally end up with anys.

That's where *object-relational mappers* (ORMs) come in. ORMs generate code from your database schema, giving you high-level APIs to express queries, updates, deletions, and so on. In statically typed languages, these APIs are typesafe, so you don't have to worry about typing things correctly and manually binding generic type parameters.

When accessing your database from TypeScript, consider using an ORM. At the time of writing, Umed Khudoiberdiev's excellent TypeORM (*https://www.npmjs.com/pack age/typeorm*) is the most complete ORM for TypeScript, and supports MySQL, PostgreSQL, Microsoft SQL Server, Oracle, and even MongoDB. Using TypeORM, your query to get a user's first name might look like this:

```
let user = await UserRepository
  .findOne({id: 739311}) // User | undefined
```

Notice the high-level API, which is both safe (in that it prevents things like SQL injection attacks) and typesafe by default (in that we know what type `findOne` returns without having to manually annotate it). Always use an ORM when working with databases—it's more convenient, and it will save you from getting woken up at four in the morning because the `saleAmount` field is `null` because you updated it to `orderAmount` the night before and your coworker decided to run your database migration for you in anticipation of your pull request landing while you were out, but then around midnight your pull request failed even though the migration succeeded, and your sales team in New York woke up to realize that all your clients' orders were for exactly `null` dollars (this happened to… a friend).

Summary

In this chapter we've covered a lot: directly manipulating the DOM; using React and Angular; adding type safety to your APIs with tools like Swagger, gRPC, and GraphQL; and using TypeORM to safely interact with your database.

JavaScript frameworks change at a rapid pace, and by the time you read this, the specific APIs and frameworks described here may be on their way to becoming museum exhibits. Use your newfound intuition for *what problems typesafe frameworks solve* to identify places where you can take advantage of someone else's work to make your code safer, more abstract, and more modular. The big idea to take away from this chapter isn't what the best framework to use in the year 2019 is, but what sorts of problems can be better solved with frameworks.

With the combination of typesafe UI code, a typed API layer, and a typesafe backend, you can eliminate entire classes of bugs from your application, and sleep better at night as a result.

Namespaces.Modules

When you write a program, you can express encapsulation at several levels. At the lowest level, functions encapsulate behaviors, and data structures like objects and lists encapsulate data. You might then group functions and data into classes, or keep them separate as namespaced utilities with a separate database or store for your data. A single class or a set of utilities per file is typical. Going up, you might group a few classes or utilities into a package, which you publish to NPM.

When we talk about modules, it's important to make a distinction between how the compiler (TSC) resolves modules, how your build system (Webpack, Gulp, etc.) resolves modules, and how modules are actually loaded into your application at runtime (`<script />` tags, SystemJS, etc.). In the JavaScript world there is usually a separate program that does each of these jobs, which can make modules hard to reason about. The CommonJS and ES2015 module standards make it easier to interoperate the three programs, and powerful bundlers like Webpack help abstract away the three kinds of resolution happening under the hood.

In this chapter we'll focus on the first of these three kinds of programs: how TypeScript resolves and compiles modules. We'll leave a discussion of how the build system and runtime loaders work with modules to Chapter 12 and talk here about:

- The different ways to namespace and modularize your code
- The different ways to import and export code
- Scaling these approaches as your codebase grows
- Module mode versus script mode
- What declaration merging is, and what you can do with it

But first, a bit of background.

A Brief History of JavaScript Modules

Because TypeScript compiles to and interoperates with JavaScript, it has to support the various module standards that JavaScript programmers use.

In the beginning (in 1995), JavaScript didn't support any sort of module system. Without modules, everything was declared in a global namespace, which made it really hard to build and scale applications. You could quickly run out of variable names, and run into collisions between variable names; and without exposing explicit APIs for each module, it's hard to know which parts of a module you're supposed to use, and which parts are private implementation details.

To help solve these problems, people simulated modules with either objects or *Immediately Invoked Function Expressions* (IIFEs), which they assigned to the global window, making them available to other modules in their application (and in other applications hosted on the same web page). It looked something like this:

```
window.emailListModule = {
  renderList() {}
  // ...
}

window.emailComposerModule = {
  renderComposer() {}
  // ...
}

window.appModule = {
  renderApp() {
    window.emailListModule.renderList()
    window.emailComposerModule.renderComposer()
  }
}
```

Because loading and running JavaScript blocks the browser's UI, as a web application grows and includes more and more lines of code, the user's browser gets slower and slower. For this reason, clever programmers started dynamically loading JavaScript after the page loaded, rather than loading it all in one shot. Nearly 10 years after JavaScript was first released, Dojo (Alex Russell, 2004), YUI (Thomas Sha, 2005), and LABjs (Kyle Simpson, 2009) shipped module loaders—ways to lazily (and often asynchronously) load JavaScript code after the initial page load has happened. Lazy and asynchronous module loading meant three things:

1. Modules needed to be well encapsulated. Otherwise, a page might be broken while dependencies are streaming in.

2. Dependencies between modules needed to be explicit. Otherwise, we don't know which modules need to be loaded and in what order.

3. Every module needed a unique identifier within the app. Otherwise, there's no reliable way to specify what modules need to be loaded.

Loading a module with LABjs looked like this:

```
$LAB
  .script('/emailBaseModule.js').wait()
  .script('/emailListModule.js')
  .script('/emailComposerModule.js')
```

Around the same time, NodeJS (Ryan Dahl, 2009) was being developed, and its creators took a lesson from JavaScript's growing pains and from other languages and decided to build a module system right into the platform. Like any good module system, it needed to satisfy the same three criteria as LABjs and YUI's loaders. NodeJS did that with the CommonJS module standard, which looked like this:

```
// emailBaseModule.js
var emailList = require('emailListModule')
var emailComposer = require('emailComposerModule')

module.exports.renderBase = function() {
  // ...
}
```

In the meantime, on the web the AMD module standard (James Burke, 2008)—pushed by Dojo and RequireJS—was taking off. It supported an equivalent set of functionality, and came with its own build system for bundling up JavaScript code:

```
define('emailBaseModule',
  ['require', 'exports', 'emailListModule', 'emailComposerModule'],
  function(require, exports, emailListModule, emailComposerModule) {
    exports.renderBase = function() {
      // ...
    }
  }
)
```

A few years after that, Browserify came out (James Halliday, 2011), giving frontend engineers the ability to use CommonJS on the frontend, too. CommonJS became the de facto standard for module bundling and import/export syntax.

There were a few problems with the CommonJS way of doing things. Among them, `require` calls are necessarily synchronous, and the CommonJS module resolution algorithm is not ideal for use on the web. On top of that, code that uses it isn't statically analyzable in some cases (as a TypeScript programmer, this should perk your ears up), because `module.exports` can appear anywhere (even in dead code branches that are never actually reached) and `require` calls can appear anywhere and contain arbitrary strings and expressions, making it impossible to statically link a JavaScript program, and verify that all referenced files really exist and export what they say they export.

Against this backdrop, ES2015—the sixth edition of the ECMAScript language—introduced a new standard for imports and exports that had a clean syntax and was statically analyzable. It looks like this:

```
// emailBaseModule.js
import emailList from 'emailListModule'
import emailComposer from 'emailComposerModule'

export function renderBase() {
  // ...
}
```

This is the standard we use in JavaScript and TypeScript code today. However, at the time of writing the standard isn't yet natively supported in every JavaScript runtime, so we have to compile it down to a format that is supported (CommonJS for NodeJS environments, globals or a module-loadable format for browser environments).

TypeScript gives us a few ways to consume and export code in a module: with global declarations, with standard ES2015 imports and exports, and with backward-compatible imports from CommonJS modules. On top of that, TSC's build system lets us compile modules for a variety of environments: globals, ES2015, CommonJS, AMD, SystemJS, or UMD (a mix of CommonJS, AMD, and globals—whichever happens to be available in the consumer's environment).

import, export

Unless you're being chased by wolves, you should use ES2015 imports and exports in your TypeScript code, rather than using CommonJS, global, or namespaced modules. They look like this—the same as plain old JavaScript:

```
// a.ts
export function foo() {}
export function bar() {}

// b.ts
import {foo, bar} from './a'
foo()
export let result = bar()
```

The ES2015 module standard supports default exports:

```
// c.ts
export default function meow(loudness: number) {}

// d.ts
import meow from './c' // Note the lack of {curlies}
meow(11)
```

It also supports importing everything from a module using a wildcard import (*):

```
// e.ts
import * as a from './a'
a.foo()
a.bar()
```

And reexporting some (or all) exports from a module:

```
// f.ts
export * from './a'
export {result} from './b'
export meow from './c'
```

Because we're writing TypeScript, not JavaScript, we can of course export types and interfaces as well as values. And because types and values live in separate namespaces, it's perfectly fine to export two things—one at the value level and one at the type level —that share the same name. Like for any other code, TypeScript will infer whether you meant the type or the value when you actually use it:

```
// g.ts
export let X = 3
export type X = {y: string}

// h.ts
import {X} from './g'

let a = X + 1          // X refers to the value X
let b: X = {y: 'z'}    // X refers to the type X
```

Module paths are filenames on the filesystem. This couples modules with the way they're laid out in the filesystem, but is an important feature for module loaders that need to be aware of that layout so they can resolve modules names to files.

Dynamic Imports

As your application gets bigger, its time to initial render will get worse and worse. This is especially a problem for frontend applications where the network can be a bottleneck, but it also applies to backend applications that take more time to start up as you import more code at the top level—code that needs to be loaded from the filesystem, parsed, compiled, and evaluated, all while blocking other code from running.

On the frontend, one way to deal with this problem (besides writing less code!) is with *code splitting*: chunking your code up into a bunch of generated JavaScript files, instead of shipping everything in a single large file. With splitting you get the benefit of loading multiple chunks in parallel, which eases the toll of large network requests (see Figure 10-1).

Name	Status	Type	Initiator	Size	Time	Waterfall	500.00 ms		1.00 s		1.50 s
QRI5Tk--LMf.js	200	script	(index)	19.5 KB	297 ms						
HYUhGIP2NS_.js	200	script	(index)	1.4 KB	232 ms						
GXV1S0CvpIB.js	200	script	(index)	595 B	233 ms						
hUbIKLhy1j0.js	200	script	(index)	28.4 KB	321 ms						
Au3a0P1wG4x.js	200	script	(index)	17.6 KB	279 ms						
jNh5JwMwDN8.js	200	script	(index)	35.4 KB	337 ms						
18rvByEMli4.js	200	script	(index)	12.0 KB	283 ms						
UjQ9vUvT4UO.js	200	script	(index)	12.6 KB	279 ms						
UdB94moa6Eu.js	200	script	(index)	13.8 KB	280 ms						
g4ZNCtvuodm.js	200	script	(index)	11.5 KB	279 ms						

Figure 10-1. Network waterfall for JavaScript loaded from facebook.com

A further optimization is to lazy-load chunks of code when they're actually needed. Really large frontend applications—like those at Facebook and Google—use this type of optimization as a matter of course. Without it, clients might be loading gigabytes of JavaScript code on the initial page load, which could take minutes or hours (not to mention that people would probably stop using those services once they received their mobile bills).

Lazy loading is also useful for other reasons. For example, the popular Moment.js (*https://momentjs.com*) date manipulation library comes with packages to support every date format used around the world, split up by locale. Each packages weighs in at around 3 KB. Loading all of these locales for each user might be an unacceptable performance and bandwidth hit; instead, you might want to detect the user's locale, then load just the relevant date package.

LABjs and its siblings introduced the concept of lazy-loading code when you actually need it, and the concept was formalized in *dynamic imports*. It looks like this:

```
let locale = await import('locale_us-en')
```

You can use `import` either as a statement to statically pull in code (as we've used it up to this point), or as a function that returns a `Promise` for your module (as we did in this example).

While you can pass an arbitrary expression that evaluates to a string to `import`, you lose type safety when you do. To safely use dynamic imports, be sure to either:

1. Pass a string literal directly to `import`, without assigning the string to a variable first.

2. Pass an expression to `import` and manually annotate the module's signature.

If using the second option, a common pattern is to statically import the module, but use it only in a type position, so that TypeScript compiles away the static import (to learn more, see "The types Directive" on page 262). For example:

```
import {locale} from './locales/locale-us'

async function main() {
  let userLocale = await getUserLocale()
  let path = ./locales/locale-${userLocale}
  let localeUS: typeof locale = await import(path)
}
```

We imported `locale` from *./locales/locale-us*, but we only used it for its type, which we retrieved with `typeof locale`. We needed to do that because TypeScript couldn't statically look up the type of `import(path)`, because `path` is a computed variable and not a static string. Because we never used `locale` as a value, and instead just scavenged it for its type, TypeScript compiled away the static import (in this example, TypeScript doesn't generate any top-level exports at all), leaving us with both excellent type safety and a dynamically computed import.

TSC Setting: module

TypeScript supports dynamic imports in `esnext` module mode only. To use dynamic imports, set `{"module": "esnext"}` in your *tsconfig.json*'s `compilerOptions`. Jump ahead to "Running TypeScript on the Server" on page 258 and "Running TypeScript in the Browser" on page 259 to learn more.

Using CommonJS and AMD Code

When consuming a JavaScript module that uses the CommonJS or AMD standard, you can simply import names from it, just like for ES2015 modules:

```
import {something} from './a/legacy/commonjs/module'
```

By default, CommonJS default exports don't interoperate with ES2015 default imports; to use a default export, you have to use a wildcard import:

```
import * as fs from 'fs'
fs.readFile('some/file.txt')
```

To interoperate more smoothly, set `{"esModuleInterop": true}` in your *tsconfig.json*'s `compilerOptions`. Now, you can leave out the wildcard:

```
import fs from 'fs'
fs.readFile('some/file.txt')
```

As I mentioned at the top of the chapter, even though this code compiles, that doesn't mean it'll work at runtime. Whichever module standard you use—import/export, CommonJS, AMD, UMD, or browser globals—your module bundler and module loader have to be aware of that format so they can package up and split your code correctly at compile time, and load your code correctly at runtime. Head over to Chapter 12 to learn more.

Module Mode Versus Script Mode

TypeScript parses each of your TypeScript files in one of two modes: *module mode* or *script mode*. It decides which mode to use based on a single heuristic: does your file have any imports or exports? If so, it uses module mode; otherwise, it uses script mode.

Module mode is what we've used up to this point, and what you'll use most of the time. In module mode, you use import and import() to require code from other files, and export to make code available to other files. If you use any third-party UMD modules (as a reminder, UMD modules try to use CommonJS, RequireJS, or browser globals, whichever the environment supports), you have to import them first, and can't use their global exports directly.

In script mode, any top-level variables you declare will be available to other files in your project without an explicit import, and you can safely consume global exports from third-party UMD modules without explicitly importing them first. A couple of use cases for script mode are:

- To quickly prototype browser code that you plan to compile to no module system at all ({"module": "none"} in your *tsconfig.json*) and include as raw <script /> tags in your HTML file.

- To create type declarations (see "Type Declarations" on page 230)

You'll almost always want to stick to module mode, which TypeScript will choose for you automatically as you write real-world code that imports other code and exports things for other files to use.

Namespaces

TypeScript gives us another way to encapsulate code: the namespace keyword. Namespaces will feel familiar to a lot of Java, C#, C++, PHP, and Python programmers.

If you're coming from a language with namespaces, note that although namespaces are supported by TypeScript, they're not the preferred way to encapsulate code; if you're not sure whether to use namespaces or modules, choose modules.

Namespaces abstract away the nitty-gritty details of how files are laid out in the file-system; you don't have to know that your .mine function lives in the schemes/scams/bitcoin/apps folder, and instead you can access it with a short, convenient namespace like Schemes.Scams.Bitcoin.Apps.mine.[1]

Say we have two files—a module to make HTTP GET requests, and a consumer that uses that module to make requests:

```
// Get.ts
namespace Network {
  export function get<T>(url: string): Promise<T> {
    // ...
  }
}

// App.ts
namespace App {
  Network.get<GitRepo>('https://api.github.com/repos/Microsoft/typescript')
}
```

A namespace must have a name (like Network), and it can export functions, variables, types, interfaces, or other namespaces. Any code in a namespace block that's not explicitly exported is private to the block. Because namespaces can export namespaces, you can easily model nested namespaces. Let's say our Network module is getting big, and we want to split it up into a few submodules. We can use namespaces to do that:

```
namespace Network {
  export namespace HTTP {
    export function get <T>(url: string): Promise<T> {
      // ...
    }
  }
  export namespace TCP {
    listenOn(port: number): Connection {
      //...
    }
    // ...
  }
  export namespace UDP {
    // ...
  }
```

---

[1] I really hope this joke ages well, and I don't end up regretting not investing in Bitcoin.

```
      export namespace IP {
        // ...
      }
    }
```

Now, all of our network-related utilities are in subnamespaces under `Network`. For example, we can now call `Network.HTTP.get` and `Network.TCP.listenOn` from any file. Like interfaces, namespaces can be augmented, making it convenient to split them across files. TypeScript will recursively merge identically named namespaces for us:

```
// HTTP.ts
namespace Network {
  export namespace HTTP {
    export function get<T>(url: string): Promise<T> {
      // ...
    }
  }
}

// UDP.ts
namespace Network {
  export namespace UDP {
    export function send(url: string, packets: Buffer): Promise<void> {
      // ...
    }
  }
}

// MyApp.ts
Network.HTTP.get<Dog[]>('http://url.com/dogs')
Network.UDP.send('http://url.com/cats', new Buffer(123))
```

If you end up with long namespace hierarchies, you can use *aliases* to shorten them for convenience. Note that despite the similar syntax, destructuring (like you do when importing ES2015 modules) is not supported for aliases:

```
// A.ts
namespace A {
  export namespace B {
    export namespace C {
      export let d = 3
    }
  }
}

// MyApp.ts
import d = A.B.C.d

let e = d * 3
```

Collisions

Collisions between identically named exports are not allowed:

```
// HTTP.ts
namespace Network {
  export function request<T>(url: string): T {
    // ...
  }
}

// HTTP2.ts
namespace Network {
  // Error TS2393: Duplicate function implementation.
  export function request<T>(url: string): T {
    // ...
  }
}
```

The exception to the no-collisions rule is overloaded ambient function declarations, which you can use to refine function types:

```
// HTTP.ts
namespace Network {
  export function request<T>(url: string): T
}

// HTTP2.ts
namespace Network {
  export function request<T>(url: string, priority: number): T
}

// HTTPS.ts
namespace Network {
  export function request<T>(url: string, algo: 'SHA1' | 'SHA256'): T
}
```

Compiled Output

Unlike imports and exports, namespaces don't respect your *tsconfig.json*'s module setting, and always compile to global variables. Let's peek behind the veil to see what the generated output looks like. Say we have the following module:

```
// Flowers.ts
namespace Flowers {
  export function give(count: number) {
    return count + ' flowers'
  }
}
```

Running it through TSC, the generated JavaScript output looks like this:

```
let Flowers
(function (Flowers) {  ❶
  function give(count) {
    return count + ' flowers'
  }
  Flowers.give = give  ❷
})(Flowers || (Flowers = {}))  ❸
```

❶ Flowers is declared within an IIFE—a function that calls itself immediately—to create a closure and prevent variables that weren't explicitly exported from leaking out of the Flowers module.

❷ TypeScript assigns the give function that we exported to the Flowers namespace.

❸ If the Flowers namespace is already globally defined, then TypeScript augments it (Flowers); otherwise, TypeScript creates and augments that newly created namespace (Flowers = {}).

Prefer Modules over Namespaces When Possible

Prefer regular modules (the import and export kind) over namespaces as a way to more closely stick to JavaScript standards and make your dependencies more explicit.

Explicit dependencies have lots of benefits for readability, enforcing module isolation (because namespaces are automatically merged, but modules are not), and static analysis, which matters for big frontend projects where stripping out dead code and splitting your compiled code into multiple files is crucial for performance.

When running TypeScript programs in a NodeJS environment, modules are also the clear choice because of NodeJS's built-in support for CommonJS. In browser environments, some programmers prefer namespaces for simplicity, but for medium- to large-sized projects, try to stick to modules over namespaces.

Declaration Merging

So far we've touched on three types of merging that TypeScript does for us:

- Merging values and types, so that the same name can refer to either a value or a type depending how we use it (see "Companion Object Pattern" on page 140)
- Merging multiple namespaces into one
- Merging multiple interfaces into one (see "Declaration Merging" on page 93)

As you might have intuited, these are three special cases of a much more general TypeScript behavior. TypeScript has a rich set of behavior for merging different kinds of names, unlocking all sorts of patterns that can otherwise be difficult to express (see Table 10-1).

Table 10-1. Can the declaration be merged?

		To							
		Value	Class	Enum	Function	Types alias	Interface	Namespace	Module
	Value	No	No	No	No	Yes	Yes	No	—
	Class	—	No	No	No	No	Yes	Yes	—
	Fnum	—	—	Yes	No	No	No	Yes	—
From	Function	—	—	—	No	Yes	Yes	Yes	—
	Type alias	—	—	—	—	No	No	Yes	—
	Interface	—	—	—	—	—	Yes	Yes	—
	Namespace	—	—	—	—	—	—	Yes	—
	Module	—	—	—	—	—	—	—	Yes

This means that if, for example, you declare a value and a type alias in the same scope, TypeScript will allow it, and infer which one you meant—the type or the value—from whether you use the name in a value or a type position. This is what lets us implement the pattern described in "Companion Object Pattern" on page 140. It also means that you can use an interface and a namespace to implement companion objects—you're not limited to just a value and a type alias. Or you can take advantage of module merging to augment a third-party module declaration (more on this in "Extending a Module" on page 278). Or you can add static methods to an enum by merging that enum with a namespace (try it!).

The moduleResolution Flag

Eagle-eyed readers may notice the moduleResolution flag available in their *tsconfig.json*. This flag controls the algorithm TypeScript uses to resolve module names in your application. The flag supports two modes:

- node: Always use this mode. It resolves modules using the same algorithm that NodeJS uses. Modules prefixed with a ., /, or ~ (like ./my/file) are resolved from the local filesystem, either relative to the current file, or using an absolute path (relative to your / directory, or whatever your *tsconfig.json*'s baseUrl is set to), depending on the prefix you use. TypeScript loads module paths that don't have a prefix from your *node modules* folder, the same as NodeJS. TypeScript builds on NodeJS's resolution strategy in two ways:

---

1. In addition to the `main` field in a package's *package.json* that NodeJS looks at to find the default importable file in a directory, TypeScript also looks at the TypeScript-specific `types` property (more on that in "Type Lookup for Java-Script" on page 242).

2. When importing a file with an unspecified extension, TypeScript first looks for a file with that name and a *.ts* extension, followed by *.tsx*, *.d.ts*, and finally *.js*.

- `classic`: You should never use this mode. In this mode, relative paths are resolved like in `node` mode, but for unprefixed names, TypeScript will look for a file with the given name in the current folder, then walk up the directory tree a folder at a time until it finds a matching file. This is really surprising behavior for anyone coming from the NodeJS or JavaScript world, and does not interoperate well with other build tools.

Summary

In this chapter we covered TypeScript's module system, starting with a brief history of JavaScript module systems, ES2015 modules and safely lazy-loading code with dynamic imports, interoperating with CommonJS and AMD modules, and module mode versus script mode. We then covered namespaces, namespace merging, and how TypeScript's declaration merging works.

As you develop applications in TypeScript, try hard to stick to ES2015 modules. TypeScript doesn't care which module system you use, but it will make it easier to integrate with build tooling (see Chapter 12 to learn more).

Exercise

1. Play around with declaration merging, to:
   a. Reimplement companion objects (from "Companion Object Pattern" on page 140) using namespaces and interfaces, instead of values and types.
   b. Add static methods to an enum.

Interoperating with JavaScript

We don't live in a perfect world. Your coffee can be too hot and burn your mouth a little when you drink it, your parents might call and leave you voicemails a little too often, that pothole by your driveway is still there no matter how many times you call the city, and your code might not be completely covered with static types.

Most of us are in this boat: though once in a while you'll have the leeway to start a greenfield project in TypeScript, most of the time it will start as a little island of safety, embedded in a larger, less safe codebase. Maybe you have a well-isolated component that you want to try TypeScript on even though your company uses regular ES6 JavaScript everywhere else, or maybe you're fed up with getting paged at 6 A.M. because you refactored some code and forgot to update a call site (it's now 7 A.M., and you're ninja-merging TSC into your codebase before your coworkers wake up). Either way, you will probably start with an island of TypeScript in a type-less sea.

So far in this book I've been teaching you to write TypeScript the right way. This chapter is about writing TypeScript the practical way, in real codebases that are in the process of migrating away from untyped languages, that use third-party JavaScript libraries, that at times sacrifice type safety for a quick hot patch to unbreak prod. This chapter is dedicated to working with JavaScript. We'll explore:

- Using type declarations
- Gradually migrating from JavaScript to TypeScript
- Using third-party JavaScript and TypeScript

Type Declarations

A *type declaration* is a file with the extension *.d.ts*. Along with JSDoc annotations (see "Step 2b: Add JSDoc Annotations (Optional)" on page 239), it's a way to attach TypeScript types to JavaScript code that would otherwise be untyped.

Type declarations have a similar syntax to regular TypeScript, with a few differences:

- Type declarations can only contain types, and can't contain values. That means no function, class, object, or variable implementations, and no default values for parameters.

- While type declarations can't define values, they can declare that there *exists* a value defined somewhere in your JavaScript. We use the special `declare` keyword for this.

- Type declarations only declare types for things that are visible to consumers. We don't include things like types that aren't exported, or types for local variables inside of function bodies.

Let's jump into an example, and take a look at a piece of TypeScript (*.ts*) code and its equivalent type declaration (*.d.ts*). This example is a fairly involved piece of code from the popular RxJS library; feel free to gloss over the details of what it's doing, and instead pay attention to which language features it's using (imports, classes, interfaces, class fields, function overloads, and so on):

```
import {Subscriber} from './Subscriber'
import {Subscription} from './Subscription'
import {PartialObserver, Subscribable, TeardownLogic} from './types'

export class Observable<T> implements Subscribable<T> {
  public _isScalar: boolean = false
  constructor(
    subscribe?: (
      this: Observable<T>,
      subscriber: Subscriber<T>
    ) => TeardownLogic
  ) {
    if (subscribe) {
      this._subscribe = subscribe
    }
  }
  static create<T>(subscribe?: (subscriber: Subscriber<T>) => TeardownLogic) {
    return new Observable<T>(subscribe)
  }
  subscribe(observer?: PartialObserver<T>): Subscription
  subscribe(
    next?: (value: T) => void,
    error?: (error: any) => void,
    complete?: () => void
```

```
  ): Subscription
  subscribe(
    observerOrNext?: PartialObserver<T> | ((value: T) => void),
    error?: (error: any) => void,
    complete?: () => void
  ): Subscription {
    // ...
  }
}
```

Running this code through TSC with the declarations flag enabled (tsc -d Observ able.ts) yields the following *Observable.d.ts* type declaration:

```
import {Subscriber} from './Subscriber'
import {Subscription} from './Subscription'
import {PartialObserver, Subscribable, TeardownLogic} from './types'

export declare class Observable<T> implements Subscribable<T> { ❶
  _isScalar: boolean
  constructor(
    subscribe?: (
      this: Observable<T>,
      subscriber: Subscriber<T>
    ) => TeardownLogic
  );
  static create<T>(
    subscribe?: (subscriber: Subscriber<T>) => TeardownLogic
  ): Observable<T>
  subscribe(observer?: PartialObserver<T>): Subscription
  subscribe(
    next?: (value: T) => void,
    error?: (error: any) => void,
    complete?: () => void
  ): Subscription ❷
}
```

❶ Notice the declare keyword before class. We can't actually define a class in a type declaration, but we can *declare* that we defined a class in the *.d.ts* file's corresponding JavaScript file. Think of declare like an affirmation: "I swear that my JavaScript exports a class of this type."

❷ Because type declarations don't contain implementations, we only keep the two overloads for subscribe, and not the signature for its implementation.

Notice how *Observable.d.ts* is just *Observable.ts*, minus the implementations. In other words, it's just the types from *Observable.ts*.

This type declaration isn't useful to other files in the RxJS library that use *Observable.ts*, since they have access to the *Observable.ts* source TypeScript file itself and can use it directly. It is useful, however, if you consume RxJS in your TypeScript application.

Think about it: if the authors of RxJS wanted to package in typing information on NPM for their TypeScript-wielding users (RxJS can be used in both TypeScript and JavaScript applications), they would have two options: package *both* source Type-Script files (for TypeScript users) and compiled JavaScript files (for JavaScript users), or ship compiled JavaScript files along with type declarations for TypeScript users. The latter reduces the file size, and makes it unambiguous what the correct import to use is. It also helps keep compile times for your application fast, since your TSC instance doesn't have to recompile RxJS every time you compile your own app (in fact, it's the reason the optimization strategy we introduce in "Project References" on page 255 works!).

Type declaration files have a few uses:

1. When someone else uses your compiled TypeScript from their TypeScript application, their TSC instance will look for *.d.ts* files corresponding to your generated JavaScript files. This tells TypeScript what the types are for your project.

2. Code editors with TypeScript support (like VSCode) will read these *.d.ts* files to give your users helpful type hints as they type, even if they don't use TypeScript.

3. They speed up compile times significantly by avoiding unnecessarily recompiling your TypeScript code.

A type declaration is a way to tell TypeScript, "There exists this thing that's defined in JavaScript, and I'm going to describe it to you." When we talk about type declarations, we often call them *ambient* in order to differentiate them from regular declarations that contain values; for example, an *ambient variable declaration* uses the `declare` keyword to declare that a variable is defined somewhere in JavaScript, while a regular nonambient variable declaration is a normal `let` or `const` declaration that declares a variable without using the `declare` keyword.

You can use type declarations for a few things:

- To tell TypeScript about a global variable that's defined in JavaScript somewhere. For example, if you polyfilled the `Promise` global or defined `process.env` in a browser environment, you might use an *ambient variable declaration* to give TypeScript a heads-up.

- To define a type that's globally available everywhere in your project, so to use it you don't have to import it first (we call this an ambient type declaration).

- To tell TypeScript about a third-party module that you installed with NPM (an *ambient module declaration*).

A type declaration, regardless of what you're using it for, has to live in a script-mode *.ts* or *.d.ts* file (recall our earlier discussion of script mode in "Module Mode Versus Script Mode" on page 222). By convention, we give our file a *.d.ts* extension if it has a corresponding *.js* file; otherwise, we use a *.ts* extension. It doesn't matter what you call the file—for example, I like to stick to a single top-level *types.ts* until it gets unwieldy—and a single type declaration file can contain as many type declarations as you want.

Finally, while top-level values in a type declaration file need the `declare` keyword (`declare let`, `declare function`, `declare class`, and so on), top-level types and interfaces do not.

With those ground rules out of the way, let's briefly look at some examples of each kind of type declaration.

Ambient Variable Declarations

An ambient variable declaration is a way to tell TypeScript about a global variable that can be used in any *.ts* or *.d.ts* file in your project without explicitly importing it first.

Let's say you're running a NodeJS program in your browser, and the program checks `process.env.NODE_ENV` (which is either `"development"` or `"production"`) at some point. When you run the program, you get an ugly runtime error:

```
Uncaught ReferenceError: process is not defined.
```

You sleuth around Stack Overflow a bit, and realize that the quickest hack to get your program running is to polyfill `process.env.NODE_ENV` yourself and hardcode it. So you create a new file, *polyfills.ts*, and define a global `process.env`:

```
process = {
  env: {
    NODE_ENV: 'production'
  }
}
```

Of course, TypeScript then comes to the rescue, throwing a red squiggly at you to try to save you from the mistake you're clearly making by augmenting the `window` global:

```
Error TS2304: Cannot find name 'process'.
```

But in this case, TypeScript is being overprotective. You really do want to augment `window`, and you want to do it safely.

So what do you do? You pop open *polyfills.ts* in Vim (you see where this is going) and type:

```
declare let process: {
  env: {
    NODE_ENV: 'development' | 'production'
  }
}

process = {
  env: {
    NODE_ENV: 'production'
  }
}
```

You're declaring to TypeScript that there's a global object `process` that has a single property `env`, that has a property `NODE_ENV`. Once you tell TypeScript about that, the red squiggly disappears and you can safely define your `process` global.

TSC Setting: lib

TypeScript comes with a set of type declarations for describing the JavaScript standard library that includes built-in JavaScript types, like `Array` and `Promise`, and methods on built-in types, like `''.toUpperCase`. It also includes global objects like `window` and `document` (in a browser environment), and `onmessage` (in a Web Worker environment).

You can pull in TypeScript's built-in type declarations using your *tsconfig.json*'s `lib` field. Jump ahead to "lib" on page 254 for a deep dive into how to dial in your project's `lib` setting.

Ambient Type Declarations

Ambient type declarations follow the same rules as ambient variable declarations: the declaration has to live in a script-mode *.ts* or *.d.ts* file, and it'll be available globally to the other files in your project without an explicit import. For example, let's declare a global utility type `ToArray<T>` that lifts T to an array, if it isn't an array already. We can define this type in any script-mode file in our project—for this example, let's define it in a top-level *types.ts* file:

```
type ToArray<T> = T extends unknown[] ? T : T[]
```

We can now use this type from any project file, without an explicit import:

```
function toArray<T>(a: T): ToArray<T> {
  // ...
}
```

Consider using ambient type declarations to model data types that are used throughout your application. For example, you might use them to make the `UserID` type we developed in "Simulating Nominal Types" on page 152 globally available:

```
type UserID = string & {readonly brand: unique symbol}
```

Now, you can use `UserID` anywhere in your application without having to explicitly import it first.

Ambient Module Declarations

When you consume a JavaScript module and want to quickly declare some types for it so you can use it safely—without having to contribute the type declarations back to the JavaScript module's GitHub repository or DefinitelyTyped first—ambient module declarations are the tool to use.

An ambient module declaration is a regular type declaration, surrounded by a special `declare module` syntax:

```
declare module 'module-name' {
  export type MyType = number
  export type MyDefaultType = {a: string}
  export let myExport: MyType
  let myDefaultExport: MyDefaultType
  export default myDefaultExport
}
```

A module name (`'module-name'` in this example) corresponds to an exact `import` path. When you import that path, your ambient module declaration tells TypeScript what's available:

```
import ModuleName from 'module-name'
ModuleName.a  // string
```

If you have a nested module, make sure you include the whole `import` path in its declaration:

```
declare module '@most/core' {
  // Type declaration
}
```

If you just want to quickly tell TypeScript "I'm importing this module—I'll type it later, just assume it's an any for now," keep the header but omit the actual declaration:

```
// Declare a module that can be imported, where each of its imports are any
declare module 'unsafe-module-name'
```

Now if you consume this module, it's less safe:

```
import {x} from 'unsafe-module-name'
x  // any
```

Module declarations support wildcard imports, so you can give a type to any `import` path that matches the given pattern. Use a wildcard (*) to match an `import` path:[1]

```
// Type JSON files imported with Webpack's json-loader
declare module 'json!*' {
  let value: object
  export default value
}

// Type CSS files imported with Webpack's style-loader
declare module '*.css' {
  let css: CSSRuleList
  export default css
}
```

Now, you can load JSON and CSS files:

```
import a from 'json!myFile'
a  // object

import b from './widget.css'
b  // CSSRuleList
```

 For the last two examples to work, you'll need to configure your build system to load *.json* and *.css* files. You can declare to Type-Script that these path patterns are safe to import, but TypeScript won't be able to build them by itself.

Jump ahead to "JavaScript That Doesn't Have Type Declarations on DefinitelyTyped" on page 246 for an example of how to use ambient module declarations to declare types for untyped third-party JavaScript.

Gradually Migrating from JavaScript to TypeScript

TypeScript was designed with JavaScript interoperability in mind, not as an afterthought. So while it's not painless, migrating to TypeScript is a good experience, letting you convert your codebase over a file at a time, opting into stricter levels of safety as you migrate, showing your boss and your coworkers just how impactful statically typing your code can be, one commit at a time.

At a high level, here's where you want to end up: your codebase should be completely written in TypeScript with strict type coverage, and third-party JavaScript libraries you depend on should come with high-quality, strict types of their own. Any bugs

---

1 Wildcard matching with * follows the same rules as regular glob pattern matching. (*https://en.wikipedia.org/wiki/Glob_(programming)*)

that could be caught at compile time are, and TypeScript's rich autocompletion halves the time it takes to write each line of code. You might have to take a few baby steps to get there:

- Add TSC to your project.
- Start typechecking your existing JavaScript code.
- Migrate your JavaScript code to TypeScript, a file at a time.
- Install type declarations for your dependencies, either stubbing out types for dependencies that don't have types or writing type declarations for untyped dependencies and contributing them back to DefinitelyTyped.[2]
- Flip on strict mode for your codebase.

This process can take a while, but you will see safety and productivity gains right away, and uncover more gains as you keep going. Let's walk through the steps one at a time.

Step 1: Add TSC

When working on a codebase that combines TypeScript and JavaScript, start by letting TSC compile JavaScript files alongside your TypeScript. In your *tsconfig.json*:

```
{
  "compilerOptions": {
  "allowJs": true
}
```

With this one change, you can now use TSC to compile your JavaScript. Just add TSC to your build process, and either run every existing JavaScript file through TSC,[3] or continue running legacy JavaScript files through your existing build process and run new TypeScript files through TSC.

With allowJs set to true, TypeScript won't typecheck your existing JavaScript code, but it will transpile it (to ES3, ES5, or whatever target is set to in your *tsconfig.json*) using the module system you asked for (in your *tsconfig.json*'s module field). First step, done. Commit it, and give yourself a pat on the back—your codebase now uses TypeScript!

---

2 DefinitelyTyped is the open source repository for JavaScript type declarations. Read on to learn more.

3 For really big projects it can be slow to run every single file through TSC. For a way to improve performance for large projects, see "Project References" on page 255.

Step 2a: Enable Typechecking for JavaScript (Optional)

Now that TSC is processing your JavaScript, why not typecheck it too? While you might not have explicit type annotations in your JavaScript, remember how great TypeScript is at inferring types for you; it can infer types in your JavaScript the same way it does in your TypeScript code. Enable this in your *tsconfig.json*:

```
{
  "compilerOptions": {
  "allowJs": true,
  "checkJs": true
}
```

Now, whenever TypeScript compiles a JavaScript file it'll do its best to infer types and typecheck as it goes, like it does for regular TypeScript code.

If your codebase is big and flipping on `checkJs` reports too many type errors at once, turn it off, and instead enable checking for a JavaScript file at a time by adding the `// @ts-check` directive (a regular comment at the top of the file). Or, if a few big files are throwing the bulk of your errors and you don't want to fix them just yet, keep `checkJs` on and add the `// @ts-nocheck` directive to just those files.

Because TypeScript can't infer everything (e.g., function parameter types), it will infer a lot of types in your JavaScript code as `any`. If you have `strict` mode enabled in your *tsconfig.json* (you should!), you may want to temporarily allow implicit `any`s while you migrate. In your *tsconfig.json*, add:

```
{
  "compilerOptions": {
  "allowJs": true,
  "checkJs": true,
  "noImplicitAny": false
}
```

Don't forget to turn `noImplicitAny` on again when you've migrated a critical mass of code to TypeScript! It will probably reveal a bunch of real errors that you missed (unless, of course, you're Xenithar, disciple of Bathmorda the JavaScript witch, able to typecheck in your mind's eye with the help of nothing but a cauldronful of mugwort).

When TypeScript runs over JavaScript code, it uses a more lenient inference algorithm than it does for TypeScript code. Specifically:

- All function parameters are optional.

- The types of properties on functions and classes are inferred from usage (rather than having to be declared up front):

```
class A {
  x = 0 // number | string | string[], inferred from usage
  method() {
    this.x = 'foo'
  }
  otherMethod() {
    this.x = ['array', 'of', 'strings']
  }
}
```

- After declaring an object, class, or function, you can assign extra properties to it. Under the hood, TypeScript does this by generating a corresponding namespace for each class and function declaration, and automatically adding an index signature to every object literal.

Step 2b: Add JSDoc Annotations (Optional)

Maybe you're in a hurry, and just need to add a single type annotation for a new function you added to an old JavaScript file. Until you get a chance to convert that file to TypeScript, you can use a JSDoc annotation to type your new function.

You've probably seen JSDoc before; it's those funny-looking comments above some JavaScript and TypeScript code with @-annotations like @param, @returns, and so on. TypeScript understands JSDoc, and uses it as input to its typechecker the same way that it uses explicit type annotations in TypeScript code.

Let's say you have a 3,000-line utilities file (yes, I know your "friend" wrote it). You add a new utility function to it:

```
export function toPascalCase(word) {
  return word.replace(
    /\w+/g,
    ([a, ...b]) => a.toUpperCase() + b.join('').toLowerCase()
  )
}
```

Without converting *utils.js* to TypeScript full sail—which would probably catch a bunch of bugs you'd then have to fix—you can annotate just your toPascalCase function, carving out a little island of safety in a sea of untyped JavaScript:

```
/**
 * @param word {string} An input string to convert
 * @returns {string} The string in PascalCase
 */
export function toPascalCase(word) {
  return word.replace(
    /\w+/g,
    ([a, ...b]) => a.toUpperCase() + b.join('').toLowerCase()
  )
}
```

Without that JSDoc annotation, TypeScript would have inferred toPascalCase's type as (word: any) => string. Now, when TypeScript compiles your code it knows toPascalCase's type is (word: string) => string. And you got some nice documentation out of it!

Head over to the TypeScript Wiki (*http://bit.ly/2YCTWBf*) to learn more about supported JSDoc annotations.

Step 3: Rename Your Files to .ts

Once you've added TSC to your build process, and optionally started typechecking and annotating JavaScript where possible, it's time to start switching over to TypeScript.

One file at a time, update your files' extensions from *.js* (or *.coffee*, *.es6*, etc.) to *.ts*. As soon as you rename a file in your code editor, you'll see your friends the red squigglies appear (the TypeError, not the kids' TV show), uncovering type errors, missed cases, forgotten null checks, and misspelled variable names. There are two strategies for fixing these errors:

1. Do it right. Take your time to type shapes, fields, and functions correctly, so you can catch errors in all the files that consume them. If you have checkJs enabled, turn on noImplicitAny in your *tsconfig.json* to uncover anys and type them, then turn it back off to make the output of typechecking your remaining JavaScript files less noisy.

2. Do it fast. Mass-rename your JavaScript files to the *.ts* extension, and keep your *tsconfig.json* settings lax (meaning strict set to false) to throw as few type errors as possible after renaming. Type complex types as any to appease the typechecker. Fix whatever type errors remain, and commit. Once this is done, flip on the strict mode flags (noImplicitAny, noImplicitThis, strictNullChecks, and so on) one by one, and fix the errors that pop up. (See Appendix F for a full list of these flags.)

If you choose to go the quick-and-dirty route, a useful trick is to define an ambient type declaration TODO as a type alias for any, and use that instead of any so that you can more easily find and track missing types. You can also call it something more specific, so it's easier to find in a project-wide code search:

```
// globals.ts
type TODO_FROM_JS_TO_TS_MIGRATION = any

// MyMigratedUtil.ts
export function mergeWidgets(
  widget1: TODO_FROM_JS_TO_TS_MIGRATION,
  widget2: TODO_FROM_JS_TO_TS_MIGRATION
): number {
  // ...
}
```

Both ways of doing it are fair game, and it's up to you which you want to go with. Because TypeScript is a gradually typed language, it's built from the ground up to interoperate with untyped JavaScript code as safely as possible. Regardless of whether you're interoperating strictly typed TypeScript with untyped JavaScript or strictly typed TypeScript with loosely typed TypeScript, TypeScript will do its best to make sure that you're doing it as safely as possible, and that on the strictly typed island that you've so carefully built, everything is as safe as it can be.

Step 4: Make It strict

Once you've migrated a critical mass of your JavaScript over to TypeScript, you'll want to make your code as safe as possible by opting into TSC's more stringent flags one by one (see Appendix F for a full list of flags).

Finally, you can disable TSC's JavaScript interoperability flags, enforcing that all of your code is written in strictly typed TypeScript:

```
{
  "compilerOptions": {
  "allowJs": false,
  "checkJs": false
}
```

This will surface the final rounds of type-related errors. Fix these, and you're left with a pristine, safe codebase that the most hardcore OCaml engineer would give you a pat on the back for (were you to ask nicely).

Following these steps will get you far when adding types to JavaScript you control, but what about JavaScript you don't control, like code you installed from NPM? To get there, we're first going to have to take a small detour…

Type Lookup for JavaScript

When you import a JavaScript file from a TypeScript file, TypeScript follows an algorithm that looks like this to look up type declarations for your JavaScript code (remember that "file" and "module" are interchangeable when we talk about TypeScript):[4]

1. Look for a sibling *.d.ts* file with the same name as your *.js* file. If it exists, use it as the type declaration for the *.js* file.

   For example, say you have the following folder structure:

   ```
   my-app/
   ├─src/
   | ├─index.ts
   | └─legacy/
   |    ├─old-file.js
   |    └─old-file.d.ts
   ```

   You then import *old-file* from *index.ts*:

   ```
   // index.ts
   import './legacy/old-file'
   ```

   TypeScript will use *src/legacy/old-file.d.ts* as the source of type declarations for *./legacy/old-file*.

2. Otherwise, if `allowJs` and `checkJs` are true, infer the *.js* file's types (informed by any JSDoc annotations in the *.js* file).

3. Otherwise, treat the whole module as an `any`.

When importing a third-party JavaScript module—that is, an NPM package that you installed to *node modules*—TypeScript uses a slightly different algorithm:

1. Look for a local type declaration for the module. If it exists, use it.

   For example, say your app's folder structure looks like this:

   ```
   my-app/
   ├─node_modules/
   | └─foo/
   ├─src/
   | ├─index.ts
   | └─types.d.ts
   ```

   And *types.d.ts* looks like this:

---

4 Strictly speaking, this is true for module-mode, but not script-mode, files. Read more in "Module Mode Versus Script Mode" on page 222.

```
// types.d.ts
declare module 'foo' {
  let bar: {}
  export default bar
}
```

If you then import foo, TypeScript will use the ambient module declaration in *types.d.ts* as the source of types for foo:

```
// index.ts
import bar from 'foo'
```

2. Otherwise, look at the module's *package.json*. If it defines a field called types or typings, use the *.d.ts* file that field points to as the source of type declarations for the module.

3. Otherwise, traverse out a directory at a time, and look for a *node modules/@types* directory that has type declarations for the module.

   For example, say you installed React:

   ```
   npm install react --save
   npm install @types/react --save-dev

   my-app/
   ├──node_modules/
   │  ├──@types/
   │  │  └──react/
   │  └──react/
   ├──src/
   │  └──index.ts
   ```

   When you import React, TypeScript will find the *@types/react* folder and use that as the source of type declarations for React:

   ```
   // index.ts
   import * as React from 'react'
   ```

4. Otherwise, proceed to steps 1–3 of the local type lookup algorithm.

That was a lot of steps, but it's remarkably intuitive once you get the hang of it.

TSC Settings: types and typeRoots

By default, TypeScript looks in *node modules/@types* in your project's folder and containing folders (*../node modules/@types* and so on) for third-party type declarations. Most of the time, you want to leave this behavior as is.

To override this default behavior for global type declarations, configure `typeRoots` in your *tsconfig.json* with an array of folders to look in for type declarations. For example, you can tell TypeScript to look for type declarations in the *typings* folder as well as *node modules/@types*:

```
{
  "compilerOptions": {
    "typeRoots" : ["./typings", "./node modules/@types"]
  }
}
```

For even more granular control, use the `types` option in your *tsconfig.json* to specify which packages you want TypeScript to look up types for. For example, the following config ignores all third-party type declarations except the ones for React:

```
{
  "compilerOptions": {
    "types" : ["react"]
  }
}
```

Using Third-Party JavaScript

I'll assume you're using a package manager like NPM or Yarn to install third-party JavaScript. And if you're one of those people that prefers to copy and paste code manually instead—shame on you.

When you `npm install` third-party JavaScript code into your project, there are three possible scenarios:

1. The code you installed comes with type declarations out of the box.

2. The code you installed doesn't come with type declarations, but declarations are available on DefinitelyTyped.

3. The code you installed doesn't come with type declarations, and declarations are not available on DefinitelyTyped.

Let's dig into each of these.

JavaScript That Comes with Type Declarations

You know that a package comes with type declarations out of the box if you `import` it with `{"noImplicitAny": true}` and TypeScript doesn't throw a red squiggly at you.

If the code you're installing is compiled from TypeScript, or its authors were kind enough to include type declarations in its NPM package, then you're in luck. Just install the code and start using it with full type support.

Some examples of NPM packages that come with built-in type declarations are:

```
npm install rxjs
npm install ava
npm install @angular/cli
```

Unless the code you're installing was actually compiled from Type-Script, you always run the risk that the type declarations it comes with don't match up to the code those declarations describe. When type declarations come packaged with source code the risk of this happening is pretty low (especially for popular packages), but it's something to be aware of.

JavaScript That Has Type Declarations on DefinitelyTyped

Even if the third-party code you're importing doesn't come with type declarations, declarations for it are probably available on DefinitelyTyped (*https://github.com/Defi nitelyTyped/DefinitelyTyped*), TypeScript's community-maintained, centralized repository for ambient module declarations for open source projects.

To check if the package you installed has type declarations available on DefinitelyTyped, either search on TypeSearch (*https://microsoft.github.io/TypeSearch/*) or just try installing the declarations. All DefinitelyTyped type declarations are published to NPM under the `@types` scope, so you can just `npm install` from that scope:

```
npm install lodash --save          # Install Lodash
npm install @types/lodash --save-dev # Install type declarations for Lodash
```

Most of the time, you'll want to use `npm install`'s `--save-dev` flag to add your installed type declarations to your *package.json*'s `devDependencies` field.

Since type declarations on DefinitelyTyped are community-maintained, they run the risk of being incomplete, inaccurate, or stale. While most popular packages have well-maintained type declarations, if you find that the declarations you're using can be improved, take the time to improve them and contribute them back to DefinitelyTyped (*http://bit.ly/2U7QYWP*) so other Type-Script users can take advantage of your hard work.

JavaScript That Doesn't Have Type Declarations on DefinitelyTyped

This is the least common case of the three. You have several options here, from the cheapest and least safe to the most time-intensive and safest:

1. *Whitelist the specific import* by adding a `// @ts-ignore` directive above your untyped import. TypeScript will let you use the untyped module, but the module and all of its contents will be typed as `any`:

   ```
   // @ts-ignore
   import Unsafe from 'untyped-module'

   Unsafe  // any
   ```

2. *Whitelist all usages of this module* by creating an empty type declaration file and stubbing out the module. For example, if you installed the rarely used package `nearby-ferret-alerter`, you could make a new type declaration (e.g., *types.d.ts*) and add to it the ambient type declaration:

   ```
   // types.d.ts
   declare module 'nearby-ferret-alerter'
   ```

   This tells TypeScript that there exists a module that you can import (`import alert from 'nearby-ferret-alerter'`), but it doesn't tell TypeScript anything about the types contained in that module. This approach is a slightly better alternative to the first, in that now there's a central *types.d.ts* file that enumerates all the untyped modules in your application, but it's equally unsafe because `nearby-ferret-alerter` and all of its exports will still be typed as `any`.

3. *Create an ambient module declaration.* Like in the previous approach, create a file called *types.d.ts* and add an empty declaration (`declare module 'nearby-ferret-alerter'`). Now, fill in the type declaration. For example, the result might look like this:

   ```
   // types.d.ts
   declare module 'nearby-ferret-alerter' {
     export default function alert(loudness: 'soft' | 'loud'): Promise<void>
     export function getFerretCount(): Promise<number>
   }
   ```

   Now when you `import alert from 'nearby-ferret-alerter'`, TypeScript will know exactly what `alert`'s type is. It's no longer an `any`, but `(loudness: 'quiet' | 'loud') => Promise<void>`.

4. *Create a type declaration and contribute it back to NPM.* If you got as far as the third option and now have a local type declaration for your module, consider contributing it back to NPM so the next person that needs type declarations for the awesome `nearby-ferret-alerter` package can use it too. To do this you can either submit a pull request to the `nearby-ferret-alerter` Git repository and

contribute the type declarations directly, or, if the maintainers of that repository don't want to be on the hook for maintaining TypeScript type declarations, contribute your declarations to DefinitelyTyped instead.

Writing type declarations for third-party JavaScript is straightforward, but how it's done depends on the type of module you're typing. There are a few common patterns that come up when typing different kinds of JavaScript modules (from NodeJS modules to jQuery augmentations and Lodash mixins to React and Angular components). Head over to Appendix D for a list of recipes for typing third-party JavaScript modules.

 Automatically generating type declarations for untyped JavaScript is an active area of research. Check out dts-gen (*https:// www.npmjs.com/package/dts-gen*) for a way to automatically generate type declaration scaffolding for any third-party JavaScript module.

Summary

There are a few ways to use JavaScript from TypeScript. Table 11-1 summarizes the options.

Table 11-1. Ways to use JavaScript from TypeScript

Approach	tsconfig.json flags	Type safety
Import untyped JavaScript	`{"allowJs": true}`	Poor
Import and check JavaScript	`{"allowJs": true, "checkJs": true}`	OK
Import and check JSDoc-annotated JavaScript	`{"allowJs": true, "checkJs": true, "strict": true}`	Excellent
Import JavaScript with type declarations	`{"allowJs": false, "strict": true}`	Excellent
Import TypeScript	`{"allowJs": false, "strict": true}`	Excellent

In this chapter we covered various aspects of using JavaScript and TypeScript together, from the different kinds of type declarations and how to use them, to migrating your existing JavaScript project to TypeScript piece by piece, to using third-party JavaScript safely (and unsafely). Interoperating with JavaScript can be one of the trickiest aspects of TypeScript; with all the tools at your disposal, you're now equipped to do it in your own project.

Building and Running TypeScript

If you've deployed and run a JavaScript application in production, then you know how to run a TypeScript application too—once you compile it to JavaScript, the two aren't so different. This chapter is about productionizing and building TypeScript applications, but there isn't much here that's unique to TypeScript apps—it mostly applies to JavaScript applications too. We'll divide it up into four sections, covering:

- The things you have to do to build any TypeScript application
- Building and running TypeScript applications on the server
- Building and running TypeScript applications in the browser
- Building for and publishing your TypeScript application to NPM

Building Your TypeScript Project

Building a TypeScript project is straightforward. In this section, we'll cover the core ideas you'll need to understand in order to build your project for whatever environment you plan to run it in.

Project Layout

I suggest keeping your source TypeScript code in a top-level *src/* folder, and compiling it to a top-level *dist/* folder. This folder structure is a popular convention, and splitting your source code and generated code into two top-level folders can make your life easier down the line, when you're integrating with other tooling. It also makes it easier to exclude generated artifacts from source control.

Try to stick to this convention when you can:

```
my-app/
├─dist/
│  ├─index.d.ts
│  ├─index.js
│  └─services/
│     ├─foo.d.ts
│     ├─foo.js
│     ├─bar.d.ts
│     └─bar.js
├─src/
│  ├─index.ts
│  └─services/
│     ├─foo.ts
│     └─bar.ts
```

Artifacts

When you compile a TypeScript program to JavaScript, there are a few different artifacts that TSC can generate for you (Table 12-1).

Table 12-1. Artifacts that TSC can generate for you

Type	File extension	tsconfig.json flag	Emitted by default?
JavaScript	.js	`{"emitDeclarationOnly": false}`	Yes
Source maps	.js.map	`{"sourceMap": true}`	No
Type declarations	.d.ts	`{"declaration": true}`	No
Declaration maps	.d.ts.map	`{"declarationMap": true}`	No

The first type of artifact—JavaScript files—should be familiar. TSC compiles your TypeScript code to JavaScript that you can then run using a JavaScript platform like NodeJS or Chrome. If you run `tsc yourfile.ts`, TSC will typecheck *yourfile.ts* and compile it to JavaScript.

The second type of artifact—source maps—is special files that link each piece of your generated JavaScript back to the specific line and column of the TypeScript file that it was generated from. This is helpful for debugging your code (Chrome DevTools will show your TypeScript code, instead of the generated JavaScript), and for mapping lines and columns in JavaScript exception stack traces back to TypeScript (tools like those mentioned in "Error Monitoring" on page 258 do this lookup automatically if you give them your source maps).

The third artifact—type declarations—lets other TypeScript projects take advantage of your generated types.

Finally, declaration maps are used to speed up compilation times for your TypeScript projects. You'll read more about them in "Project References" on page 255. We'll spend the rest of this chapter talking about how and why to generate these artifacts.

Dialing In Your Compile Target

JavaScript can be an unusual language to work with: not only does it have a quickly evolving specification with a yearly release cycle, but, as a programmer, you can't always control which JavaScript version the platform you're running your program on implements. On top of that, many JavaScript programs are *isomorphic*, meaning you can run them on either the server or the client. For example:

- If you run your backend JavaScript program on a server that you control, then you can control exactly which JavaScript version it will run on.

- If you then release your backend JavaScript program as an open source project, you don't know which JavaScript version will be supported by your consumers' JavaScript platforms. The best you can do in a NodeJS environment is declare a range of supported NodeJS versions, but in a browser environment you're out of luck.

- If you run your JavaScript in a browser, you have no idea which browser people will use to run it—the latest Chrome, Firefox, or Edge that supports most modern JavaScript features, a slightly outdated version of one of those browsers that's missing some bleeding-edge functionality, an antiquated browser like Internet Explorer 8, or an embedded browser like the one that runs on the PlayStation 4 in your garage. The best you can do is define a minimum set of features that people's browsers need to support to run your application, ship polyfills for as many of those features as you can, and try to detect when users are on really old browsers that your app won't run on and show them a message saying that they need to upgrade.

- If you release an isomorphic JavaScript library (e.g., a logging library that runs on both browser and server), then you have to support both a minimum NodeJS version and a swath of browser JavaScript engines and versions.

Not every JavaScript environment supports every JavaScript feature out of the box, but you should still try to write code in the latest language version. There are two ways to do this:

1. *Transpile* (i.e., automatically convert) applications from the latest version of JavaScript to the oldest JavaScript version that a platform you target supports. We do this for language features like `for..of` loops and `async/await`, which can be automatically converted to `for` loops and `.then` calls, respectively.

2. *Polyfill* (i.e., provide implementations for) any modern features that are missing in the JavaScript runtime you're running on. We do this for features provided by the JavaScript standard library (like `Promise`, `Map`, and `Set`) and for prototype methods (like `Array.prototype.includes` and `Function.prototype.bind`).

TSC has built-in support for transpiling your code to older JavaScript versions, but it will not automatically polyfill your code. This is worth reiterating: TSC will transpile most JavaScript features for older environments, but it will not provide implementations for missing features.

TSC gives you three settings to dial in which environments you want to target:

- `target` sets the JavaScript version you want to transpile to: `es5`, `es2015`, etc.
- `module` sets the module system you want to target: `es2015` modules, `commonjs` modules, `systemjs` modules, etc.
- `lib` tells TypeScript which JavaScript features are available in the environments you're targeting: `es5` features, `es2015` features, the `dom`, etc. It doesn't actually implement these features—that's what polyfills are for—but it does tell TypeScript that the features are available (either natively or via a polyfill).

The environment you plan to run your application in dictates which JavaScript version you should transpile to with `target` and what to set `lib` to. If you're not sure, `es5` is usually a safe default for both. What you set `module` to depends on whether you're targeting a NodeJS or browser environment, and what module loader you're using if the latter.

 If you need to support an unusual set of platforms, look up which JavaScript features your target platforms support natively in Juriy Zaytsev's (aka Kangax's) compatibility tables (*http://kangax.github.io/compat-table/es5/*).

Let's dig a little deeper into `target` and `lib`; we'll leave `module` to the sections on "Running TypeScript on the Server" on page 258 and "Running TypeScript in the Browser" on page 259.

target

TSC's built-in transpiler supports converting most JavaScript features to older JavaScript versions, meaning you can write your code in the latest TypeScript version and transpile it down to whatever JavaScript version you need to support. Since TypeScript supports the latest JavaScript features (like `async`/`await`, which is not yet supported by all major JavaScript platforms at the time of writing), you'll almost always find yourself taking advantage of this built-in transpiler to convert your code to something that NodeJS and browsers understand today.

Let's take a look at which specific JavaScript features TSC does and does not transpile for older JavaScript versions (Table 12-2 and Table 12-3).[1]

 In the past, there was a new revision of the JavaScript language released every few years, with an incrementing language version (ES1, ES3, ES5, ES6). As of 2015, the JavaScript language now has a yearly release cycle, with each language version named after the year it's released in (ES2015, ES2016, and so on). Some JavaScript features, however, get TypeScript support before they're actually slated for a specific JavaScript version; we refer to these features as "ESNext" (as in, the next revision).

Table 12-2. TSC does transpile

Version	Feature
ES2015	const, let, for..of loops, array/object spread (...), tagged template strings, classes, generators, arrow functions, function default parameters, function rest parameters, destructuring declarations/assignments/parameters
ES2016	Exponentiation operator (**)
ES2017	async functions, awaiting promises
ES2018	async iterators
ES2019	Optional parameter in catch clause
ESNext	Numeric separators (123_456)

Table 12-3. TSC does not transpile

Version	Feature
ES5	Object getters/setters
ES2015	Regex y and u flags
ES2018	Regex s flag
ESNext	BigInt (123n)

To set the transpilation target, pop open your *tsconfig.json* and set the `target` field to:

- `es3` for ECMAScript 3
- `es5` for ECMAScript 5 (this is a good default if you're not sure what to use)

---

1 If you use a language feature that TSC doesn't transpile and your target environment doesn't support it either, you can usually find a Babel plugin to transpile it for you. To find the most up-to-date plugin, search for "babel plugin <feature name>" in your favorite search engine.

- es6 or es2015 for ECMAScript 2015
- es2016 for ECMAScript 2016
- es2017 for ECMAScript 2017
- es2018 for ECMAScript 2018
- esnext for whatever the most recent ECMAScript revision is

For example, to compile to ES5:

```
{
  "compilerOptions": {
    "target": "es5"
  }
}
```

lib

As I mentioned, there's one hitch with transpiling your code to older JavaScript versions: while most language features can be safely transpiled (let to var, class to function), you still need to *polyfill* functionality yourself if your target environment doesn't support a newer library feature. Some examples are utilities like Promise and Reflect, and data structures like Map, Set, and Symbol. When targeting a bleeding-edge environment like the latest Chrome, Firefox, or Edge, you usually won't need any polyfills; but if you're targeting browsers a few versions back—or most NodeJS environments—you will need to polyfill missing features.

Thankfully, you won't need to write polyfills yourself. Instead, you can install them from a popular polyfill library like core-js (*https://www.npmjs.com/package/core-js*), or add polyfills to your code automatically by running your typechecked TypeScript code through Babel with @babel/polyfill (*https://babeljs.io/docs/en/babel-polyfill*).

 If you plan to run your application in a browser, be careful not to bloat the size of your JavaScript bundle by including every single polyfill regardless of whether or not the browser you're running your code in actually needs it—your target platform probably already supports some of the features you're polyfilling. Instead, use a service like Polyfill.io (*https://polyfill.io/v2/docs/*) to load just those polyfills that your user's browser needs.

Once you've added polyfills to your code, it's time to tell TSC that your environment is guaranteed to support the features you polyfilled—enter your *tsconfig.json*'s lib field. For example, you could use this configuration if you've polyfilled all ES2015 features plus ES2016's Array.prototype.includes:

```
{
  "compilerOptions": {
    "lib": ["es2015", "es2016.array.includes"]
  }
}
```

If you're running your code in the browser, also enable DOM type declarations for things like `window`, `document`, and all the other APIs you get when running your JavaScript in the browser:

```
{
  "compilerOptions": {
    "lib": ["es2015", "es2016.array.include", "dom"]
  }
}
```

For a full list of supported libs run `tsc --help`.

Enabling Source Maps

Source maps are a way to link your transpiled code back to the source code it was generated from. Most developer tools (like Chrome DevTools), error reporting and logging frameworks, and build tools know about source maps. Since a typical build pipeline can produce code that's very different from the code you started with (for example, your pipeline might compile TypeScript to ES5 JavaScript, tree-shake it with Rollup, preevaluate it with Prepack, then minify it with Uglify), using source maps throughout your build pipeline can make it a lot easier to debug the resulting JavaScript.

It's generally a good idea to use source maps in development, and ship source maps to production in both browser and server environments. There's one caveat, though: if you rely on some level of security through obscurity for your browser code, don't ship source maps to browsers in production.

Project References

As your application grows, it will take longer and longer for TSC to typecheck and compile your code. This time grows roughly linearly with the size of your codebase. When developing locally, slow incremental compile times can seriously slow down your development, and make working with TypeScript painful.

To address this, TSC comes with a feature called *project references* that speeds up compilation times dramatically, including incremental compile times. For any project with a few hundred files or more, project references are a must-have.

Use them like this:

1. Split your TypeScript project into multiple projects. A project is simply a folder that contains a *tsconfig.json* and some TypeScript code. Try to split your code in such a way that code that tends to be updated together lives in the same folder.

2. In each project folder, create a *tsconfig.json* that includes at least:

```
{
  "compilerOptions": {
    "composite": true,
    "declaration": true,
    "declarationMap": true,
    "rootDir": "."
  },
  "include": [
    "./**/*.ts"
  ],
  "references": [
    {
      "path": "../myReferencedProject",
      "prepend": true
    }
  ],
}
```

The keys here are:

- composite, which tells TSC that this folder is a subproject of a larger Type-Script project.

- declaration, which tells TSC to emit *.d.ts* declaration files for this project. The way project references work, projects have access to each other's declaration files and emitted JavaScript, but not their source TypeScript files. This creates a boundary beyond which TSC won't try to retypecheck or recompile your code: if you update a line of code in your subproject *A*, TSC doesn't have to retypecheck your other subproject *B*; all TSC needs to check for a type error is *B*'s type declarations. This is the core behavior that makes project references so efficient at rebuilding big projects.

- declarationMap, which tells TSC to build source maps for generated type declarations.

- references, which is an array of subprojects that your subproject depends on. Each reference's path should point either to a folder that contains a *tsconfig.json*, or directly to a TSC configuration file (if your configuration file isn't named *tsconfig.json*). prepend will concatenate the JavaScript and source maps generated by the subproject you're referencing to the JavaScript and source maps generated by your subproject. Note that `prepend` is only useful when you're using `outFile`—if you don't use `outFile`, you can ditch the `prepend`.

- `rootDir`, which explicitly specifies that this subproject should be compiled relative to the root project (`.`). Alternatively, you can specify an `outDir` that's a subfolder of the root project's `outDir`.

3. Create a root *tsconfig.json* that references any subprojects that aren't yet referenced by another subproject:

```
{
  "files": [],
  "references": [
    {"path": "./myProject"},
    {"path": "./mySecondProject"}
  ]
}
```

4. Now when you compile your project with TSC, use the `build` flag to tell TSC to take project references into account:

```
tsc --build # Or, tsc -b for short
```

At the time of writing, project references are a new TypeScript feature with some rough edges. When using them, be careful to:

- Rebuild the entire project (with `tsc -b`) after cloning or refetching it, in order to regenerate any missing or outdated *.d.ts* files. Alternatively, check in your generated *d.ts* files.

- Not use `noEmitOnError: false` with project references—TSC will always hardcode the option to `true`.

- Manually make sure that a given subproject isn't prepended by more than one other subproject. Otherwise, the doubly prepended subproject will show up twice in your compiled output. Note that if you're just referencing and not prepending, you're good to go.

Using extends to Reduce tsconfig.json Boilerplate

Because you probably want all of your subprojects to share the same compiler options, it's convenient to create a "base" *tsconfig.json* in your root directory that subprojects' *tsconfig.json*s can extend:

```
{
  "compilerOptions": {
```

```
          "composite": true,
          "declaration": true,
          "declarationMap": true,
          "lib": ["es2015", "es2016.array.include"],
          "rootDir": ".",
          "sourceMap": true,
          "strict": true,
          "target": "es5",
      }
  }
```

Then, update your subprojects to extend it using *tsconfig.json*'s extends option:

```
  {
    "extends": "../tsconfig.base",
    "include": [
      "./**/*.ts"
    ],
    "references": [
      {
        "path": "../myReferencedProject",
        "prepend": true
      }
    ],
  }
```

Error Monitoring

TypeScript warns you about errors at compile time, but you also need a way to find out about exceptions that your users experience at runtime, so that you can try to prevent them at compile time (or at least fix the bug that caused the runtime error). Use an error monitoring tool like Sentry (*https://sentry.io*) or Bugsnag (*https://bugs nag.com*) to report and collate your runtime exceptions.

Running TypeScript on the Server

To run your TypeScript code in a NodeJS environment, just compile your code to ES2015 JavaScript (or ES5, if you're targeting a legacy NodeJS version) with your *tsconfig.json*'s module flag set to commonjs:

```
  {
    "compilerOptions": {
      "target": "es2015",
      "module": "commonjs"
    }
  }
```

That will compile your ES2015 `import` and `export` calls to `require` and `module.exports`, respectively, so your code will run on NodeJS with no further bundling needed.

If you're using source maps (you should be!), you'll need to feed your source maps into your NodeJS process. Just grab the `source-map-support` (*https://www.npmjs.com/package/source-map-support*) package from NPM, and follow the package's setup instructions. Most process monitoring, logging, and error reporting tools like PM2 (*https://www.npmjs.com/package/pm2*), Winston (*https://www.npmjs.com/package/winston*), and Sentry (*https://sentry.io*) have built-in support for source maps.

Running TypeScript in the Browser

Compiling TypeScript to run in the browser involves a little more work than running TypeScript on the server.

First, pick a module system to compile to. A good rule of thumb is to stick to `umd` when publishing a library for others to use (e.g., on NPM) in order to maximize compatibility with various module bundlers that people might use in their projects.

If you just plan to use your code yourself without publishing it to NPM, which format you compile to depends on the module bundler you're using. Check your bundler's documentation—for example, Webpack and Rollup work best with ES2015 modules, while Browserify requires CommonJS modules. Here are a few guidelines:

- If you're using the SystemJS (*https://github.com/systemjs/systemjs*) module loader, set `module` to `systemjs`.
- If you're running your code through an ES2015-aware module bundler like Webpack (*https://webpack.js.org*) or Rollup (*https://github.com/rollup/rollup*), set `module` to `es2015` or higher.
- If you're using an ES2015-aware module bundler and your code uses dynamic imports (see "Dynamic Imports" on page 219), set `module` to `esnext`.
- If you're building a library for other projects to use, and aren't running your code through any additional build steps after `tsc`, maximize compatibility with different loaders that people use by setting `module` to `umd`.
- If you're bundling your module with a CommonJS bundler like Browserify (*https://github.com/browserify/browserify*), set `module` to `commonjs`.
- If you're planning to load your code with RequireJS (*https://requirejs.org*) or another AMD module loader, set `module` to `amd`.
- If you want your top-level exports to be globally available on the `window` object (as you might if you're Mussolini's great-nephew), set `module` to `none`. Note that

TSC will try to curb your enthusiasm for inflicting pain on other software engineers by compiling to `commonjs` anyway if your code is in module mode (see "Module Mode Versus Script Mode" on page 222).

Next, configure your build pipeline to compile all your TypeScript to a single JavaScript file (usually called a "bundle") or a set of JavaScript files. While TSC can do this for you for small projects with the `outFile` TSC flag, the flag is limited to generating SystemJS and AMD bundles. And since TSC doesn't support build plugins and intelligent code splitting the same way that a dedicated build tool like Webpack does, you'll soon find yourself wanting a more powerful bundler.

That's why for frontend projects, you should use a more powerful build tool from the beginning. There are TypeScript plugins for whatever build tool you might be using, such as:

- `ts-loader` (*http://bit.ly/2Gw3uH2*) for Webpack (*https://webpack.js.org*)
- `tsify` (*http://bit.ly/2KOaZgw*) for Browserify (*http://bit.ly/2IDpfGe*)
- `@babel/preset-typescript` (*http://bit.ly/2vc2Sjy*) for Babel (*https://babeljs.io*)
- `gulp-typescript` (*http://bit.ly/2vanubN*) for Gulp (*https://gulpjs.com*)
- `grunt-ts` (*http://bit.ly/2PgUXuq*) for Grunt (*https://gruntjs.com*)

While a full discussion of optimizing your JavaScript bundle for fast loading is outside the scope of this book, some brief advice—not specific to TypeScript—is:

- Keep your code modular, and avoid implicit dependencies in your code (these can happen when you assign things to the `window` global, or to other globals), so that your build tool can more accurately analyze your project's dependency graph.

- Use dynamic imports to lazy-load code that you don't need for your initial page load, so you don't unnecessarily block your page from rendering.

- Take advantage of your build tool's automatic code splitting functionality, so that you avoid loading too much JavaScript and slowing page load unnecessarily.

- Have a strategy for measuring page load time, either synthetically or, ideally, with real user data. As your app grows the initial load time can get slower and slower; you can only optimize that load time if you have a way to measure it. Tools like New Relic (*https://newrelic.com*) and Datadog (*https://www.datadoghq.com*) are invaluable here.

- Keep your production build as similar as possible to your development build. The more the two diverge, the more hard-to-fix bugs you'll have that only show up in production.

- Finally, when shipping TypeScript to run in the browser, have a strategy for polyfilling missing browser features. This might be a standard set of polyfills you ship as part of every bundle, or it might be a dynamic set of polyfills based on what features the user's browser supports.

Publishing Your TypeScript Code to NPM

It's easy to compile your TypeScript code so that other TypeScript and JavaScript projects can use it. There are a few best practices to keep in mind when compiling to JavaScript for external use:

- Generate source maps, so you can debug your own code.
- Compile to ES5, so that others can easily build and run your code.
- Be mindful about which module format you compile to (UMD, CommonJS, ES2015, etc.).
- Generate type declarations, so that other TypeScript users have types for your code.

Start by compiling your TypeScript to JavaScript with `tsc`, and generate corresponding type declarations. Be sure to configure your *tsconfig.json* to maximize compatibility with popular JavaScript environments and build systems (more on that in "Building Your TypeScript Project" on page 249):

```
{
"compilerOptions": {
  "declaration": true,
  "module": "umd",
  "sourceMaps": true,
  "target": "es5"
  }
]
```

Next, blacklist your TypeScript source code from getting published to NPM in your *.npmignore*, to avoid bloating the size of your package. And in your *.gitignore*, exclude generated artifacts from your Git repository to avoid polluting it:

```
# .npmignore

*.ts # Ignore .ts files
!*.d.ts # Allow .d.ts files

# .gitignore

*.d.ts # Ignore .d.ts files
*.js # Ignore .js files
```

If you stuck with the recommended project layout and kept your source files in *src/* and your generated files in *dist/*, your *.ignore* files will be even simpler:

```
# .npmignore

src/ # Ignore source files
# .gitignore

dist/ # Ignore generated files
```

Finally, add a "types" field to your project's *package.json* to indicate that it comes with type declarations (note that this isn't mandatory, but it is a helpful hint to TSC for any consumers that use TypeScript), and add a script to build your package before publishing it, to make sure that your package's JavaScript, type declarations, and source maps are always up to date and in sync with the TypeScript you compiled them from:

```
{
  "name": "my-awesome-typescript-project",
  "version": "1.0.0",
  "main": "dist/index.js",
  "types": "dist/index.d.ts",
  "scripts": {
    "prepublishOnly": "tsc -d"
  }
}
```

That's it! Now when you `npm publish` your package to NPM, NPM will automatically compile your TypeScript to a format usable by both people that use TypeScript (with full type safety) and people that use JavaScript (with some type safety, if their code editor supports it).

Triple-Slash Directives

TypeScript comes with a little-known, rarely used, and mostly outdated feature called *triple-slash directives*. These directives are specially formatted TypeScript comments that serve as instructions to TSC.

They come in a few flavors, and in this section, we'll cover just two of them: types, for eliding type-only full-module imports, and `amd-module`, for naming generated AMD modules. For a full reference, see Appendix E.

The types Directive

When you import something from a module, depending on what you imported, TypeScript won't always need to generate an `import` or `require` call when you compile your code to JavaScript. If you have an `import` statement whose export is only used in a type position in your module (i.e., you just imported a type from a module), TypeScript won't generate any JavaScript code for that `import`—think of it as only existing at the type level. This feature is called *import elision*.

The exception to the rule is imports used for side effects: if you import an entire module (without importing a specific export or a wildcard from that module), that import will generate JavaScript code when you compile your TypeScript. You might do this, for instance, if you want to make sure that an ambient type defined in a script-mode module is available in your program (like we did in "Safely Extending the Prototype" on page 154). For example:

```
// global.ts
type MyGlobal = number

// app.ts
import './global'
```

After compiling *app.ts* to JavaScript with `tsc app.ts`, you'll notice that that the `./global` import wasn't elided:

```
// app.js
import './global'
```

If you find yourself writing imports like this, you may want to start by making sure that your import really needs to use side effects, and that there isn't some other way to rewrite your code to make it more explicit which value or type you're importing (e.g., `import {MyType} from './global'`—which TypeScript will elide for you— instead of `import './global'`). Or, see if you can include your ambient type in your *tsconfig.json*'s `types`, `files`, or `include` field and avoid the import altogether.

If neither of those works for your use case, and you want to continue to use a full-module import but avoid generating a JavaScript `import` or `require` call for that import, use the `types` triple-slash directive. A triple-slash directive is three slashes `///` followed by one of a few possible XML tags, each with its own set of required attributes. For the `types` directive, it looks like this:

- Declare a dependency on an ambient type declaration:

    ```
    /// <reference types="./global" />
    ```

- Declare a dependency on *@types/jasmine/index.d.ts*:

    ```
    /// <reference types="jasmine" />
    ```

You probably won't find yourself using this directive often. And if you do, you may want to rethink how you're using types in your project, and consider if there's a way to rely less on ambient types.

The amd-module Directive

When compiling your TypeScript code to the AMD module format (indicated with
{"module": "amd"} in your *tsconfig.json*), TypeScript will generate anonymous AMD
modules by default. You can use the AMD triple-slash directive to give your emitted
modules names.

Let's say you have the following code:

```
export let LogService = {
  log() {
    // ...
  }
}
```

Compiling to the amd module format, TSC generates the following JavaScript code:

```
define(['require', 'exports'], function(require, exports) {
  exports.__esModule = true
  exports.LogService = {
    log() {
      // ...
    }
  }
})
```

If you're familiar with the AMD module format, you might have noticed that this is
an anonymous AMD module. To give your AMD module a name, use the amd-
module triple-slash directive in your code:

```
/// <amd-module name="LogService" />  ❶
export let LogService = {  ❷
  log() {
    // ...
  }
}
```

❶   We use the amd-module directive, and set a name attribute on it.

❷   The rest of our code is unchanged.

Recompiling to the AMD module format with TSC, we now get the following Java-
Script:

```
/// <amd-module name='LogService' />
define('LogService', ['require', 'exports'], function(require, exports) {
  exports.__esModule = true
  exports.LogService = {
    log() {
      // ...
    }
```

```
    }
})
```

When compiling to AMD modules, use the `amd-module` directive to make your code easier to bundle and debug (or, switch to a more modern module format like ES2015 modules if you can).

Summary

In this chapter we covered everything you need to know to build and run your TypeScript application in production, either in the browser or on the server. We discussed how to choose a JavaScript version to compile to, which libraries to mark as available in your environment (and how to polyfill libraries when they're missing), and how to build and ship source maps with your application to make it easier to debug in production and develop locally. We then explored how to modularize your TypeScript project to keep compilation times fast. Finally, we finished up with how to run your TypeScript application on the server and in the browser, how to publish your TypeScript code to NPM for others to use, how import elision works, and—for AMD users—how to use triple-slash directives to name your modules.

Conclusion

We're nearing the end of our journey together.

We've covered what types are and why they're useful; how TSC works; what types TypeScript supports; how TypeScript's type system handles inference, assignability, refinement, widening, and totality; the rules of contextual typing; how variance works; and how to use type operators. We've covered functions and classes and interfaces, iterators and iterables and generators, overloads, polymorphic types, mixins, decorators, and the various escape hatches you can use once in a while to sacrifice safety to get your code out before your deadline. We explored the different ways to handle exceptions safely and their trade-offs, and how to use types to make concurrent, parallel, and asynchronous programs safe. We dove into using TypeScript with popular frameworks like Angular and React, and how namespaces and modules work. We looked at using, building, and deploying TypeScript on the frontend and on the backend, and talked about how to gradually migrate code to TypeScript, how to use type declarations, how to publish your code to NPM so others can use it, how to safely use third-party code, and how to build your TypeScript projects.

I hope that I've infected you with the gospel of static types. I hope you now, at times, find yourself sketching out programs in types before implementing them, and I hope you've gained a deeply intuitive understanding of how you can use types to make your applications safer. I hope that I've changed your view of the world, at least a little bit, and that you now think in types when you write code.

You're now equipped to teach others about TypeScript. Advocate for safety, and help make your company's and your friends' code better and more fun to write.

Finally, keep exploring. TypeScript probably isn't your first language, and it probably won't be your last. Keep learning about new ways to program, new ways to think about types, and new ways to think about the trade-offs between safety and ease of use. Maybe you'll create the next big thing after TypeScript, and maybe I'll be the one to write about it someday...

Type Operators

TypeScript supports a rich set of type operators for working with types. Use Table A-1 as a handy reference for when you want to learn more about an operator.

Table A-1. Type operators

Type operator	Syntax	Use it on	Learn more
Type query	`typeof, instanceof`	Any type	"Refinement" on page 126, "Classes Declare Both Values and Types" on page 98
Keys	`keyof`	Object types	"The keyof operator" on page 134
Property lookup	`O[K]`	Object types	"The keying-in operator" on page 132
Mapped type	`[K in O]`	Object types	"Mapped Types" on page 137
Modifier addition	`+`	Object types	"Mapped Types" on page 137
Modifier subtraction	`-`	Object types	"Mapped Types" on page 137
Read-only modifier	`readonly`	Object types, array types, tuple types	"Objects" on page 25, "Classes and Inheritance" on page 83, "Read-only arrays and tuples" on page 36
Optional modifier	`?`	Object types, tuple types, function parameter types	"Objects" on page 25, "Tuples" on page 35, "Optional and Default Parameters" on page 47
Conditional type	`?`	Generic types, type aliases, function parameter types	"Conditional Types" on page 143
Nonnull assertion	`!`	Nullable types	"Nonnull Assertions" on page 149, "Definite Assignment Assertions" on page 151
Generic type parameter default	`=`	Generic types	"Generic Type Defaults" on page 79
Type assertion	`as, <>`	Any type	"Type Assertions" on page 148, "The const type" on page 123
Type guard	`is`	Function return types	"User-Defined Type Guards" on page 142

Type Utilities

TypeScript's type utilities come bundled into its standard library. Table B-1 enumerates all of the available utilities at the time of writing.

See *es5.d.ts* (*http://bit.ly/2I0Ve2U*) for an up-to-date reference.

Table B-1. Type utilities

Type utility	Use it on	Description
ConstructorParameters	Class constructor types	A tuple of a class constructor's parameter types
Exclude	Union types	Exclude a type from another type
Extract	Union types	Select a subtype that's assignable to another type
InstanceType	Class constructor types	The instance type you get from new-ing a class constructor
NonNullable	Nullable types	Exclude null and undefined from a type
Parameters	Function types	A tuple of a function's parameter types
Partial	Object types	Make all properties in an object optional
Pick	Object types	A subtype of an object type, with a subset of its keys
Readonly	Array, Object, and Tuple types	Make all properties in an object read-only, or make an array or tuple read-only
ReadonlyArray	Any type	Make an immutable array of the given type
Record	Object types	A map from a key type to a value type
Required	Object types	Make all properties in an object required
ReturnType	Function types	A function's return type

Scoped Declarations

TypeScript declarations have a rich set of behaviors needed to model types and values, and as in JavaScript, they can be overloaded in a variety of ways. This appendix covers two of these behaviors, summarizing which declarations generate types (and which generate values), and which declarations can be merged.

Does It Generate a Type?

Some TypeScript declarations create a type, some create a value, and some create both. See to Table C-1 for a quick reference.

Table C-1. Does the declaration generate a type?

Keyword	Generates a type?	Generates a value?
class	Yes	Yes
const, let, var	No	Yes
enum	Yes	Yes
function	No	Yes
interface	Yes	No
namespace	No	Yes
type	Yes	No

Does It Merge?

Declaration merging is a core TypeScript behavior. Take advantage of it to create richer APIs, better modularize your code, and make your code safer.

Table C-2 is reprinted from "Declaration Merging" on page 226; it's a handy reference for which kinds of declarations TypeScript will merge for you.

Table C-2. Can the declaration be merged?

		To							
		Value	Class	Enum	Function	Types alias	Interface	Namespace	Module
	Value	No	No	No	No	Yes	Yes	No	—
	Class	—	No	No	No	No	Yes	Yes	—
	Enum	—	—	Yes	No	No	No	Yes	—
From	Function	—	—	—	No	Yes	Yes	Yes	—
	Type alias	—	—	—	—	No	No	Yes	—
	Interface	—	—	—	—	—	Yes	Yes	—
	Namespace	—	—	—	—	—	—	Yes	—
	Module	—	—	—	—	—	—	—	Yes

Recipes for Writing Declaration Files for Third-Party JavaScript Modules

This appendix covers a few key building blocks and patterns that come up over and over again when typing third-party modules. For a deeper discussion of typing third-party code, head over to "JavaScript That Doesn't Have Type Declarations on DefinitelyTyped" on page 246.

Since module declaration files have to live in *.d.ts* files and so can't contain values, when you declare module types you need to use the declare keyword to affirm that values of the given type really are exported by your module. Table D-1 provides a short summary of regular declarations and their type declaration equivalents.

Table D-1. TypeScript and its type-only equivalents

.ts	.d.ts
var a = 1	declare var a: number
let a = 1	declare let a: number
const a = 1	declare const a: 1
function a(b) { return b.toFixed() }	declare function a(b: number): string
class A { b() { return 3 } }	declare class A { b(): number }
namespace A {}	declare namespace A {}
type A = number	type A = number
interface A { b?: string }	interface A { b?: string }

Types of Exports

Whether your module uses global, ES2015, or CommonJS exports will affect how you write your declaration files.

Globals

If your module only assigns values to the global namespace and doesn't actually export anything, you can just create a script-mode file (see "Module Mode Versus Script Mode" on page 222) and prefix your variable, function, and class declarations with declare (every other kind of declaration—enum, type, and so on—remains unchanged):

```
// Global variable
declare let someGlobal: GlobalType

// Global class
declare class GlobalClass {}

// Global function
declare function globalFunction(): string

// Global enum
enum GlobalEnum {A, B, C}

// Global namespace
namespace GlobalNamespace {}

// Global type alias
type GlobalType = number

// Global interface
interface GlobalInterface {}
```

Each of these declarations will be globally available to every file in your project without requiring an explicit import. Here, you could use someGlobal in any file in your project without importing it first, but at runtime, someGlobal would need to be assigned to the global namespace (window in browsers or global in NodeJS).

Be careful to avoid imports and exports in your declaration file in order to keep your file in script mode.

ES2015 Exports

If your module uses ES2015 exports—that is, the export keyword—simply replace declare (which affirms that a global variable is defined) with export (which affirms that an ES2015 binding is exported):

```
// Default export
declare let defaultExport: SomeType
export default defaultExport

// Named export
export class SomeExport {
  a: SomeOtherType
}

// Class export
export class ExportedClass {}

// Function export
export function exportedFunction(): string

// Enum export
enum ExportedEnum {A, B, C}

// Namespace export
export namespace SomeNamespace {
  let someNamespacedExport: number
}

// Type export
export type SomeType = {
  a: number
}

// Interface export
export interface SomeOtherType {
  b: string
}
```

CommonJS Exports

CommonJS was the de facto module standard before ES2015, and is still the standard for NodeJS at the time of writing. It also uses the export keyword, but the syntax is a bit different:

```
declare let defaultExport: SomeType
export = defaultExport
```

Notice how we assigned our exports to export, rather than using export as a modifier (like we do for ES2015 exports).

A type declaration for a third-party CommonJS module can contain exactly one export. To export multiple things, we take advantage of declaration merging (see Appendix C).

For example, to type multiple exports and no default export, we export a single namespace:

```
declare namespace MyNamedExports {
  export let someExport: SomeType
  export type SomeType = number
  export class OtherExport {
    otherType: string
  }
}
export = MyNamedExports
```

What about a CommonJS module that has both a default export and named exports? We take advantage of declaration merging:

```
declare namespace MyExports {
  export let someExport: SomeType
  export type SomeType = number
}
declare function MyExports(a: number): string
export = MyExports
```

UMD Exports

Typing a UMD module is nearly identical to typing an ES2015 module. The only difference is that if you want to make your module globally available to script-mode files (see "Module Mode Versus Script Mode" on page 222), you use the special `export as namespace` syntax. For example:

```
// Default export
declare let defaultExport: SomeType
export default defaultExport

// Named export
export class SomeExport {
  a: SomeType
}

// Type export
export type SomeType = {
  a: number
}

export as namespace MyModule
```

Notice that last line—if you have a script-mode file in your project, you can now use that module directly (without importing it first) on the global `MyModule` namespace:

```
let a = new MyModule.SomeExport
```

Extending a Module

Extending a module's type declaration is less common than typing a module, but it might come up if you write a jQuery plugin or a Lodash mixin. Try to avoid doing it when possible; instead, consider using a separate module. That is, instead of a Lodash mixin use a regular function, and instead of a jQuery plugin—wait, why are you still using jQuery?

Globals

If you want to extend another module's global namespace or interface, just create a script-mode file (see "Module Mode Versus Script Mode" on page 222), and augment it. Note that this only works for interfaces and namespaces because TypeScript will take care of merging them for you.

For example, let's add an awesome new marquee method to jQuery. We'll start by installing jquery itself:

```
npm install jquery --save
npm install @types/jquery --save-dev
```

We'll then create a new file—say *jquery-extensions.d.ts*—in our project, and add marquee to jQuery's global JQuery interface (I found that jQuery defines its methods on the JQuery interface by sleuthing through its type declarations):

```
interface JQuery {
  marquee(speed: number): JQuery<HTMLElement>
}
```

Now, in any file where we use jQuery, we can use marquee (of course, we'll want to add a runtime implementation for marquee too):

```
import $ from 'jquery'
$(myElement).marquee(3)
```

Note that this is the same technique we used to extend built-in globals in "Safely Extending the Prototype" on page 154.

Modules

Extending module exports is a bit trickier, and has more pitfalls: you need to type your extension correctly, load your modules in the correct order at runtime, and make sure to update your extension's types when the structure of the type declarations for the module you're extending changes.

As an example, let's type a new export for React. We'll start by installing React and its type declarations:

```
npm install react --save
npm install @types/react --save-dev
```

Then we'll take advantage of module merging (see "Declaration Merging" on page 226) and simply declare a module with the same name as our React module:

```
import {ReactNode} from 'react'

declare module 'react' {
  export function inspect(element: ReactNode): void
}
```

Note that unlike in our example for extending globals, it doesn't matter whether our extension file is in module mode or script mode.

What about extending a specific export from a module? Inspired by ReasonReact (*https://reasonml.github.io/reason-react*), let's say we want to add a built-in reducer for our React components (a reducer is a way to declare an explicit set of state transitions for a React component). At the time of writing, React's type declarations declare the React.Component type as an interface and a class that get merged together into a single UMD export:

```
export = React
export as namespace React

declare namespace React {
  interface Component<P = {}, S = {}, SS = any>
    extends ComponentLifecycle<P, S, SS> {}
  class Component<P, S> {
    constructor(props: Readonly<P>)
    // ...
  }
  // ...
}
```

Let's extend Component with our reducer method. We can do this by entering the following in a *react-extensions.d.ts* file in the project root:

```
import 'react' ❶

declare module 'react' { ❷
  interface Component<P, S> { ❸
    reducer(action: object, state: S): S ❹
  }
}
```

❶ We import 'react', switching our extension file into script mode, which we need to be in to consume a React module. Note that there are other ways we could have switched to script mode, like importing something else, exporting something, or exporting an empty object (export {})—we didn't have to import 'react' specifically.

❷ We declare the 'react' module, indicating to TypeScript that we want to declare types for that specific import path. Because we already installed @types/react

---

(which defines an export for the same exact 'react' path), TypeScript will merge this module declaration with the one provided by @types/react.

❸ We augment the Component interface provided by React by declaring our own Component interface. Following the rules of interface merging ("Declaration Merging" on page 93), we have to use the same exact signature in our declaration as the one in @types/react.

❹ Finally, we declare our reducer method.

After declaring these types (and assuming we've implemented the runtime behavior to support this update somewhere), we can now declare React components with built-in reducers in a typesafe way:

```
import * as React from 'react'

type Props = {
  // ...
}

type State = {
  count: number
  item: string
}

type Action =
  | {type: 'SET_ITEM', value: string}
  | {type: 'INCREMENT_COUNT'}
  | {type: 'DECREMENT_COUNT'}

class ShoppingBasket extends React.Component<Props, State> {
  reducer(action: Action, state: State): State {
    switch (action.type) {
      case 'SET_ITEM':
        return {...state, item: action.value}
      case 'INCREMENT_COUNT':
        return {...state, count: state.count + 1}
      case 'DECREMENT_COUNT':
        return {...state, count: state.count - 1}
    }
  }
}
```

As noted at the start of this section, it's good practice to avoid this pattern when possible (even though it's cool) because it can make your modules brittle and dependent on load order. Instead, try to use composition so that your module extensions consume the module they're extending, and export a wrapper rather than modifying that module.

Triple-Slash Directives

Triple-slash directives are just regular JavaScript comments that TypeScript looks for to do things like adjust compiler settings for a specific file, or indicate that your file depends on another file. Put your directives at the top of your file, before any code. Triple-slash directives look like this (each directive is a triple-slash, ///, followed by an XML tag):

```
/// <directive attr="value" />
```

TypeScript supports a handful of triple-slash directives. Table E-1 lists the ones you are most likely to use:

amd-module
> Head over to "The amd-module Directive" on page 264 to learn more.

lib
> The lib directive is a way to indicate to TypeScript which of TypeScript's libs your module depends on, which you may want to do if your project doesn't have a *tsconfig.json*. Declaring the libs you depend on in your *tsconfig.json* is almost always a better option.

path
> When using TSC's outFile option, use the path directive to declare a dependency on another file, so that the other file appears earlier in your compiled output than the dependent file does. If your project uses imports and exports, you likely won't ever use this directive.

type
> Head over to "The types Directive" on page 262 to learn more about the type directive.

Table E-1. Triple-slash directives

Directive	Syntax	Use it to...
amd-module	`<amd-module name="MyCompo` `nent" />`	Declare export names when compiling to AMD modules
lib	`<reference lib="dom" />`	Declare which of TypeScript's built-in `lib`s your type declarations depend on
path	`<reference path="./` `path.ts" />`	Declare which TypeScript files your module depends on
type	`<reference types="./` `path.d.ts" />`	Declare which type declaration files your module depends on

Internal Directives

You will probably never use the `no-default-lib` directive (Table E-2) in your own code.

Table E-2. Internal triple-slash directives

Directive	Syntax	Use it to...
no-default-lib	`<reference no-default-` `lib="true" />`	Tell TypeScript to not use any `lib`s at all for this file

Deprecated Directives

You should never use the `amd-dependency` directive (Table E-3), and instead stick to a regular `import`.

Table E-3. Deprecated triple-slash directives

Directive	Syntax	Instead use...
amd-dependency	`<amd-dependency path="./a.ts" name="MyComponent" />`	`import`

TSC Compiler Flags for Safety

For a complete list of available compiler flags, head over to the TypeScript Handbook website (*http://bit.ly/2JWfsgY*).

Each TypeScript release introduces new checks that you can enable to squeeze even more safety out of your code. Some of these flags—prefixed with strict—are included as part of the strict flag; or, you can opt into strict flags one at a time. Table F-1 lists the compiler flags related to safety that are available at the time of writing.

Table F-1. TSC safety flags

Flag	Description
alwaysStrict	Emit 'use strict'.
noEmitOnError	Don't emit JavaScript when your code has type errors.
noFallthroughCasesInSwitch	Make sure that every switch case either returns a value or breaks.
noImplicitAny	Error when a variable's type is inferred as any.
noImplicitReturns	Make sure that every code path in every function explicitly returns. See "Totality" on page 130.
noImplicitThis	Error when you use this in a function without explicitly annotating the this type. See "Typing this" on page 50.
noUnusedLocals	Warn about unused local variables.
noUnusedParameters	Warn about unused function parameters. Prefix your parameter name with _ to ignore this error.
strictBindCallApply	Enforce type safety for bind, call, and apply. See "call, apply, and bind" on page 50.

Flag	Description
strictFunctionTypes	Enforce that functions are contravariant in their parameter and `this` types. See "Function variance" on page 118.
strictNullChecks	Promote `null` to a type. See "null, undefined, void, and never" on page 37.
strictPropertyInitialization	Enforce that class properties are either nullable or initialized. See Chapter 5.

TSX

Under the hood, TypeScript exposes a few hooks for typing TSX in a pluggable way. These are special types on the `global.JSX` namespace that TypeScript looks at as the source of truth for TSX types throughout your program.

If you're just using React, you don't need to know about these low-level hooks, but if you're writing a TypeScript library that uses TSX without React, this appendix provides a helpful reference for the hooks you can use.

TSX supports two kinds of elements: built-in ones (*intrinsic elements*) and user-defined ones (*value-based elements*). Intrinsic elements always have lowercased names, and refer to built-in elements like <li>, <h1>, and <div>. Value-based elements have PascalCased names, and refer to those elements that you create with React (or whatever frontend framework you're using TSX with); they can be defined either as functions or as classes. See Figure G-1.

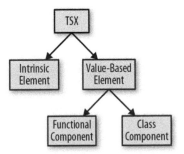

Figure G-1. The kinds of TSX elements

Using React's type declarations (*http://bit.ly/2CNzeW2*) as an example, we'll walk through the hooks TypeScript uses to safely type TSX. Here's how React hooks into TSX to type JSX safely:

```
declare global {
  namespace JSX {
    interface Element extends React.ReactElement<any> {} ❶
    interface ElementClass extends React.Component<any> { ❷
      render(): React.ReactNode
    }
    interface ElementAttributesProperty { ❸
      props: {}
    }
    interface ElementChildrenAttribute { ❹
      children: {}
    }

    type LibraryManagedAttributes<C, P> = // ... ❺

    interface IntrinsicAttributes extends React.Attributes {} ❻
    interface IntrinsicClassAttributes<T> extends React.ClassAttributes<T> {} ❼

    interface IntrinsicElements { ❽
      a: React.DetailedHTMLProps<
        React.AnchorHTMLAttributes<HTMLAnchorElement>,
        HTMLAnchorElement
      >
      abbr: React.DetailedHTMLProps<
        React.HTMLAttributes<HTMLElement>,
        HTMLElement
      >
      address: React.DetailedHTMLProps<
        React.HTMLAttributes<HTMLElement>,
        HTMLElement
      >
      // ...
    }
  }
}
```

❶ JSX.Element is the type of a value-based TSX element.

❷ JSX.ElementClass is the type of an instance of a value-based class component. Whenever you declare a class component that you plan to instantiate with TSX's <MyComponent /> syntax, its class must satisfy this interface.

❸ JSX.ElementAttributesProperty is the name of the property TypeScript looks at to figure out what attributes a component supports. For React, that means the props property. TypeScript looks for this value on a class instance.

❹ JSX.ElementChildrenAttribute is the name of the property that TypeScript looks at to figure out what types of children a component supports. For React, that means the children property.

❺ JSX.IntrinsicAttributes is the set of attributes that all intrinsic elements support. For React, that means the key attribute.

❻ JSX.IntrinsicClassAttributes is the set of attributes that all class components (both intrinsic and value-based) support. For React, that means ref.

❼ JSX.LibraryManagedAttributes specifies other places where JSX elements can declare and initialize property types. For React, that means propTypes as another place to declare property types, and defaultProps as the place to declare default values for properties.

❽ JSX.IntrinsicElements enumerates every type of HTML element that you can use in TSX, mapping each element's tag name to its attribute and children types. Because JSX isn't HTML, React's type declarations have to tell TypeScript exactly what elements someone might use in a TSX expression, and because you can use any standard HTML element from TSX, the declarations have to manually enumerate each element along with its attribute types (for an <a> tag, for example, valid attributes include href: string and rel: string, but not value) and what types of children it might have.

By declaring any of these types in the global JSX namespace, you can hook into TypeScript's typechecking behavior for TSX and customize it however you want. Unless you're writing a library that uses TSX (and doesn't use React), you'll probably never touch these hooks.

Index

Symbols

! (exclamation mark), nonnull assertion opera-
    tor, 150
& (ampersand), for intersection types, 32, 132
() (parentheses), invoking functions with, 50
* (asterisk), before function names, 52
+ (plus) type operator, 139
/// (triple-slash directives), 283
< > (angle brackets)
    enclosing generic type parameters, 67
    in type assertions, 148
? (question mark)
    for optional elements in tuples, 36
    for optional function parameters, 47
    for optional properties in objects, 27
@ts-check comment, 238
@ts-ignore comment, 246
@ts-nocheck comment, 238
[] (square brackets)
    index signature syntax, 28
    keying-in operator, 146
    retrieving enum values, 40
    in tuple declarations, 35
{} (curly braces), defining object literal types
    with, 26
| (pipe symbol), for union types, 32, 132, 190
– (minus) type operator, 139
… (ellipsis) in variadic function parameters list,
    49

A

abstract classes, 86, 88
    extending versus implementing interfaces,
    96

abstract syntax tree (AST), 5
actual parameters (see arguments)
Ahead-of-Time (AoT) compiler (Angular), 207,
    209
aliases (type) (see type aliases)
allowJs TSC flag, 237
ambient module declarations, 235
    creating for third-party JavaScript, 246
    wildcard, 236
ambient type declarations, 234
    defining TODO as type alias for any, 241
ambient variable declarations, 233
AMD module standard, 217
    consuming JavaScript module that uses, 221
amd-module directive, 264
Angular 6/7, 207-210
    components, 207
    initializing a project, 207
    installing CLI, 207
    services, 209
angularCompilerOptions, 209
any type, 19
    as overloaded function parameter type, 62
    inferred for empty array elements, 35
    JavaScript types inferred as, 238
    object versus, 25
    TODO ambient type declaration as type
        alias for, 241
    type assertions as, 148
    widening of variables initialized as null or
        undefined to, 123
APIs
    application interacting with databases, 212

event emitters, 184, 187
  using in multithreading with Web Workers, 189-194
event loop, 174-176
event queue, 175
exceptions, 159
  handling, 160
    (see also errors, handling)
  JavaScript and, 2
  returning, 163-165
  throwing, 161-163
    in Promises, 182
excess property checking, 123
executors, 179
exhaustiveness checking, 130
  (see also totality)
experimentalDecorators TSC flag, 104
exports
  CommonJS, 217
  ES2015 standard for, 218-219
  module mode versus script mode, 222
  module.exports, 217
  namespace, 223
  using CommonJS and AMD code, 221
extends keyword, 88
extends option (TSC), 257

F

factory pattern, 108
filesystem, module paths as filenames on, 219
final classes, simulating, 107
finally clause, 183
fixed-arity functions, 48
flow-based type inference, 126
folder structure for TypeScript projects, 14, 249
formal parameters (see parameters)
frameworks, 199-213
  backend, 212
  frontend, 199-210
    Angular 6/7, 207-210
    enabling DOM APIs in tsconfig.json, 199
    React, 201-207
  typesafe APIs for, 210-212
fresh object literal type, 124
fullTemplateTypeCheck TSC flag, 209
Function type, 56
functions, 45-82, 141-143
  binding generics, 70

declaring and invoking, 45-64
  call signatures, 55-58
  contextual typing, 58
  declaring with named function syntax, 46
  generator functions, 52
  invoking functions, 47
  invoking with call, apply, and bind, 50
  iterators, 53-55
  optional and default parameters, 47
  overloaded function types, 59-64
  rest parameters, 48
  typing this variable, 50
decorator, 105
improving type inference for tuples, 141
null, undefined, void and never return types, 37
overloaded ambient function declarations, 225
parameter types, 18
polymorphism, 64-80
  bounded, 75-79
  generic type defaults, 79
type-driven development, 80
user-defined type guards, 142
variance, 118
  covariant return types, 120

G

generator functions, 52
generic type parameters, 66
  (see also generic types; generics)
  as constraints, 69
  comma-separated list within angle brackets, 67
  naming conventions, 68
generic types, 67
  Promise, 180
generics, 67
  binding, when it happens, 69-72
  bounded polymorphism, 75-79
  classes and interfaces support for, 100-101
  declaring as part of a condition, 143, 145
  interface declaring, 94
  subtyping, 115
  type aliases, 73
  type defaults, 79
  type inference, 72-73
global namespace, 155, 225

global.JSX namespace, 203
globals (browser), 218, 222
gradually typed languages, 8

H

homogeneous arrays, 34
HTML templates (Angular), 208

I

immediately invoked function expressions
  (IIFEs), 216
immutable arrays, 37
implements keyword, 94
import function, 220
import statements, 155, 220
imports
  CommonJS, 217
  dynamic, 219
  ES2015 standard for, 218-219
  import elision, 263
  module mode versus script mode, 222
  module name for exact import path, 235
  using CommonJS and AMD code, 221
  whitelisting an untyped import, 246
index signatures, 28
  Record object, 137
index.ts, 13
infer keyword, 145
inferring types, 7
inheritance, 83
  simulating multiple inheritance, 101
inner nodes, 75
instance methods, 88
instanceof operator, 99
interfaces, 91-96
  Angular lifecycle hooks, 208
  binding of generics, 70
  comparison with type aliases, 91
  declaration merging, 93
  extending objects, classes, or other inter-
    faces, 92
  implementation, 94
  implementing versus extending abstract
    classes, 96
  merging, 226
  polymorphism, 101
  top-level, in type declaration files, 233
internal triple-slash directives, 284
interpreted languages, 6

intersection types, 32, 92
  array, 34
intrinsic elements (TSX), 287
invalid actions, 2
invariance, 117
isomorphic programs, 251
iterable iterators, 54
IterableIterator type, 53
iterables, 54
iterators, 53-55
  built-in, for common collection types, 55
  defined, 54

J

JavaScript, xiii
  built-in iterators for collection types, 55
  compile target for TypeScript projects,
    251-255
    language versions and releases, 253
  configuring build pipeline to compile Type-
    Script code to, 260
  engine, 6
  event loop, 174-176
  interoperating with, 229-247
    gradually migrating code to TypeScript,
      236-241
    type lookup for JavaScript, 242-244
    using third-party JavaScript, 244-247
    using type declarations, 230-236
    ways to use JavaScript from TypeScript,
      247
  latest syntax and features, xiv
  modules, brief history of, 216-218
  optimizing bundles for fast loading, 260
  type system, comparison to TypeScript,
    8-10
  TypeScript program compiled to, 250
JSDoc annotations, 239
JSON (JavaScript Object Notation)
  loading .json files, 236
JSX (JavaScript XML), 201
  React hooking into TSX to type JSX cor-
    rectly, 288
  TSX and, 202
  using TSX with React, 203-207
jsx directive, 203

K

keying-in operator, 132, 146

compiler, 5-7
   errors, handling of, 3
   gradually migrating JavaScript code to,
      236-241
      adding JSDoc annotations, 239
      adding TSC to JavaScript projects, 237
      enabling typechecking for JavaScript,
         238
      renaming files to .ts, 240
      using strict TSC flags, 241
   modules, consuming and exporting, 218
   publishing code to NPM, 261-262
   running in the browser, 259
   running on the server, 258
   setting up code editors, 11-13
   setting up projects, index.ts file, 13
   triple-slash directives, 262-265
   type system, 7-10
      comparison to JavaScript, 8-10
TypeSearch, 245

U

undefined type, 37
   example of usage, 37
   nonnull assertions, 149
   summary of usage, 38
   variables initialized to, type widening, 123
union types, 32
   adding conditional type, 144
   defining for communication among
      threads, 190
   discriminated, 128
unique symbols, 24, 153
unknown type, 20
user-defined type guards, 142

V

value-based elements (TSX), 287
value-level code, 56
value: type annotations, 7
values, xv
   classes declaring both values and types, 98
   declarations generating, 273
   merging values and types, 226
   null and undefined, 37
   top-level, in type declaration files, 233
   type declarations and, 230

var
   type declarations with, 43
   using const instead of, 22
   variable declarations with, 31
variables
   ambient variable declarations, 233
   ambient versus regular declarations, 232
   declaring, then initializing with values, 27
   immutable, no type widening, 122
   mutable, type widening, 122
   with explicitly annotated types, 7
   with implicitly inferred types, 7
variadic functions, 48
variance, 115-121
   function, 118
   kinds of, 117
   shape and array, 116
view layer of frontend applications (React), 201
void type, 37
   summary of usage, 38
VSCode, 11

W

weakly typed languages, 9
web page for this book, xvii
Web Workers, typesafe multithreading with,
   187-196
   abstracting snowflake API behind
      EvenEmitter-based API, 191
   message passing API, 188
   onmessage API, 189
   typesafe protocols, 194
widening types (see type widening)
WindowEventMap interface, 186
Without type, 145

X

XML
   JSX (JavaScript XML), 201
   tags in triple-slash directives, 283
   TSX (JSX and TypeScript), 202
   using TSX with React, 203-207

Y

yield keyword, 53

About the Author

Boris Cherny is an engineering and product leader at Facebook. Previously, he worked in VC, ad tech, and at a bunch of startups, most of which aren't around anymore. He is interested in programming languages, code synthesis and static analysis, and building user experiences that people love. In his free time, he runs the San Francisco TypeScript Meetup and writes on his personal blog, *performancejs.com*. Find him on GitHub at *https://github.com/bcherny*.

Colophon

The animal on the cover of *Programming TypeScript* is a guanaco (*Lama guanicoe*). Guanacos are the wild ancestors of llamas and are also related to camels. Before sheep were introduced to the continent, guanacos could be found throughout much of South America. They live in the dry, steep, mountainous regions, ranging as high as 13,000 feet above sea level. Most of the 600,000 guanaco live in Argentina today, specifically favoring the Patagonia region.

To survive the rocky and sloped terrain, a guanaco has two padded toes on each foot and a low center of gravity. The average height of a guanaco is under four feet at the shoulder. Their thick wool coats are light to medium, reddish brown with near white coloring underneath. Long eyelashes protect their eyes from strong winds, and big, pointed ears help them sense threats.

Guanacos travel in herds made up of several females, young under one year of age, and a single breeding male. When they feel threatened, guanacos alert their herd to flee with a high-pitched bleat that some say sounds like a barking laugh. Pumas and foxes prey on guanacos, so they take turns standing on hills and shrieking to alert the rest of the herd when it's time to run to safety. A guanaco can typically run up to 35 miles per hour. If a predator chases the herd, the male will run to the back in defense.

It takes nearly a full year for a guanaco to gestate. Once born, a *chulengo*, as they're called, needs only five minutes before it can begin to walk. After a year living with their parents, chulengos must find their own herds. This abrupt dismissal may contribute to the low survival rate among guanaco young—just 30% reach adulthood. An adult can live for 15 to 20 years.

On the rugged slopes and scrub of the guanaco habitat, grasses and vegetation are tough, thick, and a crucial source of hydration. Guanacos have three-chamber stomachs that help them digest the plants and retain the liquid for longer periods of time. Their upper lips are split in two—an adaptation that makes grabbing their food easier.

Many of the animals on O'Reilly covers are endangered; all of them are important to the world.

The cover illustration is by Karen Montgomery, based on a black and white engraving from the *Pictorial Museum of Animated Nature*. The cover fonts are Gilroy Semibold and Guardian Sans. The text font is Adobe Minion Pro; the heading font is Adobe Myriad Condensed; and the code font is Dalton Maag's Ubuntu Mono.

O'REILLY®

There's much more where this came from.

Experience books, videos, live online training courses, and more from O'Reilly and our 200+ partners—all in one place.

Learn more at oreilly.com/online-learning

Milton Keynes UK
Ingram Content Group UK Ltd.
UKHW051538210924
448609UK00002B/13